A rhetoric for
writing teachers

A rhetoric for writing teachers

ERIKA LINDEMANN

University of North Carolina
at Chapel Hill

New York   Oxford
OXFORD UNIVERSITY PRESS
1982

Library of Congress Cataloging in Publication Data

Lindemann, Erika.
  A rhetoric for writing teachers.

  Bibliography: p.
  Includes index.
  1. English language—Rhetoric—Study and
teaching.   I. Title.
PE1404.L53   808'.042'071173   82-2205
ISBN 0-19-503047-8 (pbk.)   AACR2

Printing (last digit):   9 8 7 6 5 4

Printed in the United States of America

Acknowledgments

Theron Alexander, "The Individual and Social Change," *Intellect* (December 1974).

David Bartholomae, "Teaching Basic Writing: An Alternative to Basic Skills," *Journal of Basic Writing*, Vol. 2, No. 2 (Spring/Summer 1979), pp. 85–109. Copyright 1979 by the *Journal of Basic Writing*.

James Britton et al., *The Development of Writing Abilities 11–18* (Schools Council Research Studies, Macmillan Education, 1975). Reprinted by permission.

James Britton, *Language and Learning* (Pelican Books, 1974). Copyright © James Britton, 1970. Reprinted by permission of Penguin Books Ltd.

John Broderick, *The Able Writer*. Copyright © 1982 by Harper & Row, Publishers, Inc. Reprinted by permission of Harper & Row, Publishers, Inc.

Jacob Bronowski. *The Common Sense of Science*. Copyright © 1958 by Harvard University Press.

Kenneth Burke, *A Grammar of Motives* and *A Rhetoric of Motives*. Copyright 1969 by Kenneth Burke; reprinted by permission of the University of California Press.

Kenneth Burke, "Rhetoric—Old and New," *Journal of General Education* 5 (April 1951), 203–209. Reprinted by permission of The Pennsylvania State University Press.

Forrest Burt, *The Effective Writer: A Freshman English Manual*. Copyright 1978 by Forrest Burt. Reprinted by permission.

Francis Christensen and Bonniejean Christensen, *Notes toward a New Rhetoric*, Second Edition. Copyright © 1978 by Bonniejean Christensen. Reprinted by permission of Harper & Row, Publishers, Inc.

Walter Van Tilburg Clark, *The Ox-Bow Incident* (1940). Reprinted by permission of Random House, Inc.

Richard Coe, *Form and Substance: An Advanced Rhetoric.* Copyright 1981 by John Wiley & Sons, Inc. Reprinted by permission of John Wiley & Sons, Inc.

Joseph J. Comprone, *Teaching Form and Substance: A Left-Handed Guide to Teaching Students to Read and Write* © 1976 Wm. C. Brown Company Publishers, Dubuque, Iowa. Reprinted by permission.

Conference on College Composition and Communication, "Resolution on Testing and Writing" (1978). Reprinted by permission of the National Council of Teachers of English.

Charles Cooper, "An Outline for Writing Sentence-Combining Problems," *English Journal* 62 (January 1973), 96–102, 108. Reprinted by permission of the National Council of Teachers of English.

Charles Cooper, "Responding to Student Writing," paper presented at the Annual Conference on Language Arts, State University of New York at Buffalo, 1975. Reprinted by permission.

Charles Cooper and Lee Odell, eds., *Evaluating Writing: Describing, Measuring, Judging.* Copyright 1977 by the National Council of Teachers of English. Reprinted by permission.

Edward P.J. Corbett, *The Little Rhetoric and Handbook.* Copyright © 1977 by John Wiley & Sons, Inc. Reprinted by permission of John Wiley & Sons.

Gregory Cowan and Elizabeth Cowan, *Writing.* Copyright © 1980 by John Wiley & Sons, Inc. Reprinted by permission.

Frank D'Angelo, *A Conceptual Theory of Rhetoric.* Copyright © 1975. Page 44. Reprinted by permission of Winthrop Publishers, Inc., Cambridge, Massachusetts.

Frank D'Angelo, *Process and Thought in Composition,* Second Edition. Copyright © 1980, 1977. Reprinted by permission of Winthrop Publishers, Inc., Cambridge, Massachusetts.

Peter Elbow, *Writing without Teachers.* Copyright © 1973. Reprinted by permission of Oxford University Press, Inc.

R.L. Gregory, *The Intelligent Eye.* Copyright © 1970 by R.L. Gregory. Used with the permission of McGraw-Hill Book Company.

Leonard Gross, "America's Mood Today," *Look,* June 24, 1965.

Diana Hacker and Betty Renshaw, *A Practical Guide for Writers.* Copyright © 1979. Page 20. Reprinted by permission of Winthrop Publishers, Inc. Cambridge, Massachusetts.

Edward B. Jenkinson and Donald A Seybold, "Prologue," from *Writing as a Process of Discovery.* Copyright © 1970. Reprinted by permission of Indiana University Press.

James L. Kinneavy, *A Theory of Discourse*. Copyright © 1971 by Prentice-Hall, Inc. Reprinted by permission of James L. Kinneavy.

Ann Landers, letter from "Eyes Opened" appeared in the *Miami Herald*, July 1979. Reprinted by permission of Field Newspaper Syndicate.

Richard Lanham, *Revising Prose*. Copyright © 1979 by Richard Lanham (New York: Charles Scribner's Sons, 1979). Reprinted with the permission of Charles Scribner's Sons.

Richard Larson, "Discovery through Questioning: A Plan for Teaching Rhetorical Invention," *College English* 30 (November 1968), 126–134, and "Problem-Solving, Composing, and Liberal Education," *College English* 33 (March 1972), 628–635. Copyright © 1968 and 1972 by the National Council of Teachers of English. Reprinted by permission of the publisher and the author.

Guy R. Lefrancois, *Of Children: An Introduction to Child Development*, Third Edition. Copyright © 1980 by Wadsworth, Inc. Reprinted by permission of Wadsworth Publishing Company, Belmont, California 94002.

Sinclair Lewis, *Main Street* (1920). Reprinted by permission of Harcourt Brace Jovanovich, Inc.

William E. Mahoney, *Workbook of Current English*. Copyright © 1978 by Scott, Foresman and Company. Reprinted by permission.

James Moffett, *Teaching the Universe of Discourse*. Copyright © 1968 by James Moffett. Reprinted by permission of Houghton Mifflin Company.

Donald Murray, "Internal Revision: A Process of Discovery," in *Research on Composing*, ed. Charles Cooper and Lee Odell. Copyright © 1978 by the National Council of Teachers of English. Reprinted by permission.

Donald Murray, *A Writer Teaches Writing*. Copyright © 1968 by Donald M. Murray. Reprinted by permission of Houghton Mifflin Company.

NCTE Commission on Composition, "Teaching Composition: A Position Statement," *College English* 36 (October 1974), 219–220. Copyright © 1974 by the National Council of Teachers of English. Reprinted by permission of the publisher and the author.

William T. Reilly, memorandum, 1 October 1976. Reprinted with permission.

Gilbert Ryle. *The Concept of Mind* (1949). Reprinted by permission of Harper & Row Publishers, Inc.

Mina P. Shaughnessy, *Errors and Expectations*. Copyright © 1977 by Mina P. Shaughnessy. Reprinted by permission of Oxford University Press, Inc.

Nancy Sommers, "Revision Strategies of Student Writers and Experienced Writers," *College Composition and Communication* 31 (December 1980), 378–388. Copyright © 1980 by the National Council of Teachers of English. Reprinted by permission of the publisher and author.

William Strong, *Sentence Combining: A Composing Book*. Copyright © 1973 by Random House, Inc. Reprinted by permission.

Karl Wallace, "Topoi and the Problem of Invention," *Quarterly Journal of Speech* 58 (December 1972), 387–395. Reprinted by permission of the Speech Communication Association.

Constance Weaver, *Grammar for Teachers: Perspectives and Definition*. Copyright © 1979 by the National Council of Teachers of English. Reprinted by permission.

Glenn R. Williston, *Understanding the Main Idea, Middle Level* (1976). Reprinted by permission of Jamestown Publishers.

W. Ross Winterowd, *The Contemporary Writer*, Second Edition. Copyright © 1981, 1975 by Harcourt Brace Jovanovich, Inc. Reprinted by permission.

For
Alexandra Krapels
and Keith Walters

Preface

A teacher is always a student, pleased to learn from those who limp as well as leap through their lessons. In writing this book, I have tried to remember that all teachers learn from their students. We develop our styles of teaching primarily from experience, not from books, by living in classrooms, not in libraries. But the lessons of experience can be costly, as anyone who has heard war stories told in a teacher's lounge knows. So in writing this book I have assumed, as Mina Shaughnessy did, "that we need not learn everything at our students' expense." Teachers can also profit from each other's failures and successes.

This book explicates some lessons I learned about teaching writing from students and teachers, many of them graduate teaching assistants, at the University of South Carolina–Columbia. I owe the University thanks for granting me leave from my duties as Director of Freshman English to draft the manuscript. I also thank several good friends and respected colleagues for reading sections of the manuscript, suggesting improvements, and urging me to write concisely: Robert Bain of the University of North Carolina at Chapel Hill, Tommy J. Boley of the University of Texas at El Paso, Robert Connors of Louisiana State University, Frank D'Angelo of Arizona State University, Tom Dasher of Georgia Southern College, John MacNicholas and Phillip Rollinson of the University of South Carolina at Columbia, Nancy Sommers, John Trimble of the University of Texas at Austin, Harvey Wiener of LaGuardia Community College–CUNY, and W.

Ross Winterowd of the University of Southern California. I am especially grateful to Andrea A. Lunsford, University of British Columbia, whose sensible suggestions and supportive criticism helped me rewrite the entire manuscript.

For the use of Linguistic Atlas materials, I thank Raymond O'Cain, Sara Lyles Sanders and the LAMSAS staff at the University of South Carolina at Columbia, Professor Emeritus Raven McDavid of the University of Chicago, and the University of Chicago Press, which provided the base map. The Atlas project is supported by the American Council of Learned Societies and the National Endowment for the Humanities.

For their invaluable assistance in preparing the manuscript and seeing it through production, I am grateful to Meredith Walker, Luann Moore, Ramona Cook, and especially Hilde Robinson.

From the beginning, John Wright of Oxford University Press has offered me generous support and wise counsel. Because he respects writing teachers and publishes books that help us improve our teaching, he has strengthened writing programs serving countless students.

Finally, I thank those teachers, too many to name here, who prompted me to write this book. I value their concern for students, their persistent questions, and their generosity in sharing with me what works in the classroom. They, like the two special people to whom I dedicate this book, have all been my teachers. They remain my good friends.

Chapel Hill, N.C.   E.L.
Christmas Day 1981

Contents

ONE
The composing process

1

Why teach writing?

Read not to contradict and confute; nor to believe and take for granted; nor to find talk and discourse; but to weigh and consider.

FRANCIS BACON

Teaching writing can be enormously rewarding. We may value our work for different reasons, but to give our teaching purpose, to justify our energies, we must believe that our efforts make a difference. Unfortunately, our self-esteem may be assaulted by parents, legislators, business and professional people—even other teachers—who charge that we are not doing an especially effective job. If we become preoccupied with reacting to what we perceive as criticism, we may neglect to assert the validity, even the necessity, of our work.

Experienced teachers know that writing can be taught, that it has become increasingly important to teach it well. They observe growth in their students. They read books and articles to strengthen their teaching. They try different teaching methods, searching for and refining those which work best. Dedicated teachers know failure as well as the quiet sense of accomplishment which results from a student's victory over a persistent writing problem.

Beginning teachers, however, have not had the opportunity to develop a philosophy of teaching. They remember how they were taught; they read; they listen to others suggest what writing courses ought to do—but evaluating the information is difficult. Until they develop a conceptual framework to help them sort out what they read and hear, they must teach by trial and error. They must adopt someone else's assumptions until they formulate their own.

This book should help facilitate that process. Although you will find in it unmistakable evidence of my assumptions about the teaching of writing, I do not suppose you will agree with all of them. Examine them against your own experiences as a writer, a student, and a teacher. You may want to reject some ideas, modify others, and use the rest to shape your own conceptual framework. By such a process of discovery, each of us defines for ourselves what it means to teach well.

Writing as economic power

Presumably the teaching of writing has value because using written English well is a form of power. Yet is that assumption still true in our telephone, television, multiple-choice-test society? In grade eight we tell students they will need to write well for high school classes, when in fact some students complete high school without writing much at all. In high school we tell students they will need to write term papers and book reports in college, when in fact students who eventually go to college may never write term papers and book reports, except perhaps in freshman composition classes. We tell college students they must write well to complete job applications when they graduate, when in fact someone in the personnel office most likely will fill out the forms for them. Some of our students will become members of highly paid professions without learning to write well. Lawyers often consult books of sample letters and briefs rather than write their own. Politicians outline their speeches along certain lines but leave the actual drafting to paid staff writers. Members of other professions do not compose letters, memos, or reports in written form; they dictate them. Sales reports, requests for parts and services, countless business transactions, are usually completed by filling out pre-printed forms. Although our students cannot escape all writing, many of them (more than writing teachers want to think about) do get diplomas, degrees, and jobs without needing to write much or well.

The argument that writing opens doors to many satisfying, lucrative professions no longer holds up as well as it used to. However, even though many entry-level jobs do not demand exceptional writing skills, students applying for these positions are instantly branded as illiterates if their resumes or letters contain misspelled words. Employees create similarly adverse impressions on the job if egregious errors appear in responses to memos, notes left for secretaries, and brief reports written for supervisors. The ability to write well still creates economic power. If we will examine, together with our students, the kinds of writing required in jobs that interest them, they will discover important work-related reasons to improve their skills. Many students, for example, must earn college degrees to enter their chosen field; so, they must write well enough to satisfy professors in the department of their major. Non-English faculty members regard the ability to communicate effectively as an essential professional skill: [1]

> An engineer, without the tools of communication, is unable to sell his ideas, no matter how good those ideas are. (C.L. Gilmore, Industrial Engineering)
>
> Proficiency in written English is a *must* for a public school teacher who nourishes any hope at all of establishing credibility as a professional. (David G. Armstrong, Educational Curriculum & Instruction)
>
> Most students consider English a waste of time. Yet, I get letters from former students thanking me for the strict approach I took toward writing. Probably no other trait sets out a new engineer from his contemporaries in his first assignments as does the ability to write. (D. Saylak, Civil Engineering)

Once students enter a profession, they will find important correlations between writing ability and promotions. Writing well may not guarantee advancement, but writing poorly jeopardizes success. Employers expect written communications to be clear and concise:

> Inadequate communication skills will have a direct bearing on a college graduate's promotion opportunities. (A.K. Butler, Associate Director of Personnel, Continental Oil Company [CONOCO])
>
> My major criticism of the written communications of our newly hired graduates is that they write too much or too little. The knack of effective communication is to give all that is needed for complete understanding, but no more. (Paul J. Wolfe, Executive Vice President, Mobil Oil Corporation)
>
> An individual can be brilliant, but if he lacks communication skills it is unlikely that he will be successful in the business world. (K. W. Bruder, General Manager, Swift & Company)

1. The quotations from faculty members and employers are taken from Forrest Burt, ed., *The Effective Writer: A Freshman English Manual* (Boston: American Press, 1978), back cover.

Writing as social necessity

The ability to write is important also because language is indispensable to society. Human beings are social animals and use language not only to touch others but also to make sense out of the world. We write grocery lists to help us remember what to buy at the supermarket. We take notes at meetings, during telephone conversations, as we read, to remind ourselves of significant details. Travelogues, diaries, and other first-person documents also represent ways of talking to the self, of making sense out of countless experiences we must integrate if our daily lives are to have meaning. In other words, writing aids memory and helps us organize our lives.

Writing is also an established form of social commitment. Hotel reservations and cancellations, consumer complaints, contracts, warranties, changes of address, most financial and legal transactions do not become official until the parties are notified in writing. We establish orderly, formal relationships between people with pen and paper, not by telephone or through informal conversation. Ask politicians, administrators, or bureaucrats to commit a spoken statement to paper, and they become decidedly uncomfortable. In our society, "putting it in writing" has greater force than speaking.

Writing as knowing

Writing also helps us solve problems. The "problem" may be personal, as it is in the following letter to Ann Landers:

> DEAR ANN: I'm a 26-year-old woman and I feel like a fool asking you this question, but—should I marry the guy or not? Jerry is 30, but sometimes he acts like 14. We have gone together nearly a year. He was married for three years but never talks about it. My parents haven't said anything either for or against him, but I know deep down they don't like him much.
>
> Jerry is a salesman and makes good money but he has lost his wallet three times since I've known him and I've had to help him meet the payments on his car.
>
> The thing that bothers me most, I think, is that I have the feeling he doesn't trust me. After every date he telephones. He says it's to "say an extra goodnight" but I'm sure he is checking to see if I had a late date with someone else.
>
> One night I was in the shower and didn't hear the phone. He came over and sat on the porch all night. I found him asleep on the swing when I went to get the paper the next morning at 6:30 a.m. I had a hard time convincing him I had been in the house the whole time.
>
> Now on the plus side: Jerry is very good-looking and appeals to

me physically. Well—that does it. I have been sitting here with this pen in my hand for 15 minutes trying to think of something else good to say about him and nothing comes to mind.

Don't bother to answer this. You have helped me more than you will ever know.—Eyes Opened (*The Miami Herald,* July 22, 1978)

The real audience for this letter is not Ann Landers but "Eyes Opened," who debates with herself the merits of marrying Jerry. Most of us have had similar experiences. Writing may have helped us sort out a misunderstanding with a friend, plan a vacation, or make an important decision.

The problems writing helps us solve are not necessarily subjective. Investigators usually begin research projects because some personal experience has roused their curiosity, but eventually they must explain their subject objectively. They must record their attempts to find logic in experience. Books, articles, technical reports, laws, and creeds represent solutions to problems, answers to questions human beings must ask because they are aware of their surroundings. Their need to know eventually becomes a need to share their knowledge with others. In one sense, then, all writing solves a problem: How can I communicate my understanding of this subject to someone?

Writing permits us to understand not only the world but also the self. We discover who we are by writing. College students, for example, write to acquire particular ways of communicating ideas *as* historians, economists, educators, engineers. They learn the professional dialect that their discipline sanctions and the forms of written discourse appropriate for communication among its members. In the humanities and in some academic settings (but not all), the essay remains the sanctioned form for expressing our professional selves. Rarely, however, does the essay satisfy the formal demands of writing tasks that doctors, social workers, hotel managers, and pharmacists encounter. Those professions have their jargons and characteristic forms. Mastering them enables students to *be* doctors or social workers or mechanics, enables them to understand what they read and how to communicate in writing with their colleagues.

The humanistic perspective

Writing teachers confront paradoxes. Because we acknowledge a world dominated by mass media and sometimes narrow definitions of "professionalism," we help students develop whatever writing skills will advance their careers. At the same time, however, we also recognize that writing does not serve merely a utilitarian function. That is why we encourage students to appreciate writing that discovers meaning, form, and self. Writers write because they have to; they must explore their experiences and locate themselves in relation to a complex society. *Because* other media threaten to re-create us as plastic people, Disney delusions, and Madison Avenue stereotypes, we want students to write honestly, with a kind of tough sensitivity, about subjects that matter to them.

Learning to write well, then, has value far beyond any power to bring in a paycheck or pass a course. Students will not underestimate the importance of a good salary or a diploma, but they can also come to appreciate acquiring a skill which helps them relate ideas, solve problems, make sense of their experiences, and manipulate a complex symbol system to communicate their thoughts in many voices. The uniquely human ability to use language, to create meaning, enables us to share experiences and transfer knowledge. It can also separate us, especially when our use of language creates misunderstanding or deceives. Writing teachers *must* place themselves at the center of this paradox, encouraging their students to use language effectively for a variety of purposes and audiences.

Obviously, then, we teach more than comma rules and topic sentences. We teach students how writing discovers the self and shares it with others. That is not to say that we should ignore commas and messy handwriting, but we must be just as concerned about what students say as we are about how they say it. In "Imagination and Discipline in the Writing Class," Richard Gebhardt suggests that "it makes little sense for English teachers to square off in defense of either 'lock-step instruction in prose mechanics' or 'freedom that comes from avoiding the rules.' Instead, writing teachers should realize that, in spite of differences in emphasis, the teaching of writing involves both discipline and imagination" (p. 28). We must resist any inclination to define our work too narrowly. Students who know what conjunctions are but cannot use them in a sentence need our help as much as students who have "good ideas" but present them in hopelessly written form. Both the ideas and their presentation, both the product and the process that generates it, should concern us.

The significance of this broader perspective is not so much *what* it includes, but *that* it includes everything. An effective writing teacher needs to know much more than can be found in most composition texts and grammar handbooks. The "discipline" to which we belong is housed not only in English departments but also in linguistics, psychology, sociology, foreign languages, and other fields that contribute to our understanding of how human beings communicate. We are members of an interdisciplinary profession, rooted in the humanities, certainly, but borrowing important insights from the sciences and social sciences too.

An overview of this book

What, then, must we know to teach writing well? We must know both the practical and the theoretical, two senses of "knowing" which Gilbert Ryle calls knowing *how* and knowing *that:*

> In ordinary life . . . as well as in the special business of teaching, we are much more concerned with people's competences than with their cognitive repertoires, with the operations [knowing *how*] than with the truths [knowing *that*] that they learn. Indeed even when we are concerned with their intellectual excellences and deficiencies, we are interested less in the stock of truths that they acquire and retain than in their capacities to find out truths for themselves and their ability to organise and exploit them, when discovered. (*The Concept of Mind,* p. 28; bracketed material is my addition)

Most of the chapters in this book discuss the practice of teaching writing. They describe *how* we can guide students through the composing process. The pedagogical emphasis is especially evident in Chapter 6 (Prewriting Techniques), Chapter 8 (Teaching about Words), Chapter 9 (Teaching about Sentences), Chapter 10 (Teaching Paragraphing), Chapter 11 (Shaping Discourse), and Chapter 12 (Teaching Rewriting), where our performance as teachers most crucially affects our students' performance as writers. In other words, the fact *that* paragraphs have topic sentences matters less in Chapter 10 than teaching students *how* to write topic sentences and shape paragraphs. Chapter 13 (Making and Evaluating Writing Assignments) and Chapter 14 (Designing Writing Courses) also emphasize practice, suggesting strategies for making our performance as teachers more effective.

Although *how*-knowledge may seem most useful to a writing teacher, *that*-knowledge is equally important. Understandably, we find the day-to-day practice of teaching so time-consuming that we tend to disregard theoretical concerns. Reading student papers, not theory, occupies our evenings at home. Nevertheless a theoretical understanding of what writing involves is crucial to our work. In the first place, *that*-knowledge explains why particular practices seem more appropriate than others. When we command a theoretical framework which explains our activities, we are better able to evaluate student performance, revise courses, and justify our work to interested parents and administrators.

Second, *that*-knowledge helps us solve teaching problems. Suppose, for example, that you have been teaching average college freshmen. Next semester, however, you are assigned to teach advanced composition or to tutor students in a writing laboratory. If you command a sufficiently broad theoretical understanding of your work, you can apply your knowledge to the new context and avoid wasting a semester in hit-and-miss experimentation. Or, suppose a student who has been working faithfully on sentence-combining exercises suddenly begins writing sentence fragments. With a knowledge of linguistic theory, you can diagnose the problem and help the student overcome it.

Three chapters in this book are essentially theoretical: Chapter 4 (What Do Teachers Need to Know about Rhetoric?), Chapter 5 (What Do Teachers Need to Know about Cognition?), and Chapter 7 (What Do Teachers Need to Know about Linguistics?). These chapters, of course, are not meant to be comprehensive or detailed discussions. Of necessity, they can only summarize important rhetorical, psychological, and linguistic scholarship which bears on our teaching of composition. They describe principles and methodologies in other fields so that you may understand why certain teaching practices are successful given what we know, theoretically, about how human beings communicate. Chapters 4, 5, and 7 are not intended to be substitutes for primary sources. If a particular work or point of view piques your curiosity, your next step is to consult the original texts. If those texts lead you to others, so much the better.

As you will discover in reading Chapter 2 (What Is Writing?) and Chapter 3 (What Does the Process Involve?), distinctions between theory and practice are not always clean. The theories discussed in these chapters evolved from observing how people actually write. When we apply these theories to our teaching, they help us solve practical problems. But when our teaching raises questions theories cannot answer, we must revise them to incorporate what we have observed in the practice of teaching. Theory suggests practice; practice tests theory and may spawn new theories. Both *that*-knowledge and *how*-knowledge are indispensable to writing teachers. Although theories in and of themselves make fascinating study for some people, you may be tempted to slight them to get to more practical matters discussed in other chapters. Resist the temptation if you can, for theories give coherence and direction to the practical. They demonstrate the complexities of the writing process and the importance of teaching it well.

2

What is writing?

Writing is just work—there's no secret. If you dictate or use a pen or type or write with your toes—it is still just work.

SINCLAIR LEWIS

Writing is a process of communication which uses a conventional graphic system to convey a message to a reader. Let's examine that working definition:
Writing is

- a process of communication
- which uses a conventional graphic system
- to convey a message
- to a reader.

All processes of communication have elements in common. "Who says what to whom" characterizes written messages as well as spoken ones. This chapter describes those elements, the ingredients we combine in various proportions to compose written and spoken messages. How we combine them, "the *process* of communication," is the subject of Chapter 3. Although this chapter concerns itself primarily with the rhetorical context that shapes student papers, keep in mind that teaching, like writing, is a process of communication.

Classroom talk and comments written on student papers also represent messages which teachers convey to a student audience.

The working definition of *writing* given at the beginning of this chapter specifically names three elements present in any rhetorical context: a conventional graphic system, a message, and a reader. The statement "who says what to whom" introduces a fourth element, a "who" or writer. The so-called "communications triangle" (which does not include the graphic system) introduces the subject, the larger reality (topic) from which writers draw the more narrow, specific message (thesis).

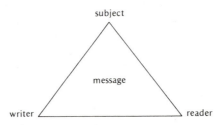

The communications triangle offers students a useful model for defining the rhetorical problem a writing assignment must solve. The terms are relatively simple, and the diagram establishes relationships between terms. In formulating questions about those relationships, we can help students plan their response to the assignment:

> What do I know about my subject? (writer-subject relationship)
>
> Who is my audience? (writer-reader relationship)
>
> What does my audience need to know to understand the subject? (reader-subject relationship)

Roman Jakobson's diagram represents a more elaborate version of the communications triangle ("Linguistics and Poetics," p. 353). His perspective is the same, but because his model contains six terms, it offers a broader view of the rhetorical context in which writing occurs. As teachers, we need a more detailed understanding of that context than we might expect of our students.

	context	
addresser	message	addressee
	contact	
	code	

Because Jakobson intended the diagram primarily to explain "factors inalienably involved in verbal communication," some of his terms differ from those used in other models. Let's examine each term as it applies specifically to writing.

The addresser

The addresser or writer composes the message. In our classes the most important addresser is the student writer, a complicated human being whose experiences, perspectives, and unique language shape every feature of written discourse. To teach well we must know as much about our students as we have time to learn and patience to discover. Otherwise, we can't determine whether our teaching enhances or interferes with their ability to write effectively.

Students, however, are not the only addressers in a classroom. Teachers too express messages, both spoken and written, and act as models for students. If we don't write, why should they? Teachers should write as frequently as they ask students to, sharing with them strategies experienced writers develop in their wars with words.

The addressee

The receiver of the message, the reader, is often ignored in traditional writing courses. Students have not had much experience writing for audiences and often have difficulty assessing even an audience of peers. Their "What do you want?" and "How long does it have to be?" reveal that they expect The Teacher to be the only reader for any writing they do. For most academic writing, the teacher really is the only audience, but students also need practice writing for themselves, for each other, for audiences outside the classroom. Teaching students how to write for increasingly diverse and complex audiences enables them to establish larger networks of social relationships. For this reason, the investigators in Britain's Schools Council Project urge writing teachers to give greater attention to the addressee:

> We want to suggest that one important dimension of development in writing ability is the growth of a sense of audience, the growth of the ability to make adjustments and choices in writing which take account of the audience for whom the writing is intended. This accommodation may be coarse or fine, highly calculated or totally intuitive, diffused through the text or explicit at particular points in it; but, whatever the form of its realization, a highly developed sense of au-

dience must be one of the marks of the competent mature writer, for it is concerned with nothing less than the implementation of his concern to maintain or establish an appropriate relationship with his reader in order to achieve his full intent. (James Britton et al., *The Development of Writing Abilities, 11–18*, p. 58)

Context

All messages come from somewhere, from some reality the writer recreates in words. *Context* refers to situations which offer the writer potential subject matter. For example, if I notice a woman stuffing a blouse into her purse on her way out of a department store, I may conclude that she stole it and out of that context frame the message "Did you pay for that?" Eventually, the experience may find its way into an editorial on shoplifting. Of course, I may have misinterpreted the experience; perhaps the woman wanted to save the store the expense of a paper bag. If so, she will respond from the context of her experience, "Yes, I paid for it. Would you like to see the receipt?" The incident now becomes potential subject matter for a discussion of appearance versus reality. Interpreting reality is a complicated process, as we will see in Chapter 5, but for now, we can define *context* to mean an entire world of subject matter or topics which writers develop into messages.

Message

Message refers to what is being said *about* the topic or subject, about the context. In a writing course the term *thesis* refers to message, to experience that is filtered, narrowed, and interpreted by the writer. When we ask students "What is the point of this essay; what is being said here?" we are asking them to restate the thesis or message. We are also discussing message whenever we talk about the organization of written discourse; its structure reflects the order we impose on our experiences in shaping what we want to say.

Contact

For communication to occur, the addresser and the addressee must somehow be in contact with each other. A physical as well as psychological connection must exist between them. In speech, contact is generally visual and auditory. Because speaker and listener occupy the same space and time, the speaker can observe signs of recognition or confusion in the listener's stance and facial expressions, revising the message to make it clearer.

In writing, contact is achieved through pen or pencil and paper, media less comfortable to use than the human voice. Some students, in fact, experience serious "writer's block" when confronted with the prospect of putting pen to paper; they freeze.[1] More than likely, their unreasonable fear stems from past teachers' finding fault with every paper. To protect themselves from making mistakes, from failing, such students simply will not write unless they fear the penalty for not writing even more than they fear writing itself. Or they may have developed poor handwriting as a defense mechanism. Realizing that they *must* write, they hope we will interpret their scrawling in their favor, reducing the number of errors they must confront when the paper is returned. Red ink, the medium for comments on student writing, also creates a strong psychological channel between student and teacher. Some students can attend to it, responding to what has become a "color of authority," while other students view it as a "color of defeat." They may be so overwhelmed by copious red marks that they cannot comprehend the message; when that happens the medium acts as a psychological barrier to communication.

Code

Code refers to the language of the message, a subject we will examine again in Chapter 7. Mathematics, braille, FORTRAN, semaphore, the International Phonetic Alphabet, Morse code, and the linguistic features of speech—all are examples of codes. The English graphic system comprises 1. alphabet letters and conventions for arranging them into words, sentences, and paragraphs; 2. a system of punctuation marks which separate the structural units of a communication—commas, periods, exclamation points, question marks, dashes, hyphens, semicolons, colons, single and double quotation marks, slash marks, apostrophes, parentheses, ellipses, brackets ([ ]), and braces ({ }); and 3. mechanical customs. Most texts define *mechanics* inadequately, but the term generally refers to matters of manuscript form rather than to conventions which express meaning. That is, mechanics determine what the text looks like rather than what it says. The writer's use of margins, indentation, italics, numerals, symbols (@

1. For a helpful discussion of "writer's block," see Mike Rose, "Rigid Rules, Inflexible Plans, and the Stifling of Language: A Cognitivist Analysis of Writer's Block," *College Composition and Communication* 31 (December 1980), 389–401.

$, %, &, and *), capital letters, abbreviations, even the convention of writing from left to right—all these belong to mechanics.

The English graphic system has a long history and, like the language itself, has changed over the years. We have gained and lost alphabet letters and redefined formal conventions. Medieval monks, for example, rarely indented their writing; parchment was simply too expensive to waste. Instead, they indicated "paragraph" by writing in a different color, adding a decorative (illuminated) letter, or changing the script. The practice of indenting paragraphs or separating blocked unindented paragraphs by a line of "white space" developed relatively recently. Conventions governing paragraph length also seem to be changing. As a rule, paragraphs tend to be shorter than they were 100 years ago, perhaps because we are accustomed to seeing overdifferentiated paragraphs in magazines, newspapers, and advertisements.

Any code is both systematic and arbitrary. The alphabet letters, punctuation marks, and mechanical customs of written English function together in predictable patterns, but the patterns are conventional. That is, we agree to use the symbols in certain ways. Other people in other times and places have communicated effectively with each other by consenting to use different graphic systems: the Cyrillic alphabet, the Germanic runic system, the ogham, the Cherokee syllabary, Hebrew script, Egyptian hieroglyphs, Sumerian cuneiform, and the Greek alphabet.

Summary and applications

Clearly our working definition, "writing is a process of communication which uses a conventional graphic system to convey a message to a reader," is not as simple as it appears. Every term, viewed in isolation, introduces a complex element to the process. The process requires a writer (addresser), a reader (addressee), a subject matter (context), one or more propositions (message) drawn from the subject matter, a channel which brings writer and reader together (contact), and a conventional system of visible marks (code). Before we examine how writers use these elements to create written discourse, the subject of Chapter 3, let me offer some suggestions for using Jakobson's diagram (or the simpler communications triangle) in the classroom.

As we have already seen, the diagram can help students plan their papers. Embedding each element in a question encourages writers to consider the dimensions of the assignment, to define a rich rhetorical problem to solve. Second, the diagram explains why writing well,

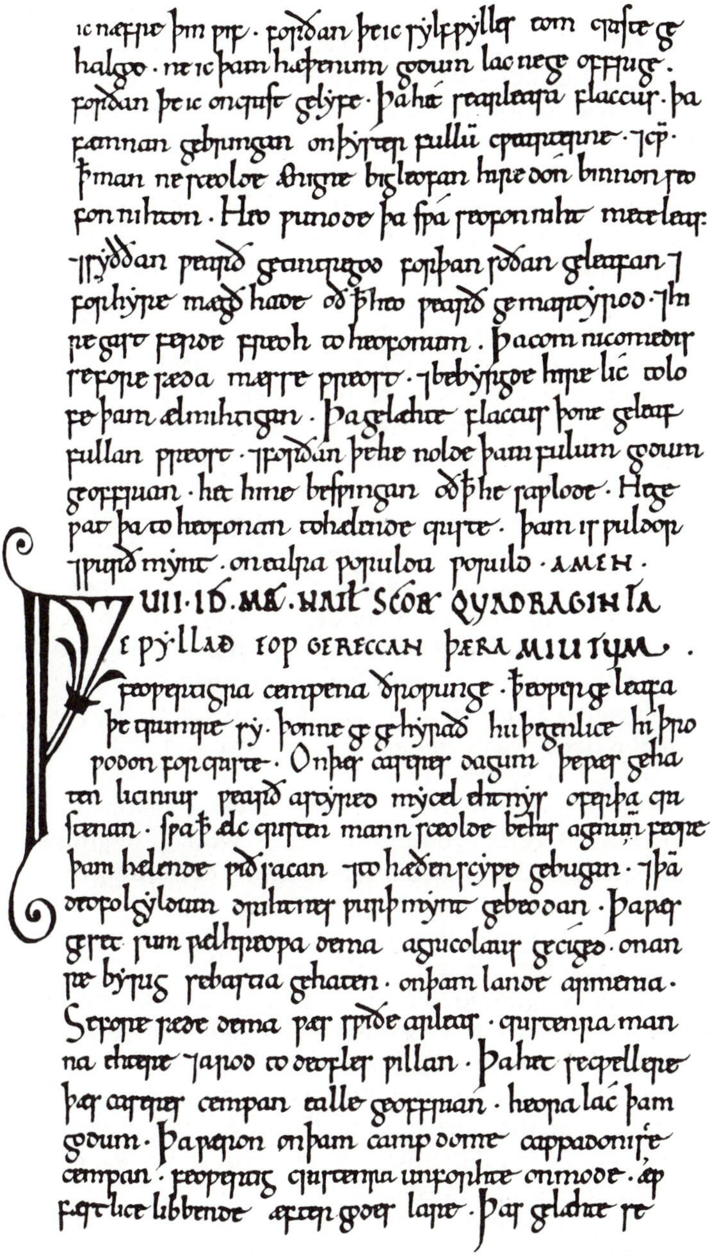

FIGURE 2.1 A page of Old English written in the early eleventh century in the Insular hand (Cotton Julius E vii f 59).

Reprinted by permission of the British Library.

balancing all of the elements effectively, is difficult. Every paper requires a slightly different balancing act. As Wayne Booth's "The Rhetorical Stance" describes, "unbalanced" stances result from a speaker's or writer's failure to adjust the subject to the needs of an audience. Students who appreciate that every assignment presents several options for treating the subject matter, audience, and so on, may also understand why there is no One Way, no Magic Pill, no single principle which solves all writing problems for all time. Third, the diagram implies that students (and teachers) must attend to all of the elements rather than focus exclusively on the code or on "good ideas." Mechanically clean papers which say nothing are as ineffective as brilliant papers which ignore the reader's expectation to find brilliance presented in reasonably punctuated sentences.

Jakobson's diagram offers a useful framework not only for explaining principles to students, but also for guiding our performance as teachers. Keeping the diagram in mind, we can draft better writing assignments, specifying more than just a topic. We can enlarge the scope of our comments on papers to address how well the student has defined a particular purpose and audience for the message. The diagram may help us correct misunderstandings which occur when we communicate with students verbally in the classroom or in conferences. Did they fail to grasp a lesson because I taught it poorly? Because they were inattentive or unprepared for class? Because the subject matter itself was difficult? Or because the code I used contained ill-defined or abstract terms?

Finally, the diagram helps us describe what Jakobson calls the "basic functions of verbal communication," which are known in traditional rhetoric as "the modes of discourse": narration, description, exposition, and argumentation. When we classify written discourse, we are saying, in effect, that the writer's purpose governed how the elements Jakobson diagrammed were combined. Although none of the elements is ignored, one may receive greater emphasis. For example, if the writer's purpose is to persuade the reader, the discourse will tend to emphasize "addressee." The traditional label for discourse which focuses primarily on the reader is *argumentation*. Jakobson claims that discourse oriented toward the addressee has a *conative* "function," while James Kinneavy in *A Theory of Discourse* maintains that it has a *persuasive* "aim."

Regardless of the label—and we have amassed a host of them over the years—we can explain various kinds of writing to students by describing which element receives the primary focus. Table 2.1 may help you organize such a discussion. The left-hand column lists each

TABLE 2.1

When the focus is primarily on the →	the purpose or aim is to →	which Jakobson calls the →	which Kinneavy calls the →	which may also be known as →	which has examples in →
writer/addresser	express the self (individual or group)	emotive function	expressive aim	"creative" writing	diaries creeds manifestos
reader/addressee	persuade the reader	conative function	persuasive aim	persuasion argument rhetoric (narrowly defined)	propaganda debates editorials sermons
reality/context	explain the world	referential function	referential aim	exposition scientific or technical writing	lab reports textbooks directions manuals
message	create a text which can be appreciated in its own right	poetic function	literary aim	narration description "imaginative" literature	movies jokes songs literary genres
contact	keep lines of communication open	phatic function			"In this paper I . . . ."
code	use language to discuss language	metalingual function		metalanguage	dictionaries grammars usage guides underlining words for emphasis*

*I am indebted to William Irmscher for pointing out that underlining words calls attention to them *as code.*

of the elements we have examined in this chapter. The sentence written across the top establishes six ways of classifying writing: by focusing on one element of the diagram; by describing the purpose or aim; by using Jakobson's terms, Kinneavy's, or those of other writers and teachers; and by citing examples. To understand how the six classification systems relate to each other, read the chart from left to right and supply the appropriate term from each column: "When the focus is primarily on the *reader/addressee,* the purpose or aim is to *persuade the reader,* which Jakobson calls the *conative function* (of discourse), which Kinneavy calls the *persuasive aim* (of discourse), which may also be called *persuasion, argument, rhetoric (narrowly defined),* and which has examples in *propaganda, debates, editorials, and sermons."*

A word of caution. Although the chart attempts to organize the many terms we use to discuss writing, it also oversimplifies matters. Most writing can't be assigned exclusively to any one category. A good dictionary may concern itself primarily with the code, but it also anticipates the needs of its readers by arranging entries in alphabetical order. An emphasis on one element doesn't deny the presence of others.

Furthermore, although the communications triangle and Jakobson's diagram conveniently list some of the *elements* present in spoken and written communication, neither diagram should be seen as a model of the *process* whereby writers make meaning.[2] Both diagrams reduce a complicated process to a few terms and ignore crucial interrelationships among the terms. Neither diagram, for example, accommodates the writer's purpose, meaning, or intention. So, although the diagrams may be helpful, they are also seductive; they can mislead us into assuming that writers translate ideas into words simply by combining "elements," like shaking together so many chemicals in a test tube. In truth, the composing process is much more complicated than that. It involves making choices, posing questions, recording and reviewing possible solutions to a writing problem, and eventually, after many tentative formulations, creating the meaning we intended to convey to a reader about our subject.

2. See especially the objections to "positivist models" that Ann E. Berthoff raises in "I.A. Richards and the Philosophy of Rhetoric," *Rhetoric Society Quarterly* 10 (Fall 1980), 195–207.

3

What does the process involve?

Writing a book was an adventure. To begin with it was a toy, an amusement; then it became a mistress, and then a master, and then a tyrant.

WINSTON CHURCHILL

What experience tells us

Writing involves not just one process but several. Most of them seem to be mental and, consequently, difficult for researchers to reconstruct. Also, the processes change depending on our age, our experiences as writers, and the kind of writing we do. Indeed, they seem as complex and varied as the people who use them. Although we are a long way from understanding completely how writers create even the simplest kinds of discourse, we can observe many activities by examining our own writing habits.

Think about the most recent significant writing you did—a letter, an article, a report, or something that required more elaborate preparation than putting together a grocery list. Try to reconstruct what you did, from beginning to end, to create the piece. What prompted you to do the writing? Why did writing serve your purposes better than speech? How much time elapsed between the "need" to write and drafting the first words? What mental processes were going on during that time?

This book, for example, evolved from my teaching. Unlike many writing tasks, the need to write it was self-imposed, prompted by reassuring comments from fellow teachers that, yes, they would find such a book helpful. But the project also gave me the chance to examine my own teaching and to read books and articles I had wanted to study. In publishing the book, I hoped to reach a large audience, many more teachers than I could speak to in a class or workshop. In the three years after I began work on the project, I digested a great deal of reading, redesigned my courses to try out new teaching methods, and talked to many writing teachers. In the process, I became a different kind of teacher, unable now to identify specifically all of the experiences and influences which shaped the ideas you are reading.

Drafting and revising the book took two years, but the procedure involved habits similar to your own. Do you complete "starting rituals"? Do you customarily begin drafting a piece in a particular place or at a particular time? Do you compose with a pen or pencil or at the typewriter? Straight through or with frequent breaks? What kinds of changes do you make as you are drafting? What kind later on? How do you determine when the piece is finished?

Most writers develop starting rituals to help them confront the blank page: cleaning house, raiding the refrigerator, sharpening pencils, tidying the desk or arranging writing materials just so, carefully copying a title onto the page. When I write, I must clear off the kitchen table, spread out books and notes I plan to use, locate an ashtray and a pack of cigarettes, and pour myself something to drink (in the mornings, coffee; in the afternoons, a diet soft drink). Although I can compose informal letters at the typewriter, I must draft significant material in pencil on long, yellow legal tablets, pausing frequently in mid-sentence to discover where the words are taking me. Like most writers, I rarely construct a formal outline, although each chapter of this book grew out of a detailed one-page list of phrases which identified the order of topics I planned to discuss. Also, like most writers, I revise as I draft, reworking sentences, substituting a word for one that doesn't quite fit, but postponing major revisions by writing marginal notes to myself. As a rule, my first draft represents agonizing effort, painstaking word-for-word labor which only here and there satisfactorily expresses what I wanted to say.

Then, I must leave the piece for a while, returning to it hours or days later to evaluate it and plan further revisions. Often, it helps me to discuss the draft with someone else. However critical another's response may be, it nevertheless suggests sources of confusion, undeveloped ideas, vague language, and alternatives for improving the piece. In the process of talking out the draft or evaluating someone else's written comments, I find my real message. If my deadline permits, I revise the piece at least twice until I'm reasonably satisfied that the words actually express what I want to say. Then I edit, proofreading for grammatical and punctuation problems. At this stage I also look up words I can't remember how to spell. At some point, however, I must stop penciling in changes and type the final draft. All the same, I make minor revisions as I type. Furthermore, when I read my "finished" work, immediately or weeks later, I always discover something else I should have attended to but didn't.

Clearly, writing is a messy business, rarely in real life as tidy as textbook descriptions portray it. We don't begin at step one, "find a topic," and follow an orderly sequence of events to "proofread the paper." Certainly, we plan what we want to say before we begin drafting, but the act of writing generates new ideas and shapes new plans. In other words, prewriting and writing can occur at the same time. So can writing (drafting) and rewriting, for we never commit words to paper without changing at least one or two here and there, in our minds as well as on the page. Unfortunately, this chapter must examine these processes sequentially, beginning from a fixed point and discussing in turn three stages of composing: prewriting, writing, and rewriting. However, as you read each section, recall your own writing experiences. They should tell you that the process isn't linear but recursive, like the forward motion of a wheel, its leading edge breaking new ground but then doubling back on itself.

Published accounts of the process

Many published sources offer information, impressions, and theories about the composing process. We can read accounts of actual writers at work—biographies, letters, writers' journals, and manuscript studies—which reveal what their authors have to say about their craft.[1] Second, we can examine theoretical discussions like those cited in Chapters 4, 5, and 7, which attempt to explain creativity and language. As teachers, however, we probably will find the most valuable information in studies which record and explain observations of student writers. Such accounts obviously have limitations. Most students can't verbalize accurately or completely what they're doing when they write; consequently, investigators can only infer from overt be-

1. See especially Malcolm Cowley, ed., *Writers at Work* (New York: Viking, 1958). Donald Murray, *A Writer Teaches Writing* (Boston: Houghton Mifflin, 1968), pp. 247–53, contains an extensive bibliography of discussions by writers about writing.

havior the feelings, attitudes, and thought processes occupying the student's mind. Even the best research design can't control or explain all of the variables, and researchers must examine considerable complex data to derive valid, reliable conclusions, often discovering that an answer to one research question raises additional problems to investigate.

Nevertheless, two studies tell us a great deal more about the composing process of students than we've ever known before. The discussion which follows is based primarily on the work of James Britton and his colleagues in Britain's Schools Council Project, *The Development of Writing Abilities, 11–18,* and on Janet Emig's *The Composing Processes of Twelfth Graders.*[2] Both investigations employ different methods, terminology, and numbers of subjects, but they substantially agree on what the process entails.

Prewriting

According to Britton, "Writing is a deliberate act; one has to make up one's mind to do it" (p. 22). The urge to write may come from within or be imposed from outside, as it is when students confront a school assignment. Nevertheless, we choose or refuse to write, either decision implying its own consequences. Deciding whether or not to write depends on the nature of the stimulus and the context. (For example, students must make a greater effort to accept a restrictive teacher-made assignment than one which permits choices.) Once aware of the need to write, we begin prewriting.

During prewriting we attempt to understand and solve the "problem" the stimulus creates for us. "In every kind of writing," maintains Britton, "defining the nature of the operation, devising ways of tackling it, and explaining its meaning and implications to oneself, are essential stages which the mind engages" (p. 90). Prewriting helps us examine what we know; we recall ideas, relate old and new information, assess what the reader expects of us, and generally explore the problem from many angles. As we stare out the window or at the blank page, our mind is consciously at work developing strategies for expressing something to somebody. We are working out answers to questions like "What is this for?" (purpose), "Who is this for?"

2. See also Sharon Pianko, "A Description of the Composing Processes of College Freshman Writers," *Research in the Teaching of English* 13 (February 1979), 5–22, and Sondra Perl, "The Composing Processes of Unskilled College Writers," *Research in the Teaching of English* 13 (December 1979), 317–36.

(audience), "What do I want to say?" (point of view on the subject), "How can I say it effectively?" (code).

Our preparations serve at least two functions. First, we begin to develop our message so that it corresponds to facts, to what we know. Second, we become comfortable with our feelings about the message, making a commitment to it that seems right for us. "An essential part of the writing process," Britton claims, "is explaining the matter to oneself" (p. 28). Planning activities seem especially crucial because they determine the writer's work in subsequent stages. Consequently, students need time to complete this stage carefully. Unfortunately, teachers often truncate prewriting, especially when they assign a paper at the beginning of a class and expect a finished product thirty minutes later. Furthermore, many teachers lack the training to suggest specific strategies that make prewriting efficient and effective. Textbooks are no help either; all but the most recent, process-centered texts scant prewriting or offer only the frustrating injunction, "Find a topic." Students are told what to do but not how. The one strategy which textbooks describe—outlining—misrepresents the practices of most writers. Like most professionals, student writers do not, as a rule, draft elaborate outlines, complete with Roman and Arabic numerals. Instead, Emig observes, they "make some kind of informal outline adapted to their individual styles of working and to the mode of the piece involved" (p. 23).

Prewriting may take anywhere from a few moments' time to many years and can be interrupted at several points, sometimes quite constructively. For example, we've all had the experience of concentrating on something else when suddenly a piece of the writing puzzle which stumped us earlier pops into our heads. That sudden insight, the "Eureka moment" or point of illumination, often occurs after we stop attending consciously to the problem and mull it over subconsciously for a while. Sometimes, what we are *not* doing during prewriting can be as significant as our conscious deliberations.

Writing

Sooner or later we begin the physical act of writing, a relatively painless decision for most people. For some, however, forcing the pencil-holding hand to make a few scrawls on the page is a torturous affair. Each letter is slowly, deliberately shaped until a certain "warm-up" period gets underway. Other writers complete "starting rituals," such as putting down a title or asking the teacher a question which may be a request for reassurance: "Can I write whatever I want?" "Does it have to be in ink?" Translation: "Getting started is a tough job for me, so please let me know that I don't have to worry about your accepting my ideas on top of everything else I'm going through just now."

> After making a start, children sometimes decide that it won't do and begin again. The strength of their conviction that a new start must be made, even though the teacher may have no complaints about what has been written, is sometimes remarkable. They are not easily persuaded to reconsider a decision to reject what they have done. Some seem to make a habit of rejecting their beginning, and rarely complete anything. These may be timid children for whom committing themselves to paper at all—"finding a tone to talk with" and "being oneself in talking"—imposes a severe strain. (*The Development of Writing Abilities, 11–18,* p. 34)

Once students make a "good start," they seem to resent interruptions from outside and concentrate intensely on their work. However, they frequently interrupt themselves, pausing for periods of three to thirty seconds on the average. During this time, facial expressions and gestures reveal frustration or pleasure with what is appearing on the page. The pauses which punctuate the act of writing serve several functions for the writer. First, they enable us to scan the text so that we can make minor alterations or write notes about major changes to make later. Second, pausing helps us look forward to plan the next idea or rephrase a thought we've begun to express. Emig notes that many experienced writers prefer to write drafts in longhand, instead of at the typewriter. Writing by hand, she suggests, slows the process down constructively so that the pauses permit half-formed ideas to develop and unexpected ideas to surface.[3]

One of the constraints on composing is the number of words or phrases we can hold in our short-term memory. Five to seven items, what we have written and what we intend to write, can be suspended until we have determined what meaning they will take:

> The fluent writer . . . can hold not only whole words and phrases, but meanings as well, and possibly even general intentions (which

3. Janet Emig, "Hand, Eye, Brain: Some 'Basics' in the Writing Process," in *Research on Composing: Points of Departure,* ed. Charles Cooper and Lee Odell (Urbana, Ill. NCTE, 1978), p. 61. Writing by hand may also be aesthetically important to some writers: "We may be able to make personal statements initially or steadily only in our own personalized script, with all of its individualities, even idiosyncrasies" (p. 61).

can scarcely be thought of as items), so that it is much easier for what is written to have coherence. If, on the other hand, the teasing out of the thought becomes particularly difficult, all the resources of the short-term memory may have to be concentrated on a few words. That is when a writer may lose the track of his thoughts, omit or repeat words, misconnect or blunder in some way. (*The Development of Writing Abilities, 11–18*, p. 45)

Britton also confirms the experience of many writers who are some-times "taken over" by their material; an idea, image, sound pattern, or sentence rhythm affects them so strongly that it controls to a de-gree what is written. This may explain the practice of some students who occasionally link all sentences with *and* (although habitual use of *and* may suggest that the student hasn't learned other varieties of sentence combining).

The act of writing principally involves expressing the message in words. Yet for most of us, the second stage requires difficult, intense work. Psychologically, we must overcome our fear of the blank page, communicate with an unresponsive piece of paper, and struggle en-tirely on our own to create meaning. Furthermore, we have to juggle several complex operations almost simultaneously, for the second stage combines writing with prewriting and rewriting. In the process of expressing our ideas, we also reshape them and plan the next brief stretch of discourse.

Rewriting

Having drafted the discourse (or a substantial section of it), most writers begin what Emig calls "reformulation," a process which in-cludes everything from correcting minor mechanical errors to chang-ing the entire piece substantially. The term *rewriting* incorporates both *revising* and *editing* (or proofreading). When we ask students to cor-rect errors in a paper, check spellings, solve subject-verb agreement problems, and straighten out punctuation, we are asking them to edit, not revise, their work. True revision involves reseeing, rethinking, and reshaping the piece, resolving a tension between what we in-tended to say and what the discourse actually says. In revising we assess the "fit" among the elements of Jakobson's diagram, and where we notice incongruities, we stop to untangle them. Both revising and editing, then, are necessary to rewriting a draft.

In rewriting, we must shift our perspective, which up to this point has focused solely on generating the text. Now we become alterna-tively a detached reader, substituting for our intended audience, and an involved reader, discovering how well we said what we hoped to. Donald Murray calls these activities external and internal revision.[4] External revision requires us to become an outsider, to be concerned with the "exterior appearance" of the discourse, its language, punctuation, and style, its overall effectiveness on the intended audience. Internal revision, the kind writers spend the most time on, requires us to please ourselves, to discover what we intended to say and where our subject, language, and voice have led us.

> During the process of internal revision, writers are not concerned with correctness in any exterior sense. They read what they have written so that they can deal with the questions of subject, of adequate information, of structure, of form of language. They move from a revision of the entire piece down to the page, the paragraph, the sentence, the line, the phrase, the word. And then, because each word may give off an explosion of meaning, they move out from the word to the phrase, the line, the sentence, the paragraph, the page, the piece. Writers move in close and then move out to visualize the entire piece. Again and again and again. ("Internal Revision: A Process of Discovery," p. 92)

As we shuttle back and forth between our two roles as readers, we change the text either to satisfy our audience or ourselves.

Most students have little experience with rewriting as we have defined it broadly here. They know to correct errors but rarely concern themselves with more than the exterior appearance of the paper. For them, rewriting is punishment, a process of correcting errors *after* the paper receives a grade. Unfortunately, writing teachers encourage this view. If we insist that all writing be neat, we unintentionally discourage students from performing the messy draftwork essential to rewriting. If our comments on student papers address only spelling, punctuation, and sentence errors, in effect we are saying that they matter most. Even if we believe that honest, logically organized, fully developed ideas are as important as correctness, students will infer our real priorities from what we mark in evaluating their work. If we fail to give students specific instruction in rewriting or classtime to work on drafts *before* they're due, we shouldn't be surprised to discover that the final paper represents only a first draft. When what we say is inconsistent with what we do, students develop mistaken notions about the importance of rewriting.

4. Donald Murray, "Internal Revision: A Process of Discovery," in *Research on Composing: Points of Departure*, ed. Charles Cooper and Lee Odell (Urbana, Ill.: NCTE, 1978), pp. 85–103.

When we have finished rewriting, the composing process ends. We stop because a deadline is at hand or because we've worked out all the possibilities that interest us in the piece. Sometimes we contemplate our work with considerable satisfaction and pride. Our students, however, do not. Emig notes that, for her twelfth-grade subjects, stopping "is a mundane moment devoid of any emotion but indifference and the mildest of satisfactions that a task is over" (p. 87). No matter how students may have viewed their achievements in the past, they seem to have learned that school-sponsored writing always "fails." It's always returned with at least one defeating comment. Lynn, one of the students in Emig's study, may be typical of others who find little pleasure in contemplating the finished work: "She seems to mean first that her teachers, on the whole, write evaluative comments that do not deal with what she is really trying to say; and that they are not really interested in reading and evaluating any reformulation she might attempt" (p. 68). Students like Lynn accuse us, perhaps justifiably, of failing to keep our readers in mind as we comment on their papers.

For better or worse, we exert a significant influence on our students' writing. To improve it, we ought to know what writers do and appreciate how complex the composing process is for most people. Because classrooms are busy places, we often lack the time to observe carefully how individual students create written messages. That is why in this chapter we've examined the process in some detail. Good writing instruction supports writing-as-process and directs attention not only to *what* students write but also to *how* they manage prewriting, writing, and rewriting. To teach well, we must concern ourselves with both the product and the process which generated it.

TWO

Rhetorical theory and practice

4

What do teachers need to know about rhetoric?

[Rhetoric] is rooted in an essential function of language itself, a function that is wholly realistic, and is continually born anew; the use of language as a symbolic means of inducing cooperation in beings that by nature use symbols.

KENNETH BURKE

Preliminary questions

The history of rhetoric covers almost 2500 years, beginning with the work of Corax of Syracuse in the fifth century B.C. and extending to present-day discussions by those who study language "as a symbolic means of inducing cooperation." Throughout its history, the discipline has accumulated principles which reflect the changing needs of those who practice it. It has experienced countless shifts of emphasis. For most of its history, rhetoric has also been associated with education. A prominent discipline in the schools for centuries, rhetoric embraces the work of teachers who studied the tradition and taught others to practice it. As writing teachers, we are part of that tradition. Consequently we ought to understand its broader currents and crosscurrents.

We also need to know about rhetoric for other reasons. It is, first of all, a compelling subject to study. Of course, many of us could teach writing without ever having read Aristotle; knowing what he said won't necessarily make us better teachers. But we shouldn't feel reluctant to study rhetoric for its own sake. We can appreciate Aristotle simply because he had important things to say. Second, a knowledge of rhetoric helps us understand our world. Kenneth Burke's definition of the art, quoted at the beginning of this chapter, asserts that all human beings practice rhetoric and come under its influence. Every day we use words to shape attitudes and encourage people to act in certain ways. In one sense, then, teaching represents a rhetorical art. We can also find language used "as a symbolic means of inducing cooperation" in literature, advertising, broadcast journalism, politics, religion, art, films, and conversation. Not all communication, of course, has a rhetorical purpose, but much of what we say, hear, read, and do involves somebody's influencing somebody else to make choices. Rhetoric is a humanistic discipline which enables us to understand those choices and the processes whereby we make them.

Important though they may be, none of these reasons for studying rhetoric applies to this chapter. Although the chapter surveys a great deal of history, that isn't its primary purpose. Nor will the chapter help you understand, except perhaps incidentally, how rhetoric functions in contemporary society. Instead, we will examine here a few significant developments which have influenced how we were taught, and how we teach, composition. As part of a centuries-old rhetorical tradition, these developments explain many contemporary teaching practices.[1] And because our profession has seen a resurgence of in-

---

1. One of the best, brief historical surveys of rhetorical developments up to the twentieth century is Edward P.J. Corbett, *Classical Rhetoric for the Modern Student,* 2nd ed. (New York: Oxford University Press, 1971), pp. 594–630. For longer surveys of rhetorical theories from the Greeks to modern times see James L. Golden, Goodwin F. Berquist, and William E. Coleman, *The Rhetoric of Western Thought,* 2nd ed. (Dubuque, Ia.: Kendall Hunt, 1978); George A. Kennedy, *Classical Rhetoric and Its Christian and Secular Tradition from Ancient to Modern Times* (Chapel Hill, N.C.: University of North Carolina Press, 1980); and Aldo Scaglione, *The Classical Theory of Composition from Its Origins to the Present: A Historical Survey* (Chapel Hill, N.C.: University of North Carolina Press, 1972).

Specific applications of rhetorical principles to contemporary teaching practices are too numerous to cite here; however, several essays in Gary Tate's *Teaching Composition: Ten Bibliographical Essays* (Fort Worth, Tex.: Texas Christian University Press, 1976) cite important works which chart the influence of the rhetorical tradition on teaching, especially Richard Young's "Invention: A Topographical Survey," pp. 1–43; Edward P.J. Corbett's "Approaches to the Study of Style," pp. 73–109; and Jim W. Corder's "Rhetorical Analysis of Writing," pp. 223–40. See also Richard M. Coe, "Rhetoric 2001," *Freshman English News* 3 (Spring 1974), 1–13; Edward P.J. Corbett, "The Usefulness of Classical Rhetoric," *College Composition and Communication* 14 (October 1963), 24–26; Robert M. Gorrell, ed., *Rhetoric: Theories for Application* (Champaign, Ill.: NCTE, 1967); Andrea Lunsford, "Aristotelian Rhetoric: Let's Get Back to the Classics," *Journal of Basic Writing* 2 (Fall/Winter 1978), 2–12; and Barry Ulanov, "The Relevance of Rhetoric," *English Journal* 55 (April 1966), 403–8.

terest in the rhetorical tradition, we need to understand something of the history of rhetoric. Specifically, we want to answer the following questions:

> What is *rhetoric* (and why do people say bad things about it)?
>
> Why do we discuss writing in terms of writer-reader-subject?
>
> What is a topic?
>
> Where did the five-paragraph theme come from?
>
> What is *style* and what explains our preference for plain, clear writing?
>
> Why do traditional courses concern themselves with grammar instruction, imitating models of good prose, and studying literature?
>
> What is a mode?
>
> How is "new" rhetoric different from classical rhetoric?

Keep these questions in mind as you read. The chapter examines each of them in order, even though the discussion focuses on major figures in the history of rhetoric. You will find that many current definitions and teaching practices were first codified thousands of years ago. Other developments evolved fairly recently. Still other customs significantly reinterpret earlier practices. Understanding these principles from a historical perspective helps us teach them effectively. More important, a sense of the past prevents us from becoming trapped by the tradition and allows us to see rhetoric as an ongoing process, meeting the needs of different cultures in different ways.

What is rhetoric?

In 2500 years the word *rhetoric* has taken on a wide range of meaning. People may use the term to refer to skillful, but often deceptive, eloquence. They point to the empty pomposity of political oratory, the slick language of advertising, or the verbal sparring of heated discussions and claim, "That's all rhetoric, empty hot air with no substance behind it." Rhetoric, so defined, is a fraudulent practice intended to give some people an advantage over others by appealing to their emotions or prejudices, but not to their intelligence. Allied with this view is the notion that rhetoric deals exclusively with language rather than with ideas. Flowery figures of speech and double-talk give the appearance of substance, while the "real questions" go unanswered. "The rhetoric was impressive," some people might say, "but he didn't tell us much." This view has had formidable support, most notably from Socrates and from Plato, who claims in the *Gorgias,* "The rhetorician need not know the truth about things; he has only to discover some way of persuading the ignorant that he has more knowledge than those who know." Although many people still attach negative connotations to the term *rhetoric,* most scholars do not. They now regard all uses of language as inherently suasive, in effect removing the onus of deception or manipulation evident in earlier discussions of the art.

Historically, *rhetoric* has also had positive connotations, suggesting a commendable skill with words. The Declaration of Independence, for example, eloquently expresses the consensus of a people persuaded to uphold certain self-evident truths. Similarly, writers of great literature have employed language powerfully to make us cry, to poke fun at our human frailties, and to command our support for important causes. Those who believe that rhetoric has a useful function see it as a tool, inherently neither good or bad. A deceitful person will use the art to deceive; an ethical person, to make truth and justice prevail. Aristotle, who regards rhetoric as a practical art, defines it in the *Rhetoric* as "the faculty [power] of discovering in the particular case . . . the available means of persuasion" (p. 7). When rightly practiced, Aristotle argues, rhetoric serves an honest and useful purpose; "we apply the term 'rhetorician' alike to describe a speaker's command of the art and a speaker's moral purpose" (p. 7).

As we will see, every historical period has characterized the tradition differently, sometimes focusing on oral discourse, sometimes on written texts. Some rhetoricians have concerned themselves exclusively with style (narrowly defined), or delivery, or invention, while others have enlarged the discipline to include many arts and forms of communication. Currently, the term *rhetoric* can even refer to books—"Open your rhetorics to page 109"—and courses—"She teaches freshman rhetoric"—which may not, in fact, treat rhetorical principles at all or which subordinate them to the study of grammar and literature.

Given the multiplicity of meanings *rhetoric* has accumulated, it may be foolish to attempt a working definition here. Yet the term identifies a discipline fundamental to this book, as its title makes clear. To insure that we are attaching roughly similar connotations to the word, let me spell out five assumptions governing my use of the term:

1. Rhetoric is both a field of humane study and a pragmatic art; that is, we can read about it as well as practice it.

2. The practice of rhetoric must be viewed as a culturally determined, interdisciplinary process. Rhetoric enables writers and speakers to design messages for particular audiences and purposes. Since people in various cultures and historical periods are likely to adopt different perspectives on what makes communication effective, rhetoric will accommodate the needs of those who practice it. Although Aristotle's description of the art is still relevant, we must not assume that rhetorical principles articulated in the past *necessarily* determine or reflect contemporary practices.

3. When we practice rhetoric, we use language, either spoken or written, to "induce cooperation" in an audience.

4. The purpose of rhetoric, inducing cooperation, involves more than mere persuasion, narrowly defined. Discourse which affects an audience, which informs, moves, delights, and teaches, has a rhetorical aim. Not all verbal or written communication aims to create an effect in an audience; the brief exchanges between people engaged in informal conversation usually do not have a rhetorical purpose. But when we use language in more formal ways, with the premeditated intention of changing attitudes or behaviors, of explaining a subject matter, of expressing the self, or of calling attention to a text which can be appreciated for its artistic merits, our purpose is rhetorical.

5. Rhetoric implies choices, for both the speaker or writer and the audience. When we practice rhetoric we design the message, first by making decisions about our subject, audience, point of view, and purpose. Then, we select our best ideas, the best order in which to present them, and the best resources of language to express them. In other words, we develop strategies for creating an effect in our audience. However, the notion of choice carries with it an important ethical responsibility. Our strategies must be reasonable and honest. Furthermore, the audience must have a choice in responding to the message, must be able to adopt, modify, or reject the message. A burglar who holds a gun to my head and calmly expresses an intention to rob me may induce my cooperation, but not by means of rhetoric. Similarly, a formal argument which urges human beings not to age is not rhetorical. Many modern rhetoricians agree that rhetoric doesn't exist when the audience lacks the power to respond freely to the message.

Classical rhetoric

In classical (Greek and Roman) rhetoric lie the sources for many contemporary practices in the teaching of writing.[2] Aristotle's three appeals—to the good will of the speaker, to the nature of the audience, to the logic of the subject matter—suggest the writer-reader-subject relationship we discussed in Chapter 1. Aristotle also introduces the term *topic,* still in use today, although our definition of it differs from Aristotle's. Classical rhetoricians consider style as one of the five "departments" of rhetoric, and by Cicero's time, three levels of style had evolved, each intended to achieve a different purpose. Even in this early period, we find a school of rhetoricians, the sophists, whose emphasis on style prompted Plato's criticism that rhetoric amounted to no more than deceitful flattery. The notion of prewriting, discussed in Chapter 3, also has its roots in classical rhetoric, for invention or ways of discovering lines of argument is another one of rhetoric's five departments. Finally, we can discover similarities between the five-paragraph theme, the staple of many writing classes, and formulas the classical rhetoricians proposed for structuring arguments. Corax of Syracuse (fl. 465 B.C.), generally thought to have composed the first written rhetoric to help Sicilian landowners win title to disputed property, proposed that legal arguments have four parts. Aristotle adopted the same four divisions, and Cicero expanded them to six. Although no classical rhetorician suggests precisely five sections, the principle *that* speeches be arranged in clearly defined sections was firmly established in the classical period.

Classical rhetoric is characterized by certain practices which distinguish it from the rhetorics of other periods. First, it was primarily a spoken, not a written, art. Second, it focused primarily on persuasive discourse, as it is traditionally defined. Rhetoric enabled politicians, lawyers, and statesmen to argue court cases (forensic or judicial rhetoric), shape political decisions about the nation's future (deliberative rhetoric), or make speeches of praise or blame on ceremonial occasions (epideictic rhetoric). When classical rhetoricians codified what had already become accepted practice, they divided rhetoric into five parts or departments: invention (*inventio,* ways of discovering relevant ideas and supporting evidence), arrangement (*dispositio,* ways of organizing the parts of a discourse), style (*elocutio,* ways of ornamenting discourse), memory (*memoria,* mnemonic techniques), and

---

2. Useful histories of Greek and Roman rhetoric are George Kennedy, *The Art of Persuasion in Greece* (Princeton, N.J.: Princeton University Press, 1963) and his *The Art of Rhetoric in the Roman World* (Princeton, N.J.: Princeton University Press, 1972).

delivery (*pronuntiatio*, techniques for practicing and giving oral speeches). The most influential works which describe the practice of classical rhetoricians are the *Rhetoric* of Aristotle (384–322 B.C.), Cicero's *De inventione* and *De oratore,* and Quintilian's *Institutio oratoria.*

Aristotle's *Rhetoric* is divided into three books, which treat respectively the nature of rhetoric, of invention, and of arrangement and style. For Aristotle, universal and verifiable truths belong to the science of logic; rhetoric, he maintains, deals with *probable* truth, with opinions and beliefs that can be advanced with greater or lesser certainty. He groups all arguments into two categories based on the kinds of proof used to support what the speaker believes to be true. Inartistic proofs make use of external evidence such as witnesses, contracts, evidence based on torture. Artistic proofs, on the other hand, rely on three means of persuasion. The speaker may argue from his own personal qualities as a sensible, moral man of good will (*ethos*). Or, he may appeal to the character or mental state of the audience (*pathos*). Or, he may argue from the subject matter (*logos*) by using the inductive logic of examples and the deductive logic of enthymemes.

Aristotle's *Rhetoric* also introduces the notion of topics (*topoi* or commonplaces). However, by *topoi* (Greek for "places") Aristotle means not a list of subjects, but ways in which arguments applying to any subject matter can be discovered. In Book Two of the *Rhetoric,* Aristotle illustrates twenty-eight *topoi* for inventing enthymemes. The *topoi* represent lines of inquiry—such as arguing from opposites, from cause and effect, from the definitions of words, from parts to the whole, and so on. These discovery procedures receive further elaboration in Aristotle's *Topics,* a work which Cicero later interpreted to include topics-as-subjects as well as topics-as-methods-of-inquiry. Much later, in Renaissance England, the *topoi* came to mean "commonplaces," subjects to write about. The usual definition of *topic* in today's English classes is "subject for writing about," not "way of approaching any subject."

In Book Three Aristotle maintains that arguments should have two parts; the first part states the case, and the second proves it. At most, arguments should have only four sections: the introduction (*proem*), the outline or narration of the subject (*statement* of the case), the proofs for and against the case (the *argument*), and the summary (*epilogue*). Believing that a discourse persuades by reason rather than by calling attention to itself as a work of art, Aristotle advocates a plain or natural style which exhibits the virtues of clarity, dignity, propriety, and correctness. This view of style contrasts significantly with rhetorical traditions that precede and follow Aristotle—the Greek sophistic tradition of the fifth and fourth centuries B.C. and the Ciceronian tradition. The sophists emphasized style above all. It is to this dependence on ornamentation that Plato responds in the *Gorgias* by castigating rhetoric as an ignoble deceit, an attempt to flatter the audience. For Aristotle, though, rhetoric in itself was neither good nor bad; its tools could be used for good or evil purposes.

Cicero (106–43 B.C.), a brilliant Roman politician, philosopher, and speaker, expected the orator to command a broad understanding of culture:

> no one should be numbered with the orators who is not accomplished in all those arts that befit the well-bred; for though we do not actually parade these in our discourse, it is none the less made clear to demonstration whether we are strangers to them or have learned to know them. (*De oratore,* p. 100)

The orator must know a great deal about human experience in order to defend the political state eloquently. For Cicero, rhetoric is a branch of political science, if we define *political science* broadly, as "the liberal arts."

Cicero composed at least seven rhetorical treatises, one on invention when he was only nineteen years old. He also wrote numerous orations and epistles, which generations of students studied as models of the theoretical principles he outlined. He expanded the parts of an argument from four to six, dividing Aristotle's section on the proofs into separate categories: *exordium* (introduction), *narratio* (a discussion of what has occurred to generate the issue to be resolved), *partitio* (a division of the argument or outline of the points to be proven), *confirmatio* (proofs "for" or confirmation of the argument), *refutatio* (proofs disproving the opponent's arguments), and *conclusio* (a review of the argument and a final appeal to the audience). Because the *Rhetorica ad herennium* for centuries was thought to have been written by Cicero, we credit him with having suggested three levels of style—high, middle, and low—intended respectively to move, delight, and teach the audience. Cicero's treatises tend to emphasize forensics, the use of rhetoric to argue legal cases, but because he believed that the orator needed to know many subjects, Cicero's influence had special significance during the Renaissance, with its emphasis on the humanistic training of clergy and statesmen.

Quintilian (A.D. 35–96) was born in Spain but later became a prominent teacher of rhetoric in Rome. He agrees with Cicero that the rhetor must be broadly educated but asserts that he must also be a good and moral man. Educational institutions from the Middle Ages to the twentieth century reflect Quintilian's insistence on the moral as well as the intellectual training of students. Although books three through twelve of Quintilian's *Institutio oratoria* represent traditional Ciceronian discussions of the five departments of rhetoric, books one and two detail an educational program for training the ideal orator of strong moral character.

As soon as he was able to read and write, the child received instruction in grammar, which was for Quintilian a twofold science that encompassed speaking and writing correctly as well as interpreting the poets. The grammar teacher (*grammaticus*) taught rules for proper word order, agreement, and word choice, and gave lectures on every kind of writer. In this way students could learn by imitation to recite and comment on literature, noting the type of feet in a metrical line, the parts of speech in a line, and so on. Then, students proceeded to write their own imitations of fables and verse as well as aphorisms, character sketches, and moral essays. Paraphrasing or imitating models was the major method of teaching grammar. After the child completed grammar instruction, the *rhetoricus,* a second teacher, then managed the student's education. The *rhetoricus* taught more advanced rhetorical studies and assigned exercises in epideictic speaking and disputation. In general, he taught students to master the five departments of classical rhetoric. Grammatical studies, then, gave students an understanding of what correct discourse and poetic interpretation entails (knowledge of *what*); rhetorical studies equipped them to accomplish things by action (knowledge of *how*).

Quintilian's curriculum sounds similar to some contemporary writing courses, doesn't it? Even though classical rhetoric excluded grammar (grammar, like logic, was a separate discipline), Quintilian codified a hierarchy of instruction which began with grammar and proceeded to rhetorical studies. Nowadays many people still believe that students must study formal grammar before they can take writing courses. Notice too that Quintilian incorporates writing into the curriculum; he valued training in writing as a means of reinforcing speaking skills. Then, as now, literature served an important function in the classroom, for the most important methods Quintilian used to develop writing skill were imitating, translating, or paraphrasing literary models. Quintilian's model certainly isn't the only design for a writing course, and many contemporary writing teachers give the study of grammar and literature much less prominence than Quintilian did. Nevertheless, most of us probably were taught to write by methods at least indirectly traceable to Quintilian.

Medieval and Renaissance rhetoric

Although the classical tradition survived more or less intact throughout the Middle Ages and the Renaissance, two developments especially interest us as writing teachers. First, rhetoric became both a practical art and an academic subject. Rhetorical treatises and commentaries were studied by Scholastic philosophers. Cicero was favored as a classical authority until about the thirteenth century, when Aristotle's *Rhetoric* was recovered in a Latin translation. As a practical art, rhetoric served the clergy, whose sermons persuaded congregations to accept Christianity, and secular or ecclesiastical courts, where letter-writing was an essential means of conducting legal and diplomatic transactions. Second, style (*elocutio*) began to assume greater importance, together with delivery dominating the other four departments of classical rhetoric. Through the influence of Christianity, invention became less significant, for biblical truths were inspired or "invented" by God; principles of style, however, helped men study God's Word and explain it to others. This attention to the Bible as a text, aided later by the development of the printing press, gave rhetoric a new focus. Whereas classical rhetoric had been concerned primarily with spoken discourse, medieval and Renaissance scholars increasingly applied rhetorical principles to written discourse.

In the Middle Ages, undergraduate students pursuing the bachelor of arts degree studied the *trivium:* grammar (*ars poetria* or verse-writing), logic, and rhetoric. Graduate students received additional training in the disciplines which made up the *quadrivium:* arithmetic, astronomy, music, and geometry. The study of rhetoric was divided into two arts, letter-writing (*ars dictaminis*), and preaching (*ars praedicandi*).[3] Both arts were heavily influenced by the so-called "Second Sophistic Tradition" (ca. A.D. 100–500) and writers like Cassiodorus and Bishop Isidore of Seville.

Cassiodorus (A.D. 490–586), minister to an illiterate Italian king, compiled twelve books of letters under the title *Variae*. Kings and nobles during this period often depended on literate servants to compose, write down, and deliver orally any messages of considerable

---

3. For a fuller discussion of medieval rhetoric, consult James F. Murphy, *Rhetoric in the Middle Ages* (Berkeley, Calif.: University of California Press, 1974).

political importance. Students in the Middle Ages studied model letters like those of Cassiodorus and learned how to imitate their formulas and stylistic embellishments.

Style is also the chief concern of Bishop Isidore of Seville (ca. A.D. 570–636). His work, known variously as *Origenes* or *Etymologiae*, devotes considerable attention to summarizing the arts of grammar, rhetoric, and dialectic. "Like other encyclopedists," writes James Murphy, "he was trying merely to salvage what he could from the ancient heritage" (*Rhetoric in the Middle Ages*, p. 76). In cataloguing many traditional rhetorical figures, Isidore slights invention and arrangement and altogether ignores memory and delivery.

The sophists' concern with ornamentation can be traced back to the three Ciceronian levels of style: the grand style intended to move an audience, the middle style intended to delight an audience, and the plain style intended to teach an audience. To move a congregation to accept Christianity or to teach Christian precepts, the clergy ornamented sermons and letters with "figures" which had been conveniently catalogued in many stylistic compendia. The anonymously authored *Rhetorica ad herennium* (ca. 86 B.C.) enjoyed enormous popularity as a standard list. Although the "doctrine of figures" had been well established in Quintilian's day, the tradition has defied the attempts of scholars to trace its shifting, growing classifications. Essentially, the figures were of two kinds: 1. *tropes* or figures of thought or sense (e.g., metaphor, metonymy, synecdoche), and 2. *schemes* or figures of words and arrangement (e.g., amplifying or repeating an idea, alliteration, assonance). The figures weren't merely ornamental; they often reflected strategies of invention and arrangement.

As Corbett points out in *Classical Rhetoric for the Modern Student* (p. 605), Renaissance rhetoricians were also preoccupied with words, particularly with the distinction between words and the "things" they stood for, between *verba* and *res*, form and matter. Sister Miriam Joseph divides Renaissance rhetoricians into three groups: the traditionalists, the figurists, and the Ramists. The differences among them, she suggests, center on whether they viewed the topics of invention as belonging to rhetoric, to logic, or to both—a moot question really, since "notwithstanding the variety of opinion as to the number of topics or places, there was complete unanimity among all Renaissance groups as to their nature, use, and importance" (*Rhetoric in Shakespeare's Time*, p. 30).

The traditionalists, among them Desiderius Erasmus and Thomas Wilson, tended to appreciate the importance of all five departments of rhetoric. Erasmus' *De Copia* (1512) is divided into two parts, the first teaching students how to vary their arguments by means of schemes and tropes and the second encouraging students to master lines of inquiry (topics) in order to be able to invent subjects in a variety of ways. Even though words and things, form and matter, are treated separately, there is a close Aristotelian connection between them. Erasmus was probably the first to advocate constant practice in writing rather than rote drill as a teaching technique. He encouraged students to keep commonplace books as an aid to invention, to express the same argument in a variety of styles, and to treat the same topic along several lines of reasoning. Thomas Wilson's *Arte of Rhetorique* (1553) presents the whole classical tradition in its five parts. It reintroduces a discussion of memory and delivery, often slighted in earlier works, and because it was one of the first rhetorics written in English rather than in Latin, it enjoyed considerable popularity as a model of English prose style.

The second group of rhetoricians, the figurists, subordinated logic to rhetoric, emphasizing above all the importance of style. George Puttenham's *The Arte of English Poesie* (1589), which treats 107 figures, and Henry Peacham's *The Garden of Eloquence* (1577), which catalogues 184 figures, are important representatives of this tradition. A third group, the Ramists, tended to subordinate rhetoric to logic. By assigning invention, arrangement, and memory to logic, and grouping style and delivery under rhetoric, in effect they created a dichotomy between matter and form, between processes which they said belonged to the intellect (logic) and those which sprang from the imagination (rhetoric).

Both Corbett and Joseph conclude that Renaissance rhetoricians were master classifiers and cataloguers concerned primarily about the matter of *copia,* literally "abundance." *Copia* refers not only to various techniques for embellishing the argument, but also to the many ways in which arguments could be invented. The poets and prose writers who studied these techniques produced a literature as rich in imagery and sound patterns as it was thoughtful and deeply rooted in logic.

The Renaissance to the twentieth century

In the centuries following the Renaissance several approaches to rhetoric held the field in what W. Ross Winterowd calls "the war between the plain, unadorned method of human discourse and the elegant and ornate" (*Rhetoric: A Synthesis,* p. 46). The war centered on a difference of opinion among prominent scholars who sought to adapt classical principles to new developments in literature and the sciences. In blending the old and new, however, they tended to emphasize different elements of the tradition. Throughout this period, at least three points of view shape rhetorical theory: the scientific, elocutionary, and literary perspectives. Although our current methods of teaching writing were not significantly influenced by any of these perspectives except perhaps the literary, all three support the principle that rhetoric is a dynamic process. It finds its roots not only in the past but also in contemporary concerns. People change the art to suit their purposes.

The scientific perspective stresses the importance of invention and advocates a plain style. It represents an attempt to adapt rhetoric to the emerging natural and social sciences. Although Francis Bacon (1561–1626) wrote no rhetorical treatises, many of his writings suggest new directions for rhetoric in the service of scientific studies. Bacon separates logic and rhetoric, reason and imagination, as distinct faculties which nevertheless must work harmoniously. "The duty and office of Rhetoric is to apply Reason to Imagination for the better moving of the Will," writes Bacon in *Advancement of Learning*. In redefining invention, he minimizes the classical penchant for the deductive enthymeme, giving greater significance to inductive processes and memory, which help the scientist unlock knowledge stored in the mind. Bacon also advocates a "Senecan Style," characterized by relatively short sentences, simple words, and little ornamentation. In his view, the style should suit the subject matter and the audience. A plain style, a code similar to mathematics, best expresses the precise, objective observations of scientists.

In some ways, George Campbell (1719–96) also approaches rhetoric scientifically by incorporating principles from what we now call the social and behavioral sciences. Although upholding many precepts of classical rhetoric, Campbell's work is also influenced by Bacon, Locke, Hume, and Hartley, writers who attempted to explain the workings of the human mind. As the first sentence of Campbell's *Philosophy and Rhetoric* (1776) reveals, rhetoric is a process of effecting change in an audience: "In speaking there is always some end proposed, or some effect which the speaker intends to produce on the hearer." To be effective, rhetoricians must understand human nature, must analyze the audience they hope to influence. Elaborating on Locke and Hume's discussions, Campbell proposes a hierarchy of four mental "faculties" common to all human beings: an understanding, an imagination, passions, and a will. Although the speaker may have one predominant purpose—"to enlighten the understanding, to please the imagination, to move the passions, or to influence the will"—a speech may introduce secondary rhetorical aims which enhance its persuasive power. Campbell is best known for reestablishing an important connection between rhetoric and psychology, between the arts of eloquence a speaker uses and their effect on an audience. Nevertheless he also explored the use of wit, humor, and ridicule as rhetorical strategies; examined the limitations of the deductive syllogism; enlarged the kinds of evidence which could be used to support arguments, including common sense, experience, analogy, testimony, and "calculations concerning chances"; and established what is now known as the "doctrine of usage," which suggests that generalizations about language should be based not on classical "authorities" but on the contemporary practices of reputable English authors.

A second perspective on rhetoric emphasized delivery. Like Bacon and Campbell, the elocutionists hoped to give classical rhetoric a contemporary focus, but the principle aim of the elocutionary movement was to advance the art of public speaking. For too long, elocutionists claimed, rhetoricians had ignored delivery and emphasized the written word. But now public lectures, oral reading, parliamentary debates, and pulpit oratory offered numerous opportunities to express ideas orally. Thomas Sheridan's *Lectures on Elocution* (1762) and John Walker's *Elements of Elocution* (1781) offered speakers advice about pronunciation, gestures, voice control, and accent. Other elocutionary texts listed tropes and schemes for ornamenting speeches and provided models, often in the form of letters, for addressing various audiences in an elegant, genteel style. Very often prose and verse passages were included to give students practice reading material aloud. Although elocutionists didn't ignore invention altogether, in effect they reduced rhetoric to delivery and style and limited its practice to formal spoken contexts. As public speaking declined in importance, so did the elocutionary movement. Nevertheless, the elocutionists demonstrated that delivery could be studied seriously, and not only studied, but practiced. Although nowadays courses in public speaking tend to lie buried in theater or speech departments, we might well improve our teaching performance by investigating the more significant principles the elocutionary movement advanced.

The third perspective focused not so much on public speaking or the new science as on literary texts. The literary perspective, however, encompasses a spectrum of views concerning style. First, the neoclassicists, men like Jonathan Swift (1667–1745) and Jonathan Ward (d. 1758), revered the ancients and sought to reassert principles of taste built on classical precepts. A good writer, they maintained, studies classical authors and then imitates their style. The works of Horace, Homer, Virgil, and Cicero represented especially significant models. A good style, said the neoclassicists, need not show complete originality, need not be "modern." Rather, it should be relatively unadorned, free of ambiguity, and "correct," conforming to the style of Greek and Latin models. *Propriety* and *perspicuity* were the watchwords, and rhetorical choices tended to be primarily a matter of doctrine and rule. In reestablishing the importance of classical learning, these prominent men of letters hoped to give the English language the same power of expression they admired so much in Greek and Latin literature. Unfortunately, by slavishly adhering to classical principles and denigrating modern tastes, many of them reduced style to absolute law.

At the other end of the scale were literary scholars who admired the ornate style and revived the study of invention. They claimed as their authority Longinus, a third-century Roman whose treatise *On the Sublime* had been translated into English in 1674. Longinus recognized enthusiasm as a respectable source of ideas. Rhetoric, he claimed, need not merely persuade audiences; it could also transport them. Writers like Joseph Addison (1672–1719) and Edmund Burke (1729–97) placed great emphasis on sublimity of thought as well as style. The "sublime" that Longinus discussed arises from contemplating greatness, from permitting the beautiful to act on the mind through the senses. Sublimity of style moves an audience with irresistible power, grand thoughts, and eloquent expression. The followers of Longinus yielded to their emotions, to forces of enthusiasm, in order to create, especially through metaphor, expressions which would transport their audience.

In between these two groups, the proponents of enthusiasm and the advocates of propriety, we find a large group of rhetoricians who blended the old and the new. They combined rhetoric and poetics, which the classical tradition had treated as separate verbal arts. They illustrated rhetorical principles, not by quoting Greek and Latin models, but by citing English literature. They looked to classical theories but also took into account contemporary discussions concerning genius, reason, and imagination. This synthesis represents the beginning of modern literary criticism and is best illustrated in the work of Hugh Blair (1718–1800).

Blair, a well-known preacher, was Regius Professor of Rhetoric and Belles Lettres at the University of Edinburgh for more than twenty years, retiring in 1783. *Lectures on Rhetoric and Belles Lettres* was published in the same year. "Blair explains in the preface that many students, relying on superficial notes, were circulating imperfect copies of his lectures. The purpose of the volume, therefore, was to give to the public an accurate account of his teachings."[4] Addressing his forty-seven lectures to beginners, Blair presents a systematic overview of rhetoric-as-verbal-art. He deals with matters of taste and aesthetics, surveys classical and contemporary rhetoric, reviews grammar, offers a history of elocution, and explains stylistic principles by analyzing the prose of Addison and Swift. Although he prefers the plain style, he doesn't refute the Longinians' emphasis on the sublime. The sublime, he maintains, rests not in words but in things, not in stylistic adroitness but in noble and pleasurable ideas. For their time Blair's lectures offered the most comprehensive survey of the rhetorical tradition. They were enormously popular. In addition to summarizing the old, however, they also forge a new alliance between rhetoric and other verbal arts. For Blair, rhetoric doesn't focus merely on style, plain or ornate, but on culture, on human beings and how they use language to communicate with different audiences for different purposes.

Blair's *Lectures on Rhetoric and Belles Lettres* served as a popular textbook in colleges and universities, not only in England and Scotland but in America as well. Yale adopted it in 1785, Harvard in 1788, and Dartmouth in 1822.[5] The study of English in American universities, however, is a relatively recent development, generally considered to have begun in 1806, when John Quincy Adams became Boyleston Professor of Rhetoric and Oratory at Harvard. Throughout the first half of the nineteenth century, the impetus to add courses in English to the college curriculum was supported by scholarly developments in philology, the forerunner of modern linguistics, and by a popular interest in public lectures and debates. At first, these courses emphasized oratory, rhetoric, and the study of language and logic; as a rule, they were taught by clergymen, historians, or philosophers. In addition to Blair's *Lectures,* other texts enjoyed considerable influence: Thomas Sheridan's *Lectures on Elocution* (1762), Richard Whateley's *Elements of Rhetoric* (1828), and Alexander Bain's *English Composition and Rhetoric* (1866). Although courses in the reading and

4. Golden, Berquist, and Coleman, p. 95; see also James L. Golden and Edward P.J. Corbett, eds., *The Rhetoric of Blair, Campbell, and Whately* (New York: Holt, Rinehart and Winston, 1968).

5. William Riley Parker, "Where Do English Departments Come From?" in *The Writing Teacher's Sourcebook,* ed. Gary Tate and Edward P.J. Corbett (New York: Oxford University Press, 1981), p. 8.

analysis of English literature were not to become part of the curriculum until the second half of the nineteenth century, by 1883 forty college teachers, representing twenty institutions, met in New York to establish the Modern Language Association. Most of the faculty members present taught modern foreign languages, but English teachers joined them in asserting "the disciplinary value of the modern as compared with the ancient languages" [Latin and Greek].[6] By the end of the century, the contributions of British and Scottish rhetoricians and philosophers to the centuries-old history of rhetoric had found a place in the curriculum of most major American universities.

Contemporary rhetoric

The twentieth century has seen a resurgence of interest in rhetoric. Modern scholars have continued to build on centuries-old traditions, reinterpreting them to assert the importance of human communication here and now. Authors like I.A. Richards, Kenneth Burke, Chaim Perelman, Richard Weaver, Stephen Toulmin, and Marshall McLuhan view rhetoric from quite different perspectives, but they're all principally concerned with the uses of language in a complex society. Some focus on questions of meaning, on how we use language and other media to make sense of our world. Others, like Weaver, concern themselves with ethics: "As rhetoric confronts us with choices involving values, the rhetorician is a preacher to us, noble if he tries to direct our passion toward noble ends and base if he uses our passion to confuse and degrade us" (*Language Is Sermonic*, p. 179). Still others value rhetoric as a means of knowing. For them, language is crucial to thinking, to advancing human knowledge. Toulmin, for example, who finds formal syllogistic logic impractical, develops a model for arguments which uses language not so much to proclaim truth but to foster understanding. Finally, some contemporary rhetoricians explore the impact of language on political and social relationships, viewing rhetoric as an instrument of social change. In some ways, of course, the "new" rhetoric isn't new; it reaches back to the classical tradition. But it also incorporates recent perspectives from linguistics, anthropology, psychology, philosophy, semantics, politics, and even advertising to synthesize the arts of rhetoric our culture now practices.

We won't survey here all of the significant contemporary develop-

6. [George Winchester Stone], "The Beginning, Development, and Impact of the MLA as a Learned Society: 1883–1958," *Publications of the Modern Language Association of America* 73 (December 1958), 25.

ments in rhetoric. Some of them will be discussed later, when we can examine particular teaching strategies in light of current theories. So, although prewriting, for example, reflects a renewed interest in invention, we'll examine that contemporary development more closely in Chapters 5 and 6. In this section the discussion focuses on two individuals often cited in the professional literature English teachers read, Kenneth Burke and James Kinneavy.

Kenneth Burke (1897–   ) has had the greatest impact on rhetoric in the twentieth century. Since the publication of *Counter-Statement* (1931), a succession of books articulate Burke's concern with the problem of language. "To his thorough knowledge of classical tradition," writes Marie Hochmuth, "he has added rich insights gained from serious study of anthropology, sociology, history, psychology, philosophy, and the whole body of humane letters."[7] Although essentially a philosopher, Burke views rhetoric so comprehensively that social scientists and humanists, especially literary critics, find his work valuable. Instead of placing inordinate emphasis on persuasion, or style, or literary criticism, Burke enlarges the scope of rhetoric to include all of the "symbolic means of inducing cooperation in beings that by nature respond to symbols" (*A Rhetoric of Motives*, p. 43).

Human beings, asserts Burke, are linguistic animals, using and misusing symbols. Rhetoric is a function of language which enables human beings to overcome the divisions separating them. Since human beings are, most of the time, at odds with one another, language permits them to "induce cooperation," to identify themselves with other individuals:

> If I had to sum up in one word the differences between the "old" rhetoric and a "new" (a rhetoric reinvigorated by fresh insights which the "new sciences" contributed to the subject), I would reduce it to this: The key term for the old rhetoric was "persuasion" and its stress was upon deliberate design. They key term for the "new" rhetoric would be "identification," which can include a partially "unconscious" factor in appeal. "Indentification" at its simplest is also a deliberative device, as when the politician seeks to identify himself with his audience. In this respect, its equivalents are plentiful in Aristotle's *Rhetoric*. But identification can also be an end, as when people earnestly yearn to identify themselves with some group or other. Here they are not necessarily being acted upon by a conscious external

7. Marie Hochmuth, "Kenneth Burke and the 'New Rhetoric,' " *Quarterly Journal of Speech* 38 (April 1952), p. 144; the essay offers an excellent overview of Burke's work and serves as my principal source for the following discussion.

agent, but may be acting upon themselves to this end. ("Rhetoric— Old and New," p. 63)

Identification is a key concept in Burke's theory of rhetoric; it explains why human beings act rhetorically on one another—to promote social cohesion.

The central question Burke investigates is, "What is involved, when we say what people are doing and why they are doing it?" (*A Grammar of Motives*, p. xv). In other words, he concerns himself with attributing motives to human actions. Instead of viewing motive in simple, mechanistic terms like "cause and effect" or "stimulus and response," Burke approaches the study of motivation through the analysis of drama. *Motive* acts as a kind of shorthand term for *situation*:

> In a rounded statement about motives, you must have some word that names the *act* (names what took place, in thought or deed), and another that names the *scene* (the background of the act, the situation in which it occurred); also, you must indicate what person or kind of person (*agent*) performed the act, what means or instruments he used (*agency*), and the *purpose*. Men may violently disagree about the purposes behind a given act, or about the character of the person who did it, or how he did it, or in what kind of situation he acted; or they may even insist upon totally different words to name the act itself. But be that as it may, any complete statement about motives will offer *some kind of* answers to these five questions: what was done (act), when or where it was done (scene), who did it (agent), how he did it (agency), and why (purpose). (*A Grammar of Motives*, p. xv)

These five terms—act, scene, agent, agency, and purpose—become the "pentad" for examining human motivation dramatistically, in terms of action and its ends.

Burke's rhetoric of motives helps us understand human relations in terms of "signs," not just spoken language but also nonverbal communication which achieves identification. For example, regardless of what a department head may say to me when he visits my office, the visit itself represents a symbolic, nonverbal action associated with administrative rhetoric. Meeting me on my "territory" suggests that he identifies himself with my concerns, a rhetorical strategy more likely to induce my cooperation than if he had summoned me to his office. Similarly, the tendency toward identification is reflected in symbolic actions like signing a petition, attending a social function because we ought to make an appearance, remembering someone's birthday, or carefully selecting the clothes we wear on the first day of class.

Burke's major contribution to rhetorical theory is his attempt to broaden its scope. In *A Rhetoric of Motives*, he redefines *persuasion*: "All told, persuasion ranges from the bluntest quest of advantage, as in sales promotion or propaganda, through courtship, social etiquette, education, and the sermon, to a 'pure' form that delights in the process of appeal for itself alone, without ulterior purpose" (p. xiv). More important, Burke reasserts the importance of rhetoric at a time when most people have become conscious of the dehumanizing influence of technology. Rhetoric functions, he argues, not to ornament arguments or even to assert truths. Rather, it uses symbols as a means whereby human beings act out with each other the drama of life.

Much more limited in scope, James Kinneavy's *A Theory of Discourse* (1971) nevertheless brings together with extraordinary comprehensiveness classical and contemporary developments in rhetoric. His theory is essentially Aristotelian, but it also incorporates the perspectives of modern linguists, logicians, semioticians, propaganda analysts, literary critics, philosophers, information theorists, and social scientists. Kinneavy avoids the term *rhetoric*, primarily because it has taken on meanings as broad as "the general science or art of communication" and as restricted as "style." He focuses instead on the term *discourse*, "the full text . . . of an oral or written situation."[8] His work gives us a framework for understanding what is produced when people practice rhetoric, using language purposefully to communicate ideas to an audience. His theory certainly includes a discussion of rhetoric-as-persuasion, but it also examines other purposes for oral and written communication.

Beginning with the communication triangle (encoder, decoder, reality, signal), Kinneavy divides the field of English into three areas of study, which explain human experience with some element of the triangle. (See Fig. 4.1). Only one of these areas, pragmatics, concerns us here. Pragmatics studies the actual *use* of meaningful signals by encoders and decoders. Viewed as the study of texts, pragmatics de-

8. James Kinneavy, *A Theory of Discourse* (Englewood Cliffs, N.J.: Prentice-Hall, 1971), p. 4. Kinneavy summarizes his *Theory of Discourse* and compares it to James Moffett's *Teaching the Universe of Discourse*, Frank D'Angelo's *A Conceptual Theory of Rhetoric*, and James Britton's *The Development of Writing Abilities, 11–18* in "A Pluralistic Synthesis of Four Contemporary Models for Teaching Composition," in *Reinventing the Rhetorical Tradition*, ed. Aviva Freedman and Ian Pringle (Conway, Ark.: L & S Books, 1980), pp. 37–52.

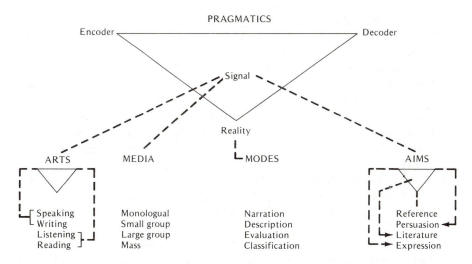

FIGURE 4.1   Pragmatics: The Study of Texts

Adapted from James Kinneavy, *A Theory of Discourse* (Englewood Cliffs, N.J.: Prentice-Hall, 1971).

pends on all four terms in the communication triangle because every discourse, every spoken or written text, is characterized by an author who uses signals to communicate a reality for a particular purpose.

Kinneavy subdivides pragmatics into the arts, media, modes, and aims of discourse. The arts—speaking, writing, listening, and reading—reflect differences in the kinds of signals that encoders and decoders use and how they process these signals. The media define the *channels* through which the signal is transmitted. "In other words, arts of discourse are signals transmitted through various media of discourse" (p. 33). Media can be classified according to the number of encoders and decoders using the channels at a given time. From monologual to mass media, Kinneavy's classification includes lectures, soliloquies, telephone calls, counseling sessions, panels, questionnaires, conventions, newspapers, and television.

The term *mode* is difficult to define because it has accumulated multiple meanings over the years. Alexander Bain, in *English Composition and Rhetoric* (1866), established five modes, four of which are still found in many contemporary textbooks: narration, description, exposition, and argumentation. In all probability, Bain's modes were adaptations of the classical "topics" of invention which, in time, came to denote ways of arranging material. However, Kinneavy notes that argumentation or persuasion is not a mode, but an aim of discourse, not a method or way of discussing reality, but a reason or purpose for using language. Consequently, he revises the traditional classification of modes to include narration, description, evaluation, and classification.

For Kinneavy, the term *mode* denotes the kinds of realities discourse refers to. Modes answer the question, "What is this text about?" We're naming modes when we respond to this question with "It's a story (narration)," "It's a description of my dog," "It's a criticism (evaluation) of President Reagan's energy policy," or "It's a discussion of the types (classification) of college students." Each mode, Kinneavy maintains, is grounded in a principle of thought which permits us to view reality a certain way. "Therefore," he claims, "each of the modes has its own peculiar logic. It also has its own organizational patterns and, to some extent, its own stylistic characteristics" (p. 37). Furthermore, the modes of discourse overlap; a given text may have a dominant mode, but "in actuality, it is impossible to have pure narration, description, evaluation, or classification" (p. 37).

Having defined the arts, media, and modes of discourse, Kinneavy devotes the rest of the book to a discussion of aims. The aims of discourse reflect the writer's or speaker's purpose for using language. They are perhaps the most significant subdivision of pragmatics in Kinneavy's theory because purpose determines everything else about the discourse. When our purpose is to discuss reality, we may produce what Kinneavy calls *reference discourse*. There are three kinds of reference discourse. If we know the reality and simply want to relay facts about it we use language to inform; Kinneavy cites weather reports, news stories, and telephone directories as examples of informative discourse. Second, "if this information is systematized and accompanied by demonstrative proof of its validity, there is a scientific use of language" (p. 39); some literary criticism and much history represents scientific discourse. Third, if we don't know the reality but our purpose is to explore it, we stress the exploratory use of language; exploratory discourse may include interviews, questionnaires, and some seminars.

Whereas reference discourse is reality-centered, the other three aims of discourse focus on different components of the communication triangle. (See Fig. 4.2.) Persuasive discourse uses language to persuade the audience; our primary purpose is to prompt a response in the reader or listener. Literary discourse calls attention to itself as a text; our primary purpose is to create artifacts "worthy of contemplation in their own right" (p. 39). Expressive discourse emphasizes the encoder, either a person or a group, using language to assert the self. The four aims, like the four modes, overlap. We may use language

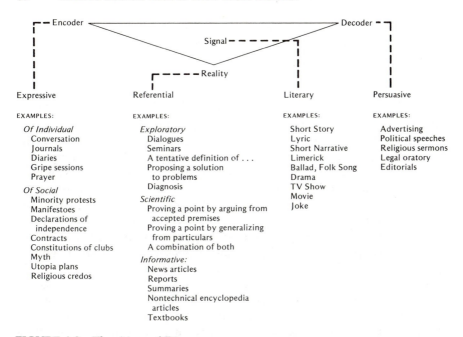

FIGURE 4.2   The Aims of Discourse

From James Kinneavy, *A Theory of Discourse* (Englewood Cliffs, N.J.: Prentice-Hall, 1971).

primarily to emphasize one element of the communication triangle, but that doesn't deny the presence of lesser purposes and other uses of language: "Persuasion as a matter of course incorporates information about the product [to be advertised], maybe even some valid scientific proof of its superiority, and it may use such literary techniques as rhythm, rhyme, and alliteration in its slogan" (p. 60).

Each of these four uses of language, governed by the writer's or speaker's purpose, has its own logic, organizational patterns, and stylistic peculiarities. Kinneavy's discussion of these distinguishing characteristics occupies most of his book. Essentially, he applies the traditional departments of rhetoric—especially invention, arrangement, and style—to the four aims, consequently generating four "rhetorics." Rhetoric, traditionally viewed as the art of persuasion, is for Kinneavy only one use of language, only one aspect of a much larger study which describes how human beings use language to realize certain purposes in communicating with each other:

> Language is like a windowpane. I may throw bricks at it to vent my feelings about something; I may use a chunk of it to chase away an intruder; I may use it to mirror or explore reality; and I may use a

stained-glass windowpane to call attention to itself. Windows can be used expressively, persuasively, referentially, and artistically. (*A Theory of Discourse*, p. 40)

Conclusion

We must now return to the question the title of this chapter poses: What do teachers need to know about rhetoric? In and among the historical summaries you've read lie terms, principles, and emphases writing teachers need to understand. Why? Because they shaped the courses we took to become teachers. Because the texts we use as well as the literature of our profession make assumptions about rhetoric we need to understand if we want to teach well. Because we all practice rhetoric, composing written and spoken discourse for a variety of rhetorical purposes. And perhaps, in reading this chapter, you've gained other insights which will benefit your teaching.

One conclusion you might have reached is that the terms associated with rhetoric change. *Rhetoric* itself is difficult to define, for it denotes both a practice and a body of knowledge which describes the practice. We need to understand what people mean when they use the term. Are they referring to a theory? If so, whose? To a practice? If so, from what perspective do they view its use? Similarly, when we hear words like *persuasion, communication, style,* and *mode,* what do they mean? Does *style* simply refer to the kinds of words writers use or does it rather embody all of the rhetorical choices they make? We need to remember that the concern for stylistic "correctness" or "propriety" represents only one view of the rhetorical tradition, and a relatively recent view at that. We should also recognize that texts which urge students to "be clear, precise, and concise" reflect a neoclassical preference for the plain style.

These terms have taken on different meanings because the rhetorical tradition has experienced shifts in emphasis. As we have seen, classical rhetoric forms the foundation which subsequent rhetoricians modified. They practiced the art to meet their own needs and developed rhetorical theories which reflect a unique cultural perspective. As a result, various departments of rhetoric fluctuated in prominence. In the Middle Ages and the Renaissance, then again in the eighteenth century, rhetoricians focused primarily on style. Elocutionists concerned themselves principally with delivery. Longinians asserted the primacy of sublime thoughts or invention (as well as sublimity of style). In the twentieth century, especially among writing teachers, there has been a resurgence of interest in invention or prewriting, in part to counter an excessive preoccupation with the written product.

We can note other changes too. Historically some rhetoricians sought to combine rhetoric with other verbal arts: logic, grammar, and poetics. Writing courses which devote considerable time to the study of grammar or literature represent such a blending of the arts; in fact, such courses, whatever else they may do, probably do not give students much practice in rhetoric. We should remember too that literature (or belles-lettres) hasn't always served as the model for teaching rhetorical principles. From time to time other forms of oral and written discourse—letters, sermons, debates, lectures, disputations on points of law—helped students understand rhetorical theory and practice.

Perhaps the most important conclusion to be drawn from this chapter is that rhetoric changes. People change it as they use language to communicate with each other. For some time now, the narrower definition of rhetoric as the art of persuasion has failed to describe how we use language. That is why in this century the definition has been enlarged to incorporate other aims of discourse. Knowing that rhetoric is a dynamic process permits us to question assumptions which presume rhetoric "has always been thus" or "ought to treat such and such." It makes no more sense to assume that rhetoric is principally concerned with persuasion, or with stylistic flair, or with literary analysis than it would to assert that our students must demonstrate the elocutionary skills of medieval preachers. If we view rhetorical theory and practice as some irrelevant archaism, we will become trapped by the tradition. Instead, we must understand the varied and changing purposes people have for using language so that we can teach intelligently the arts of rhetoric our culture now practices.

5

What do teachers need to know about cognition?

> We do not write in order to be understood, we write in order to understand.
>
> C. DAY LEWIS

Most students believe that good writers are born, not made. Some have the gift; some don't. For those who do, the right words somehow move magically from the mind to the page. For those who don't, writing is pretty tough work. Most students think they belong to this latter group. Since writing is a struggle, they assume they must lack the talent for it. Their teachers, unfortunately, often agree with them. "My students just can't think," protests one. "Susan has absolutely no imagination," complains another. Such statements, born of frustration, shouldn't be taken literally, of course, but they suggest that writing has a great deal to do with creativity.

This chapter explores the creative process. It explains how seeing and thinking help writers generate ideas, and why prewriting is crucial to the composing process. The discussion is by no means comprehensive. In the first place, we know very little about how the mind functions. In the second place, a single chapter can't summarize what we do know. However, it can help us understand why "finding a topic" may not be as simple as most textbooks assume. We may also discover tentative answers to other questions: How do people learn to think? How do writers interpret experience? Why do people who've been through the same experience describe it differently? How can we sequence writing instruction to develop our students' powers of observation and thinking?

Creativity

Many scholars, particularly in this century, have sought to explain creativity. Janet Emig summarizes several important discussions of the creative process in Chapter One of *The Composing Processes of Twelfth Graders*. Her review suggests two ways of viewing creativity: 1. as a tension or moment of intersection between two or more opposing variables, and 2. as a series of several aligned stages. The second perspective is best illustrated by Graham Wallas's *The Art of Thought* (1926), which defines four stages of creative problem-solving. In the first stage, called *preparation,* we become aware of the problem, exploring and investigating its dimensions. In the second stage, *incubation,* we mull the problem over subconsciously. At the point of *illumination,* a sudden insight or "Eureka moment" propels us toward a possible solution. Finally, we test the potential or hypothetical solution in the fourth stage, *verification.* Viewed as a sequence of stages, creativity involves several mental operations. They enable us to become conscious of a problem, to explore it from various angles as we search for some unknown. When we discover it, we make an imaginative leap toward a solution which can be tested or verified.

Although we still have much to learn about how the brain functions, current theories agree on one significant point: "To create" is not beyond the capacity of any normal human being. If creativity is somehow a special ability, it is special for us all. With the possible exception of brain-damaged individuals, we all develop modes of consciousness which have physiological origins in the brain. Our culture tends to place greater emphasis on cognitive modes of thought, on logic, reason, and "literacy." However, imagination and feeling, affective modes, also represent an important way of thinking. Writers must respect both the affective and cognitive dimensions of thought, developing a feeling for and an intuition about their work as well as a sense of its logic.

The subject of this chapter, however, is *cognition,* which means "knowing." Psychologists generally use the term to describe at least two kinds of knowledge: 1. knowledge through awareness, seeing, or perception, and 2. knowledge through judgment, thinking, or conception. To separate cognition into seeing and thinking forces an artificial distinction between two processes which must work together. Many textbooks foster a similar division when they suggest, for example, that descriptive writing emphasizes the writer's powers of observation, whereas persuasive writing focuses on the ability to reason. Such a division fails to consider that writers see and think regardless of their aim or mode of discourse. Nevertheless, by examining separately these two cognitive processes, perception and conception, we may better understand what they contribute to the composing process. Both the eye and the brain serve as essential tools for writers.

Perception

Perception or seeing is far more complex than most of us consciously realize.[1] Almost everyone has seen a deck of playing cards, for example. Stop reading and try to sketch the five of hearts *from memory.* Now, compare your drawing to the actual card (it is reproduced on p. 63). Very few people can draw the five of hearts accurately on the first try. Why? Must we conclude that reasonably intelligent human beings can't remember what they've obviously seen many times? Not really. Gestalt psychologists maintain that we don't just perceive stimuli; we impose patterns on stimuli. We compose them.

At this moment your eyes are taking in thousands of bits of data, but reading specialists tell us that we don't read every word, much less every letter. It's impossible for us to comprehend so many stimuli at once. If we had to see every line and curve of every letter in every word, we could only read about one word every 1.75 seconds, or roughly 35 words per minute.[2] Fluent readers, however, comprehend anywhere from 180 to 600 words per minute, depending on their familiarity with the material.[3] That's because we don't allow masses of stimuli to overwhelm us; instead, we select those which are significant and ignore or deemphasize what doesn't matter at the moment. We compose the selected stimuli into patterns consistent with other patterns we have created from other stimuli. We build categories, making choices about what to highlight and what to place into the background. That's why different people can observe the same phenomenon—an automobile accident, a film, a Rorschach drawing—and see them differently.

Let's consider another example. What do you see in the drawing at the top of page 61, a goblet or two faces?

1. For many of the principles discussed in this section and for the five-of-hearts exercise, I am indebted to Richard Coe for making available preliminary manuscript material of his book *Form and Substance: An Advanced Rhetoric* (New York: John Wiley & Sons, 1981).
2. Paul A. Kolers, "Experiments in Reading," *Scientific American* 227 (July 1972), 13.
3. Charles Cooper and Anthony R. Petrosky, "A Psycholinguistic View of the Fluent Reading Process," *Journal of Reading* 19 (December 1976), 194.

FIGURE 5.1   The Goblet and Two Faces

What you see depends on whether you select white or black as the background for the picture. Similar choices determine how we see "Day and Night," a woodcut by Maurits Escher, who produced fascinating art by manipulating principles of perception. By forcing black into the background at the top of the picture, we observe white geese flying east through the night sky. Reversing fields by selecting white as the background, we see black geese flying west in the daytime.

FIGURE 5.2   Maurits C. Escher, "Day and Night" (color woodcut, 1938)
Yale University Art Gallery. Gift of George Hopper Fitch, B.A., 1932 and Mrs. Fitch.

Not only do we compose stimuli into patterns; we also translate two-dimensional images into hypotheses about three-dimensional realities. The Necker cube illustrates this principle.[4]

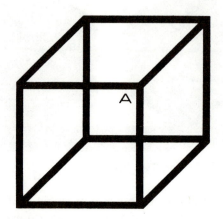

FIGURE 5.3   The Necker Cube

If you look steadily at corner A, you may see it two ways, as part of the front of the cube or as part of the back. The first view you decide on may actually interfere with your seeing the cube from the other perspective. Neither view is right or wrong; the drawing just represents two valid hypotheses about three-dimensional cubes. We simply don't get enough contextual information from the drawing to relate the pattern of stimuli to a familiar surrounding.

The decisions we make about which stimuli to select and what patterns to impose on them are based largely on what we already "know." James Britton describes this decision-making process as follows:

> I look at the world in the light of what I have learned to expect from past experience of the world. That is to say, there is on the one hand my world representation—the accumulated record of my past experience—and there is on the other hand the process of representing to myself whatever of the world confronts me at any given moment. It is as though, in confrontation, my world representation were a body of expectations from which I select and match: the selecting and

4. The goblet and two faces and the Necker cube appear in R.L. Gregory, *The Intelligent Eye* (New York: McGraw-Hill, 1970), a detailed, thoroughly illustrated discussion of perception.

matching being in response to whatever cues the situation offers (but influenced also by my mood of the moment). What takes place in the confrontation may contradict or modify or confirm my expectations. My expectations are hypotheses which I submit to the test of encounter with the actual. The outcome affects not only my representation of the present moment, but, if necessary, my whole accumulated representation of the world. *Every encounter with the actual is an experimental committal of all I have learned from experience.* (*Language and Learning,* p. 15)

Who we are, then, determines how we see. And who we are, in turn, depends on how we have been socialized. In our culture, for example, we have come to associate the color black with death, dirt, and predominantly unfavorable images. Writers may consciously play up this color stereotype to create various moods and symbols in their works. In Japan, however, and in some African tribes white is the color of death. Because different cultures dissect the universe in different ways, our perceptions are influenced by the culture we live in. To some extent we share perceptual patterns with everyone else in our culture.

Context also determines what we see. Since the mind can't sort all of the stimuli the eye sees, we select those bits of information which have meaning for us *in a certain context.* Your attempt to draw the five of hearts illustrates this principle.

FIGURE 5.4

Your picture probably didn't reproduce every detail of the card, even though you had seen it many times. However, most people who attempt to draw it do include the heart symbol and some way of representing the notion "five." That's because, in the context of card games, the number and suit matter most to us. We have sorted the information from our perceptions into categories necessary to playing card games. The person who designed the card, however, kept in mind something we rarely consider: for convenience, the suit and number should appear at the "top" of the card regardless of how the player holds it. In other words, your drawing suggests that context assumes greater importance than the evidence of your senses.

The same principle—context overrides visual evidence—can also be illustrated by other drawings (see Fig. 5.5).

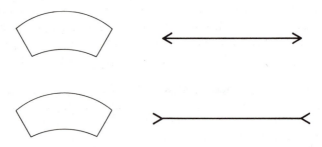

FIGURE 5.5
Reprinted from R.L. Gregory, *The Intelligent Eye* (New York: McGraw-Hill, 1970).

Try as we might, we have a difficult time believing that the curved figures are identical in size or that the two horizontal lines are equal in length.

So far we have examined sensory or visual contexts which determine what we see, but verbal contexts also shape perceptions. As Stuart Chase explains, "We cut up the seamless web of nature, gather the pieces into concepts, because, within our speech community, we are parties to an agreement to organize things that way, an agreement codified in the patterns of language" ("How Language Shapes Our Thoughts," p. 33). Language shapes our view of reality, and according to Benjamin Lee Whorf, people who speak different languages see the world differently. An investigator for an insurance company, Whorf describes a fire which was caused by language, because a workman responded to the way a situation was named, not the way it really was.

> An electric glow heater on the wall was little used and for one workman had the meaning of a convenient coathanger. At night a watch-

man entered and snapped a switch, which action he verbalized as "turning on the light." No light appeared, and this result he verbalized as "light is burned out." He could not see the glow of the heater because of the old coat hung on it. Soon the heater ignited the coat, which set fire to the building.[5]

I've had a similar experience in which language determined my view of reality. Needing 100 copies of a handout, I placed the original into the photocopier and set the dial on C, which I interpreted as the Roman numeral 100 or "centum." Ten minutes later, the machine was still spitting out copies of the handout, so I concluded that it must have been malfunctioning and turned it off. By that time, it had already copied the handout 245 times! When I reported the problem to the secretary, she laughed. "Oh, there's nothing wrong with the machine. C means 'continuous'; the machine just keeps making copies until you turn it off."

Different languages express reality in different ways. The world of color, for example, may be the same reality for all people, but other languages dissect the color spectrum in ways English doesn't. Zuñi, a Southwestern American Indian language, uses a single word for our *yellow* and *orange*. Other realities—actions, kinship, the parts of the body—are also treated differently by speakers of other languages. The English word *eat,* for example, names an activity which, in German, represents two distinct actions: *essen,* "to eat like a human being," and *fressen,* "to eat like an animal."

5. Coe, p. 224. See also Benjamin Lee Whorf, *Language, Thought and Reality,* ed. John B. Carroll (Cambridge, Mass.: The MIT Press, 1967).

FIGURE 5.6

By permission of Johnny Hart and Field Enterprises, Inc.

Whorf isn't the only one to suggest that verbal contexts determine how we perceive the world. Francis Bacon in *Novum Organum* (1620) views language, the Idol of the Market, as an obstruction to thinking: "For men believe that their reason governs words; but it is also true that words react on the understanding." George Orwell's *Nineteen Eighty-Four* proposes a society in which the thoughts of individuals can be controlled by controlling their language. Politicians and advertisers also attempt to shape our thoughts and experiences through language.

We need to know much more about the complex relations between language, perception, and thought. Sometimes we seem to think in words, talking to ourselves as we sort out a problem or grope for an idea. At other times, we seem to think nonverbally, in pictures. All of us, for example, have experienced the feeling that we know what we mean but can't put it into words. Similarly, a colleague of mine, whose hobby is woodworking, "thinks" in terms of the materials he works with: "When I design a piece of furniture, I do not think in words, but in images of the areas to be joined, and I solve problems of construction by manipulating images of the pieces to be joined."

Sometimes we control language, and at other times it controls us. We succumb to linguistic, cultural, and perceptual stereotypes as well as break through them now and then. Prewriting helps us question these stereotypes. When we probe a subject matter thoroughly and systematically, we begin to see it differently. We examine the topic from various perspectives. We place it in different contexts, breaking out of the sensory, verbal, emotional, or cultural limitations on what we see. The specific prewriting activities in Chapter 6 invite students to question perceptual patterns, to see the subject from many angles so that they can discover a message which is truly their own.

Conception

Not only does prewriting encourage students to see their subject and envision an audience, perceptual problems all writers must solve, it also aids thinking. It helps us relate perceptions, to understand differences and similarities in what we observe, to make inferences. Although seeing and thinking are closely related, for our purposes here, thinking or conception refers to a more abstract process. In perception the eye and the mind collect, sort out, and impose patterns on visual, verbal, and auditory stimuli. In conception, the mind relates those patterns to other patterns, enlarging, reinterpreting, and giving meaning to our experiences and observations. "By 'thinking,' " writes D. Gordon Rohman, "we refer to that activity of mind which *brings forth* and develops ideas, plans, designs, not merely the entrance of an idea into one's mind [perception]; an active, not a passive enlistment in the 'cause' of an idea; conceiving, which includes consecutive logical thinking but much more besides; essentially the imposition of pattern upon experience" ("Pre-Writing," p. 106).

Whenever we complain "My students can't think," we imply that conceptual processes are crucial to composing. Furthermore, we expect "thought-provoking," "it's-the-thought-that-really-counts" papers from our students. Perhaps if we understood conceptual processes better, we might be able to show students how to probe their topics more efficiently, how to make effective choices, how to think through a writing assignment.

Unfortunately, experts can't tell us much about conception. They haven't yet been able to identify, much less explain, the complex mental processes we call "thinking." But we do know a few things about how children grow to be thinkers, about intellectual development. Social scientists, especially those who conduct research in several subspecialties of psychology and education, insist that human intellectual development never occurs in isolation. It remains inextricably bound to physical, social, and emotional growth, and to language acquisition. Both heredity and environment shape conceptual processes; furthermore, those processes change as we grow older. A four-year-old thinks differently from a twelve-year-old. The "logic" of a college freshman also probably differs from the modes of thought an experienced, older teacher uses in an academic setting. Describing systematically and chronologically the intellectual development of human beings has been the life's work of one man and his students—Jean Piaget.

Piaget

Perhaps no other single individual has made a greater impact on educational theory in this century than Jean Piaget (1896–1980). His research concerns itself with two questions: What mechanisms permit human beings to adapt efficiently to their environment? How can we classify the progressively complex adaptations human beings make as they grow older?

Problem-solving is one technique Piaget uses to study intellectual developments. A typical problem for children eleven years old or older requires them to supply a missing letter, figure, or object in a collection.[6] Can you determine what symbol belongs in the blank section of the circle below?

Solving the problem made me feel like a slow seven-year-old because my perceptions inhibited my powers of reasoning. The difficulty lies in classifying the letters to determine how they correspond to each other. To solve the problem I must recognize that the symbols I, V, and X represent Roman numerals, that A and J represent the first and tenth letters of the alphabet, and that the alphabet letters and Roman numerals are arranged in an "opposite to" relationship within the circle. Thus, the letter opposite Roman numeral V must be the fifth letter of the alphabet or E. To arrive at that conclusion requires a complicated understanding of space, numbers, letters, correspondences, sequences, and relationships.

Were we born with this understanding? It seems not. We learn these concepts slowly, generally through flexible processes of trial and error. As infants, we gradually learned to recognize sizes and shapes, and not until much later did we learn that objects have permanence. Two underlying processes explain how we learn these things and thereby gradually adapt to our environment. First, we use the environment to learn a new behavior, a process Piaget calls *assimilation*. Second, the environment modifies behaviors we have already learned, a process called *accommodation*. In other words, we are constantly drawing the environment to us or adapting ourselves to it. We must balance these two processes, finding an equilibrium between them that meets the demands of a particular situation or environment. When we manage the equilibrium we are demonstrating, according to Piaget, intelligent behavior.

A specific example may make the two processes clearer. Infants are born with a sucking reflex, one of very few reflexes Piaget's theory

6. Ruth M. Beard, *An Outline of Piaget's Developmental Psychology for Students and Teachers* (Students Library of Education; London: Routledge and Kegan Paul, 1969), pp. 1–2.

admits, and an "urge" to adapt to the environment in order to survive. But the sucking reflex is quite unsophisticated; any stimulation of the lips or mouth will prompt some kind of sucking.

> The infant is unsure of just how to hold his mouth and how to accommodate his sucking to the particular size and shape of the object presented. He will starve to death unless he assumes the correct posture. Thus, an act as simple as sucking a nipple requires more than assimilation; the child must also accommodate. The environment demands a balance between these two processes, since aspects of the child's reflexive sucking behavior are clearly appropriate and should be retained; other aspects of that behavior are unsuitable for obtaining milk from the nipple and must be modified. The result is a simple adaptation—a manifestation of intelligence. (Guy R. Lefrancois, *Of Children: An Introduction to Child Development*, p. 47)

By repeatedly responding to our environment, assimilating it or accommodating ourselves to it, we organize our behavior into habits, sequences of actions which Piaget calls *schemes*. We incorporate new experiences into these schemes (assimilation) until the environment presents some unfamiliar problem which requires us to modify, extend, or combine the schemes (accommodation).

Piaget defines four stages of intellectual development. Each stage is characterized by schemes the child learned during the previous stage as well as by new adaptations which prepare for the next stage. Like blowing up a balloon, we progress through each stage with schemes we have already organized, adjusting them gradually to incorporate new concepts. Table 5.1 describes the major characteristics of each stage.

High school and college teachers, of course, are most interested in the fourth stage, the stage of formal operations, but before we examine its characteristics, let's survey what children can already do by the time they are eleven or twelve. They have acquired language, and they can comprehend all of its uses. They can reverse thoughts or actions, whereas younger children can't; if two-year-old Jimmy, *in the process* of pulling on a sock, is asked to take it off, he can't do it. Older students can also symbolize. They can construct classifications, and they recognize that objects belonging to the same class have unique identities; preschool children can't, which is why they can still believe in Santa Claus even though they've seen several different Santas, several members of the class, on the same day in the same department store.

Older children have also learned what Piaget calls *conservation*, that objects don't change unless something's been added or taken away.

TABLE 5.1   Piaget's Stage of Cognitive Development

Stage	*Approximate Age*	*Some Major Characteristics*
Sensorimotor	0–2 years	Motoric intelligence. World of the here and now. No language, no thought in early stages. No notion of objective reality.
Preoperational Preconceptual Intuitive	2–7 years 2–4 years 4–7 years	Egocentric thought. Reason dominated by perception. Intuitive rather than logical solutions. Inability to conserve.
Concrete Operations	7–11 or 12 years	Ability to conserve. Logic of classes and relations. Understanding of number. Thinking bound to concrete. Development of reversibility in thought.
Formal Operations	11 or 12 to 14 or 15 years	Complete generality of thought. Propositional thinking. Ability to deal with the hypothetical. Development of strong idealism.

Source: Guy R. Lefrancois, *Of Children: An Introduction to Child Development,* p. 47.

Preoperational children wouldn't be able to reason that Figures A and B below contain the same number of dots, even though they have merely been rearranged; children able to "conserve" wouldn't make that mistake.

By the time they are twelve, children have developed rules of logic governing numbers, area, volume, liquids, and so on. They can construct series, order classes into hierarchies, imagine perspectives other than their own, make substitutions, and combine operations in various ways to yield the same result. They are also less egocentric and, instead of playing by themselves, demonstrate increased cooperation with and interest in others. Although they can reason inductively and deductively, their thinking is still tied to the concrete, to this world or to objects easily imagined.

During the period of formal operations, young adults develop abilities to use logic as we usually define it, inductive and deductive reasoning from the concrete to the abstract and vice versa. They can now express and test hypotheses, accept assumptions for the sake of argument, deal with more complex concepts (including "infinity," "correlation," and "probability"), and compare ideal or imagined concepts with actuality. This ability to reason from the real to the possible prompts the intense idealism and frustration of adolescents. They now become aware of discrepancies between the actual world and the utopia they contemplate, between who they think they are and who they want to be. Although intellectual as well as emotional turmoil seems unavoidable at this stage (at least in western cultures), young adults spend most of their teens applying their recently developed inductive and deductive powers to the problems they perceive in themselves and in their world. They are practicing conceptual processes which, in increasingly efficient, effective ways, help them adapt to an ever more complex environment, the world of an independent adult.

Piaget's work urges us to reexamine our teaching and the assumptions on which it is based so that we foster rather than frustrate the progress of children learning to adapt to their world. Since children don't develop the ability to do operational thinking until they are teenagers, we can't expect them to be able to do certain kinds of writing until then.

Prior to about the ninth grade, writing courses should emphasize self-expressive writing, description, simple stories, fairly concrete subject matters. As Piaget tells us, students at this age tend to be preoccupied with themselves and concerned with their immediate environment. They are their own best audience. After grade nine, however, they can reason in progressively abstract ways either from memory or from present phenomena. It makes sense then to focus on more complex categories of writing to reinforce the development of operational thinking.

However, some kinds of writing will present difficulties even for high school and college students. Generally they handle descriptive and narrative modes of discourse confidently, but evaluation, classification, persuasion, writing for a mixed audience, and topics which require theorizing, abstracting, or predictions about the future can be troublesome. We shouldn't expect college freshmen to write cleverly organized, cogently argued syllogistic essays because they don't yet command conceptual processes essential to completing the assignment brilliantly. That doesn't mean they should avoid challenging assignments. On the contrary, practicing difficult modes of thought encourages their mastery. Nevertheless, some abstractions and kinds of logic which seem "so natural" to us involve conceptual processes our students have only recently begun to exercise. They do not yet command securely the "logics" of the academic world which took us four years of college and perhaps a few years of graduate school to master.

To summarize Piaget's themes is to list clichés, but the clichés raise important questions writing teachers must answer.

1. People do not live in a vacuum; they interact with their world. Are our writing classes an "English vacuum" or do they encourage interaction with the world outside the academic setting?

2. Thinking is based on experience. Do our writing assignments urge students to assess their own experiences or are we confining student writers to fields of specialized experiences?

3. People know more than they can verbalize. How can a piece of writing help us understand the difference between what students know and what they can do?

4. Intellectual growth occurs when people are required to exercise high-level thinking ("high" relative to their own stage of development, but not so high as to represent a stage the child has not yet attained). How can we sequence writing courses and assignments to encourage "high-level thinking" without frustrating intellectual growth?

5. People possess an intrinsic, internal "need to know." How can we harness this internal energy to make student writers self-motivating?

A writing class offers excellent opportunities to reinforce our students' cognitive development. In our haste to teach a subject matter, we sometimes forget that we're teaching, first and foremost, a complex human being. We shouldn't be concerned as much with the facts we want students to know as with those processes that help students learn whatever facts they have a need to know. We need to teach thinking, not things to think about. By posing unfamiliar problems which require students to see, talk, think, and write, we encourage them to modify the Piagetian schemes they have developed and to adopt progressively more complex thinking strategies.

Although Piaget's work doesn't directly suggest specific teaching techniques, other investigators, working from Piaget's description, have developed curricula and instructional materials which foster cognitive development. English teachers are especially fortunate in finding many of Piaget's principles applied to the teaching of writing in James Moffett's work.

Moffett

James Moffett's *Teaching the Universe of Discourse* presents a rationale for a student-centered, process-oriented language arts curriculum. A companion volume, *Student-Centered Language Arts and Reading, K–13: A Handbook for Teachers,* translates Moffett's theory of discourse into practice, offering specific suggestions for teaching techniques, classroom activities, and instructional materials. For Moffett, communication is a process of overcoming an imbalance in knowledge by means of a symbol system, "and the great thing to learn about symbol systems is how to manipulate them, not how to analyze them" (*Teaching the Universe of Discourse,* p. viii). He laments approaches which dissect the traditional subject matters of English classes into elements, categories, and units—he calls it "the particle approach"—rather than seeing things holistically. Students learn to write by writing, Moffett maintains, not by talking about writing. The student consequently is the backbone of Moffett's curriculum.

When Moffett suggests that writing "overcomes an imbalance in knowledge" he means that communication requires adjusting the relationships among writer, reader, and subject.

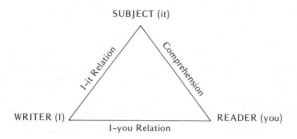

If you are to comprehend my message, I must effectively manipulate two relationships, how I view my subject matter and how I view you. Moffett calls the relation between writers and their subject the "I-it" or referential relation. To adjust this relationship, I must exercise perception, memory, and reason. The I-it relation becomes increasingly abstract as I select, incorporate, and reorganize the features of the subject, as I generalize about it or create hierarchies of classes and subclasses, as I extend it into time and space, and as I remember my experiences. For example, if I were discussing with another teacher how a student's paper is organized, there wouldn't be much distance between me and the experience. I am participating in a drama, recording the event through my perceptions of it.

However, if months or years later I were to combine what I remember of that experience with recollections of other experiences, I would be generalizing from the events, drawing conclusions from them at a fairly high level of abstraction. Now my memory, not my perceptual apparatus, is selecting the details.

Moffett describes a spectrum of four I-it relations, each one at a higher level of abstraction. The lowest level, "what is happening," corresponds most nearly to the reality of the experience itself and entails the least processing of events by the mind. Higher levels of abstraction require more complex conceptual processes and manipulations of logic; the "subject becomes less and less matter and more and more idea" ("I, You, and It," p. 246). The list below represents the continuum of I-it relations by questions with different verb tenses, "which indicate when events occurred in relation to when the speaker is speaking of them" (p. 244). Each level also corresponds to a form of discourse (which symbolizes the experience) and to abstractive processes (which define the logic of each level).

What may happen?	Argumentation	Theorizing about experience
What happens?	Exposition	Generalizing from experience
What happened?	Narrative	Reporting experience
What is happening?	Drama	Recording experience

Moffett's I-you relation, on the other hand, defines degrees of distance, not between writer and subject, but between writer and reader. "We abstract not only from something," Moffett claims, "but for someone" (p. 246). Beginning with self-verbalization, in which "I" and "you" are the same person (Piaget's "egocentric speech"), the spectrum of I-you relations expands to include audiences in the same time or place as the writer or in progressively distant times and places. The audience may also grow to include more than one reader. Each kind of discourse becomes more and more public and offers less and less immediate feedback for the writer. Moffett suggests that students need to develop, in an orderly fashion, "voices" and rhetorical stances which can be used to address a variety of audiences. Unfortunately most students are not really writing for a "you." They have learned to address most of their academic writing to an "it," an abstraction of an authority figure they presume to be The English Teacher.

To produce authentic discourse, writers must mesh both the I-it and I-you relationships. They must practice increasing the distance between themselves and their audience, simultaneously adjusting the abstractive attitude between themselves and the subject matter. A writing curriculum, in Moffett's view, should move students through a spiral of writing assignments which require progressively complex cognitive processes and progressively larger or more distant audiences. Students would first record the drama of "what is happening" for several kinds of audiences, re-creating the experience for themselves, for a close friend sitting within speaking distance, in a letter to someone they know, in a formal essay addressed to a public audience. Then, students would move to the next level of the spiral, reporting the narrative of "what happened" for a variety of audiences. And so on. In Moffett's curriculum, each turn of the spiral builds on the previous one and leads to the next. As students speak, read, and write progressively more abstract discourse, they learn to differentiate and integrate the mental operations each kind of discourse requires. "The movement is from self to world, from a point to an area, from a private world of egocentric chatter to a public universe of discourse" ("I, You, and It," p. 246), from concrete experience to abstract idea, from first-person observation to third-person theorizing.

In Moffett's view, writing teachers must have as their primary aim encouraging a student's intellectual and social development. They act as one kind of audience, offering a point of view which helps the student manipulate effectively the I-you and I-it relations. They provide important feedback for the writer who has encountered problems or can't see what the problem is. Instead of assuming roles as a "parental substitute, civic authority, and the wielder of marks" (*Teaching the Universe of Discourse*, p. 193), instead of explaining what's in the textbook, teachers using Moffett's student-centered curriculum encourage students to teach each other. Writing assignments aren't restricted to academic prose practical only in schools; students practice writing many forms of discourse, for many audiences.

Conclusion

Moffett returns us to the communications triangle and the balancing act writers perform. To mesh the I-it and I-you relations successfully requires making choices, but as we have seen, those choices are generally determined more by who we are than by our ability to make unbiased observations based on "facts." What we write has a lot to do with what we see, how we interpret experiences, how we relate them to other experiences. Although we need to know much more about these perceptual and conceptual processes, they are far more complex than most of us consciously realize. And because they are so habitual, so conditioned by our unique past and our culture, it helps to slow them down, to focus consciously on our subject matter, our audience, our ideas and feelings. Prewriting triggers these mental processes, permitting us to find ideas—or let them find us.

6
Prewriting techniques

This is the first requirement for good writing: truth; not *the* truth . . . but some kind of truth—a connection between the things written about, the words used in the writing, and the author's real experience in the world he knows well—whether in fact or dream or imagination.

KEN MACRORIE

The prewriting techniques discussed in this chapter help students assess the dimensions of a rhetorical problem and plan its solution. They trigger perceptual and conceptual processes, permitting writers to recall experiences, break through stereotyped thinking, examine relationships between ideas, assess the expectations of their audience, find an implicit order in their subject matter, and discover how they feel about the work.[1] Some prewriting activities enable writers

---

1. An indispensable bibliographical essay which surveys methods of invention as well as the history of the art is Richard Young, "Invention: A Topographical Survey," in *Teaching Composition: Ten Bibliographical Essays,* ed. Gary Tate (Fort Worth, Tex.: Texas Christian University Press, 1976), pp. 1–43. As Young points out, the term *prewriting* technically should be restricted to denote the techniques of invention developed by D. Gordon Rohman and Albert O. Wlecke—journals, meditation, and analogy—which emphasize creative thinking and the "self-actualization" of the writer [cf. D. Gordon Rohman and Albert O. Wlecke, *Pre-Writing: The Construction and Application of Models for Concept Formation in Writing* (USOE Cooperative Research Project No. 2174; East Lansing, Mich.: Michigan State University, 1964)]. However, I use *prewriting* throughout this book as a synonym for "invention," primarily because current usage among writing teachers assigns the term broader meaning than Rohman and Wlecke intended.

to probe the subject matter from several perspectives; others help writers assess their relationship to an audience. Some use pictures, talk, or pantomime to generate ideas, while others ask students to write lists, notes, and scratch outlines.

As a rule, the more time students spend on a variety of prewriting activities, the more successful the paper will be. In working out all the possibilities an assignment suggests, students discover what they honestly want to say and resolve some of the decisions they must make if the paper is to express a message effectively. Writing the first draft becomes easier because some writing—notes, lists, freewritings—has already taken place. Drafting also becomes more productive because students are less preoccupied with formulating ideas from scratch and freer to discover new messages as the words appear on the page.

Often, the outline represents the only prewriting technique students find in composition texts. Although writers rarely construct elaborate outlines, informal outlines serve a useful purpose. Outlining can help students shape raw material generated by other prewriting activities. Outlining can also serve revision because, when students outline a draft, they may discover digressions, inconsistencies, or other organizational problems to work on in subsequent drafts. Nevertheless, outlining represents only one of many prewriting activities which help students plan their work.

Since prewriting is a means to an end, I don't grade the notes, lists, and miscellaneous scratchwork my students turn in with their final drafts. I look through the material, however, to discover which students need help generating more support for their topics or making prewriting work more efficiently for them. I also involve students in several prewriting activities, not just one, for each paper I assign. The series of activities encourages them to explore their subjects thoroughly, planning their response to an assignment carefully as they move closer to a first draft. Eventually, students modify and combine in whatever ways work best for them the techniques discussed in this chapter. All of them offer writers places to begin, keys of different shapes and sizes which grant access to experience, memory, and intuition.

Perception exercises

Thinking games, "conceptual blockbusting," and sense-scrambling activities encourage students to think about how they think. By analyzing the steps they go through to "have ideas" or solve problems, they discover barriers which block perceptions.[2] Much of the material in Chapter 5, including the five of hearts exercise, can prompt a discussion of these perceptual, cultural, emotional, and intellectual barriers. To demonstrate these principles, you might ask students to pair up and by turns lead each other blindfolded on a tour of the building or some other familiar place. Deprived of their visual orientations, they can appreciate perceptions gained through other senses: smell, touch, hearing. Students might also discuss pictures, a busy city street for example, and then draw the scene from various perspectives. What would a bird's-eye view of the picture look like? How would you draw it if you were looking out from under the manhole cover? If you were standing at the right-hand side of the picture looking left? After students have compared their drawings and discussed the differences in perspective, the class can move to other prewriting activities which elaborate plans for a descriptive writing assignment.

For many students, arts and media which don't involve writing offer a comfortable place to begin probing a subject. Pantomime and role-playing encourage students to act out the subject before they translate it into written form. Especially when an "issue" admits several points of view or when an audience may hold diverse opinions about a subject, role-playing clarifies the options and choices students must consider. Persuasive papers can begin with impromptu debates, which might then be worked into brief written dialogues and from there into more formal kinds of discourse. Similarly, reading assignments, pictures, or music can be translated from one medium to another, then to a third and finally to a written form. The assumption behind these activities is that similar principles govern communication in various media. When students practice the "language" of pictorial art, of gesture, and of music, they also learn principles which reinforce their use of the spoken and written word. Furthermore, in responding to cartoons, music, pantomime, students become more sensitive observers of their world.

Not every piece of writing, of course, finds a convenient beginning in art, music, or drama, but all writing can begin with speech, a comfortable means of expression for most people. As Robert Zoellner and others have suggested, talking out a rhetorical problem helps

2. James L. Adams, *Conceptual Blockbusting: A Pleasurable Guide to Better Problem Solving* (San Francisco: W.H. Freeman, 1974) is a useful discussion of how to cultivate thinking and problem-solving abilities. The book analyzes barriers to thinking and suggests strategies for breaking through them.

students define and solve it: "Since students have a greater fluency in speaking than in writing because they practice it more, speaking can be used as a stage prior to writing and can provide the basis for moving through increasingly adequate written versions of a unit of discourse."[3] All students, especially those whose fear of failure makes writing anything, even scratch notes, difficult, need opportunities to explain their plans to themselves or discuss them with other students, a sympathetic teacher, or even a tape recorder.

Brainstorming

Brainstorming is an unstructured probing of a topic. Like free association, brainstorming allows writers to venture whatever comes to mind about a subject, no matter how obvious or strange the ideas might be. When the entire class brainstorms a topic, the teacher generally writes on the board as many words and phrases as the students suggest. When students brainstorm topics on their own, they list whatever details occur to them. As a rule, general or superficial observations head the list, but as students are forced to examine the subject more closely, useful and interesting details begin to appear. To be useful, of course, the list must contain abundant raw material.

Sometimes, however, brainstorming yields only rambling, unfocused, or repetitive generalizations. Why? The teacher may have presented the technique in such a way that students conclude, "Okay, she wants a list of 100 details, so I'll give her a list of 100 details." The purpose of brainstorming is neither list-making nor reaching a precise number of details. As Donald Murray advises in *A Writer Teaches Writing*, "The teacher must, in such lists as this, begin to encourage honesty, to have the student look into himself and into his subject with candor and vigor. The list also gives the teacher a chance to defeat the cliché and the vague generalization by saying to the student, 'What does that mean? Can you be more specific?' The teacher should praise a student when he gets a good concrete detail which has the ring of reality" (p. 78). At least initially, students need guidance so that brainstorming generates *useful* details and enough of them to permit the writer to discard those which don't say much. Students also need to be reminded that making lists serves a larger purpose, exploring the subject thoroughly and discovering what about it interests them.

3. Young, p. 37; cf. Robert Zoellner, "A Behavioral Approach to Writing," *College English* 30 (January 1969), 267–320.

Teachers can go over these lists with individual students in brief conferences during the class period, or an especially rich list can be discussed with the entire class. What details seem most forceful? In what ways could details be grouped? What patterns have emerged in the list? What dimensions of the subject seemed to attract the writer's interest? What details must be left out at this point if the first draft is to have unity? A discussion along these lines helps students discover organizational possibilities in the raw material and suggests options for developing the paper. Following such a discussion, students might develop a "subject chart," regrouping items on the list into a branching tree diagram. The subject chart in Fig. 6.1 grew out

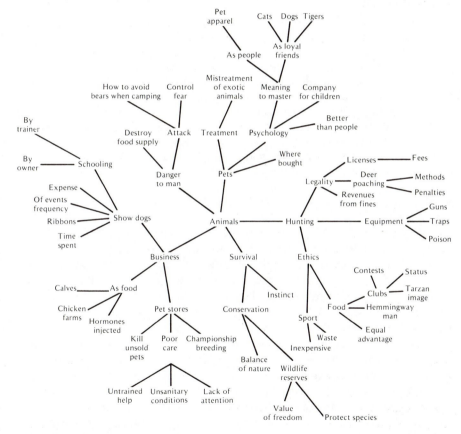

FIGURE 6.1   The Subject Chart

From Adrienne Robins, *The Writer's Practical Rhetoric* (New York: John Wiley and Sons, 1980). Reprinted by permission of John Wiley and Sons, Inc.

of a brainstorming session on the topic "animals." Any branch of the subject chart could be developed into a thesis statement. If students discover that one area of their diagram still looks skimpy, they could brainstorm it again for additional material (or abandon it altogether if it doesn't interest them).

Freewriting

Freewriting, a technique advocated by Peter Elbow and Ken Macrorie, offers students a risk-free way of getting words onto a page without having to worry about their correctness. Elbow explains the technique this way:

> The idea is simply to write for ten minutes (later on, perhaps fifteen or twenty). Don't stop for anything. Go quickly without rushing. Never stop to look back, to cross something out, to wonder how to spell something, to wonder what word or thought to use, or to think about what you are doing. If you can't think of a word or a spelling, just use a squiggle or else write, "I can't think of it." Just put down something. The easiest thing is just to put down whatever is in your mind. If you get stuck it's fine to write "I can't think what to say, I can't think what to say" as many times as you want: or repeat the last word you wrote over and over again: or anything else. The only requirement is that you *never* stop." (*Writing without Teachers*, p. 3)

Elbow recommends that students do freewriting exercises at least three times a week. Freewritings, he insists, should *never* be graded. Their primary purpose is to get something on paper, and "it's an unnecessary burden to try to think of words and also worry at the same time whether they're the right words" (p. 5). Macrorie advocates freewriting because it produces honest writing, writing that is free from phoniness or pretension. The writer must write fast enough to use "his own natural language without thinking of his expression" (*Telling Writing*, p. 9).

Some teachers do not constrain freewriting in any way; others offer a word or phrase to help students get started. Teachers can also sequence freewriting exercises in several ways to move students closer to more formal drafts. For example, after students have completed a freewriting, they can look it over to find words, phrases, a sentence or two which seem especially appealing. These words then offer a place to begin a second freewriting. The second freewriting may suggest ideas for a third and so on.

Murray sequences freewritings by incorporating student response at each stage.[4] First, students write freely for five minutes or so. Then, working in pairs, they discuss the freewriting by answering a question about it: "What appeared on the page that you didn't expect?" After a few minutes of discussion, students complete a second freewriting and stop to discuss it: "What idea do you want to develop in the next freewriting?" The procedure is repeated six or seven times. Guiding the discussion by means of questions helps students focus on what has appeared naturally, spontaneously on the page. They begin to see where the composing process is taking them. Teachers and students may substitute their own questions to guide the discussion, but they should focus on the writing, at the same time leaving students free to let their own language take charge of the page: What is the writing telling you? How do you (the writer) feel about what is appearing on the page? What do you (the reader) need to know that I haven't told you yet?

Freewriting often helps students overcome their fear of the blank page and their stifling preoccupation with correctness. The technique encourages play with language and uses language as an aid to thinking. A freewriting represents a writer talking out an idea; it is not a polished communication intended for an outside audience. Needless to say, if teachers grade freewritings, they are no longer "free." Threatened by grades, students will shift their attention from generating and developing ideas to editing a finished product.

Journals

Journals, commonplace books, or writer's notebooks have been indispensable tools for many writers, the famous and not so famous. Some journals, like diaries, record experiences and observations meant only to be read by their authors. Other journals, like Virginia Woolf's *Writer's Diary* and Ralph Waldo Emerson's *Journals,* contain such significant information about the life and work of their authors that they reach a large public audience. Many professional writers use journals to sketch out, organize, draft, and revise their work before they submit it for publication. Murray reports that his book, *A Writer Teaches Writing,* "is the distillate of boxes and files of materials. It was writ-

---

4. Donald Murray, workshop presentation, South Carolina English Teachers Conference, University of South Carolina, October 21, 1978. See also "The Listening Eye: Reflections on the Writing Conference," *College English* 41 (September 1979), 13–18. "Looping" and "cubing," additional ways of encouraging students to complete series of freewritings, are described in Gregory Cowan and Elizabeth Cowan, *Writing* (New York: John Wiley and Sons, 1980), pp. 9–26.

ten from sixteen two-inch thick notebooks, almost 300 pages drawn from perhaps 4,800 pages" (p. 6).

The journal has several uses in a writing class. Many teachers set aside the first ten minutes or so of every class period for journal writing. While the teacher checks the roll, returns papers, or reviews the lesson plan, students use the time to write whatever they want in their journals. The procedure settles the class down to work and gives students daily writing practice. Writing assignments develop the material students record in their journals. Journals can also become workbooks for the course. In them, students may practice freewriting, work out plans for papers, complete sentence-combining exercises, work on revisions, experiment with stylistic effects, keep track of spelling demons, and note which writing problems have been conquered and which still need work.

Unaccustomed to writing without some teacher-made assignment in front of them, students may protest that they can't think of anything to write in their journals, or they may devote several entries to deliberately "detached" topics: "I got up at eight, skipped breakfast, and went to class. Nothing much happened today." When this happens, teachers can suggest that they explore their reactions to some recent experience, capture a feeling in words, or speculate about some imaginary, "what if" situation. If these open-ended, deliberately vague suggestions don't work, the following list might help, at least until students become comfortable pursuing their own interests.[5]

1. Speculate. Why do you spend so much time in a certain place? Why do you read a certain book or see a particular movie more than once?
2. Sketch in words a person who doesn't know you're watching: someone looking at his or her reflection in a store window, a spectator at a sports event, a student studying desperately.
3. Record some observations about a current song, book, movie, television program.
4. React to something you've read recently. Was it well written? Why or why not? What strategies did the writer use to get you to like or dislike the piece?
5. Try to capture an incident of night fear—when a bush became a bear, for example—so that a reader might feel the same way you did.

5. Adapted from a list developed by Connie Pritchard, University of South Carolina, Fall 1977. See also Macrorie, *Telling Writing,* pp. 122–33.

6. Explain an important lesson you learned as a child.
7. If peace were a way of life and not merely a sentiment, what would you have to give up?
8. Describe your idea of paradise or hell.
9. Write a nasty letter complaining about some product that didn't work or some service that was performed poorly.
10. Pretend you're the consumer relations official for the company in number 9. Write a calm, convincing response to your complaint in which you blame someone else for the problem.
11. If you were an administrator in this school, what's the first change you'd make? Why?
12. Tell what season of the year brings the things you like best.
13. You have been given the power to make one person, and only one, disappear. Whom would you eliminate and why?

Most teachers check their students' journals periodically but, wisely, don't grade them. Journals offer students a place to write out ideas without fear of making mistakes or facing criticism for what they have to say. As a rule, comments on journal entries should be positive, encouraging further exploration of an idea: "I felt that way too when my best friend misunderstood what I said." "It must have taken courage to tell your parents this; why not write an entry as if you were telling the story from their point of view?" Students should feel free to write "Do not read" across the top of any entry they don't want to share with a teacher. A teacher unable to resist temptation should ask students to remove personal entries before the journals are turned in.

When I read a set of journals, occasionally I'll come across an entry full of obscenities. They're meant to shock me. Generally, I ignore them the first time around; if they appear again, I usually discuss the journal with the student. In a fit of pique, I once asked a student to write another entry defining one of the four-letter words he'd used. He never did. Much more common are the touchingly painful accounts of personal traumas students sometimes share with their English teachers. If I ignore the entry because it makes me uncomfortable, the student will conclude that I can't handle honest, sensitive topics and prefer to read only about "safe," academic subjects. If I write some gratuitous comment in the margin, I belittle the experience. When I discover students working out difficult experiences by writing them down in a journal, I generally encourage them to tackle the problem in several entries. They may have detected an irony in the experience, a weakness or strength in themselves, or a serious flaw in their idealistic notions about people. They need to examine further what they have found, first to understand it for themselves and perhaps later to share it with a larger audience. Precisely because such entries contain honest statements about important problems, they deserve to be treated seriously.

Heuristics

Heuristics derive ultimately from the *topoi* of classical rhetoric. In Book Two of the *Rhetoric,* Aristotle discusses twenty-eight "universal topics for enthymemes on all matters," among them, arguing from opposites, dividing the subject, exploring various senses of an ambiguous term, examining cause and effect. Although the classical *topoi* represent lines of reasoning speakers might pursue to invent arguments, heuristics prompt thinking by means of questions. The questions are ordered so that writers can explore the subject systematically and efficiently, but they are also open-ended to stimulate intuition and memory as well as reason. Most students are already familiar with the heuristic procedure journalists use: Who? What? When? Where? How? These questions help reporters compose effective lead paragraphs in news stories. Conditioned by years of testing, students often think the questions must have right and wrong answers; they don't. They increase the possibilities for probing a topic thoroughly, and they usually generate provisional answers. Ideally, those tentative answers should lead to formulating new questions which can be investigated some more.

In *Writing* (pp. 34–43), Gregory and Elizabeth Cowan present a heuristic derived from the classical *topoi* "definition," "comparison," "relationship," "testimony," and "circumstance." The authors encourage students to take the questions one at a time, thoughtfully, replacing the blank with a subject they want to explore and writing brief notes in answer to the questions. If students get stuck on a question, they should move on. When they have finished the entire list, they should reread their notes, starring material that looks the most promising.

> Definition
> 1. How does the dictionary define _____?
> 2. What earlier words did _____ come from?
> 3. What do *I* mean by _____?
> 4. What group of things does _____ seem to belong to? How is _____ different from other things in this group?

5. What parts can _____ be divided into?
6. Does _____ mean something now that it didn't years ago? If so, what?
7. What other words mean approximately the same as _____?
8. What are some concrete examples of _____?
9. When is the meaning of _____ misunderstood?

Comparison
1. What is _____ similar to? In what ways?
2. What is _____ different from? In what ways?
3. _____ is superior to what? In what ways?
4. _____ is inferior to what? In what ways?
5. _____ is most unlike what? (What is it opposite to?) In what ways?
6. _____ is most like what? In what ways?

Relationship
1. What causes _____?
2. What are the effects of _____?
3. What is the purpose of _____?
4. Why does _____ happen?
5. What is the consequence of _____?
6. What comes before _____?
7. What comes after _____?

Testimony
1. What have I heard people say about _____?
2. Do I know any facts or statistics about _____? If so, what?
3. Have I talked with anyone about _____?
4. Do I know any famous or well-known saying (e.g., "A bird in hand is worth two in the bush") about _____?
5. Can I quote any proverbs or any poems about _____?
6. Are there any laws about _____?
7. Do I remember any songs about _____? Do I remember anything I've read about _____ in books or magazines? Anything I've seen in a movie or on television?
8. Do I want to do any research on _____?

Circumstance
1. Is _____ possible or impossible?
2. What qualities, conditions, or circumstances make _____ possible or impossible?
3. Supposing that _____ is possible, is it also feasible? Why?
4. When did _____ happen previously?
5. Who has done or experienced _____?

6. Who can do _____?

7. If _____ starts, what makes it end?

8. What would it take for _____ to happen now?

9. What would prevent _____ from happening?

The dramatistic pentad is a heuristic derived from Kenneth Burke's rhetoric of human motives discussed in Chapter 4:

What was done? (act)

Where or when was it done? (scene)

Who did it? (agent)

How was it done? (agency)

Why was it done? (purpose)

Although Burke originally posed these questions to explore the complicated motives of human actions, most composition teachers use the heuristic with a simpler aim in mind: to help students generate descriptive or narrative material. As a prewriting technique, the pentad works well for investigating literary topics, historical or current events, and biographical subjects.

Another series of questions, adapted from Richard Larson's problem-solving model, suggests ways to engage issues-oriented subjects, the sort teachers often assign for persuasive papers. Students may also find the heuristic useful in sorting through other problems: personal difficulties, writing problems, or the problem posed by a writing assignment.

What is the problem?

Why is the problem indeed a problem?

What goals must be served by whatever action or solution that is taken?

Which goals have the highest priority?

What procedures might attain the stated goals?

What can I predict about the consequences of each possible action?

How do the actions compare with each other as potential solutions to the problem?

Which course of action is best?

In answering these questions, students define the problem, analyze it, formulate several hypotheses which might solve it, and select the best solution. "In every problem," writes Edward Corbett, "there are some things that you know or can easily find out, but there is something too that you don't know. It is the *unknown* that creates the problem. When confronted with a problem, you have to take note of all the things you do know. Then, by a series of inferences from the known, you try to form a hypothesis to determine whether your theory leads you to discover the unknown that is causing the problem" (*The Little Rhetoric and Handbook,* p. 44). Teachers, too, can employ the heuristic to define, analyze, and solve teaching problems or conduct research.

Since most writing courses are also reading courses, a heuristic for analyzing, interpreting, and evaluating literature can pose useful questions to guide students as they read literary texts or plan papers on literary topics. Corbett devised the series of questions shown in Fig. 6.2a–c, which have been adapted from *The Little Rhetoric and Handbook* (p. 186–221).

Obviously, students don't need to answer all the questions every time they read a literary work. Dragging the class routinely through each question would be pointless, boring busywork. The questions have value only insofar as they guide reading, or suggest new ideas to explore in the work, or encourage a closer examination of the text. The questions can be broken apart, altered, or culled selectively. At some point, students need to frame their own questions to explain their response to the work.

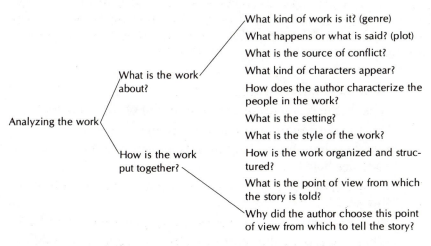

FIGURE 6.2a

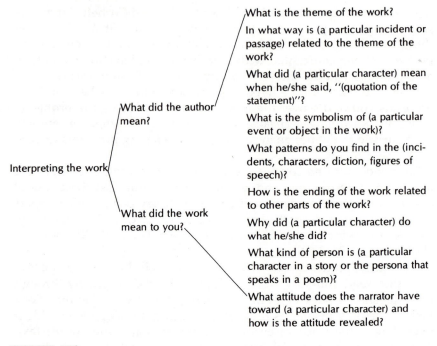

Interpreting the work

What did the author mean?

What did the work mean to you?

What is the theme of the work?

In what way is (a particular incident or passage) related to the theme of the work?

What did (a particular character) mean when he/she said, "(quotation of the statement)"?

What is the symbolism of (a particular event or object in the work)?

What patterns do you find in the (incidents, characters, diction, figures of speech)?

How is the ending of the work related to other parts of the work?

Why did (a particular character) do what he/she did?

What kind of person is (a particular character in a story or the persona that speaks in a poem)?

What attitude does the narrator have toward (a particular character) and how is the attitude revealed?

FIGURE 6.2b

Since most textbooks devote little attention to audience, a heuristic may help students make decisions, not about the content of a piece, but about its tone and point of view. The following questions, suggested by Karl R. Wallace's "*Topoi* and the Problem of Invention," mention several characteristics of audiences:

How old is the audience?

What is the economic or social condition of the audience?

What is the educational status of the audience?

What general philosophies of government or politics does the audience hold?

What values and beliefs would be common to an audience of this age?

What economic or social values is the audience likely to hold?

What value does the audience place on education, religion, work?

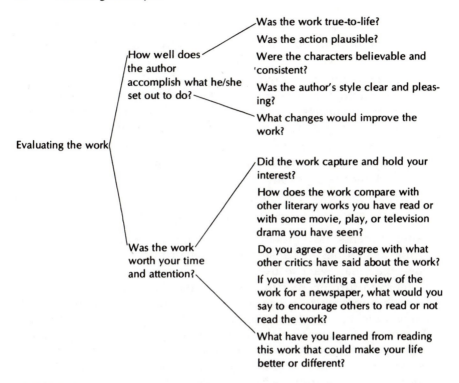

Evaluating the work

How well does the author accomplish what he/she set out to do?

- Was the work true-to-life?
- Was the action plausible?
- Were the characters believable and 'consistent?
- Was the author's style clear and pleasing?
- What changes would improve the work?

Was the work worth your time and attention?

- Did the work capture and hold your interest?
- How does the work compare with other literary works you have read or with some movie, play, or television drama you have seen?
- Do you agree or disagree with what other critics have said about the work?
- If you were writing a review of the work for a newspaper, what would you say to encourage others to read or not read the work?
- What have you learned from reading this work that could make your life better or different?

FIGURE 6.2c

Which of these values—economic, social, political, educational—is most important to the audience? Least important?

In general, how does the audience feel about its heritage or events that happened in the past? That are going on in the present? What hopes for the future does the audience hold?

In general, does the audience expect certain patterns of thought in what it reads? Should I include a lot of data to convince the audience of my point? What authorities would be most convincing? Does the audience need to see the causes and effects of my proposals? Would stories and analogies confuse my readers or encourage them to understand what I want to say? What terms will I need to define, and what terms can I assume are already understood?

What sorts of issues most frequently make the audience angry or defensive?

What things can I say without antagonizing my audience?

What options do I have for presenting unpopular opinions to my audience?

What is the *most* convincing appeal I could make? Should I try to convince by being reasonable and logical? Should I appeal to the emotions? Or should I demonstrate that I am an honest, trustworthy, sympathetic expert whom the audience can trust?

Have I stereotyped my audience, overlooking individuals who may hold views that are different from those the rest of my audience believes in?

Am I just saying what my audience wants to hear or am I also saying what I honestly believe to be true?

After students have grown comfortable with relatively simple prewriting techniques—brainstorming, freewriting, brief lists of questions—they may want to use more elaborate heuristics to probe the subject even further. Richard Larson's discovery questions represent one such approach.[6] To use it, students must first determine what kind of topic they are dealing with, for Larson's questions are grouped into two major categories: 1. topics that invite comment (single items, events, parts of a process, concepts, collections of items, groups of events), and 2. topics to which comments have already been attached (statements or questions which invite the writer's response). Once students have located the appropriate category, they can proceed to investigate the questions just as they would with any other heuristic. For example, the topic "guppies" lends itself to questions in group IA and ID, whereas the questions in IIB could be used to probe a topic like "What sort of connection do you see between grammar instruction and writing instruction?"

I. "Topics" That Invite Comment

    A. Writing about Single Items (in present existence)

    What are its precise physical characteristics (shape, dimensions, composition, etc.)?

    How does it differ from things that resemble it?

    What is its "range of variation" (how much can we change it and still identify it as the thing we started with)?

6. Richard L. Larson, "Discovery Through Questioning: A Plan for Teaching Rhetorical Invention," *College English* 30 (November 1968), 126–34. Although few heuristics direct specific attention to persuasive discourse, a helpful sequence of questions is Tommy J. Boley's "A Heuristic for Persuasion," *College Composition and Communication* 30 (May 1979), 187–91.

Does it call to mind other objects we have observed earlier in our lives? Why? In what respects?

From what points of view can it be examined?

What sort of structure does it have?

How do the parts of it work together?

How are the parts put together?

How are the parts proportioned in relation to each other?

To what structure (class or sequence of items) does it belong?

Who or what produced it in this form? Why?

Who needs it?

Who uses it? For what?

What purposes might it serve? How can it be evaluated, for these purposes?

B. Writing about Single Completed Events, or Parts of an Ongoing Process (These questions can apply to scenes and pictures, as well as to works of fiction and drama.)

Exactly what happened? (Tell the precise sequence: Who? What? When? How? Why? Who did what to whom? Why? What did what to what? How?)

What were the circumstances in which the event occurred? What did they contribute to its happening?

How was the event like or unlike similar events?

What were its causes?

What were its consequences?

What does its occurrence imply? What action (if any) is called for?

What was affected (indirectly) by it?

What, if anything, does it reveal or emphasize about some general condition?

To what group or class might it be assigned?

Is it (in general) good or bad? By what standard? How do we arrive at the standard?

How do we know about it? What is the authority for our information? How reliable is the authority? How do we know it to be reliable? (or unreliable?)

How might the event have been changed or avoided?

To what other events was it connected? How?

To what kinds of structure (if any) can it be assigned? On what basis?

C. Writing about Abstract Concepts (e.g., "religion," "social-ism")

To what specific items, groups of items, events, or groups of events does the word or words connect, in your experience or imagination?

What characteristic must an item or event have before the name of the concept can apply to it?

How do the referents of that concept differ from the things we name with similar concepts (e.g., "democracy" and "social-ism")?

How has the term been used by writers whom you have read? How have they implicitly defined it?

Does the word have "persuasive" value? Does the use of it in connection with another concept seem to praise or condemn the other concept?

Are you favorably disposed to all things included in the con-cept? Why or why not?

D. Writing about Collections of Items (in present existence) (These questions are in addition to the questions about single items, which can presumably be asked of each item in the group.)

What, exactly, do the items have in common?

If they have features in common, how do they differ?

How are the items related to each other, if not by common characteristics? What is revealed about them by the possibility of grouping them in this way?

How may the group be divided? What bases for division can be found?

What correlations, if any, may be found among the various possible subgroups? Is anything disclosed by the study of these correlations?

Into what class, if any, can the group as a whole be put?

E. Writing about Groups of Completed Events, Including Pro-cesses (These questions are in addition to questions about sin-gle completed events; such questions are applicable to each event in the group. These questions also apply to literary works, principally fiction and drama.)

What have the events in common?

If they have features in common, how do they differ?

How are the events related to each other (if they are not part of a chronological sequence)? What is revealed by the possibility of grouping them in this way (these ways)?

What is revealed by the events when taken as a group?

How can the group be divided? On what bases?

What possible correlations can be found among the several subgroups?

Into what class, if any, can the events taken as a group fit?

Does the group belong to any other structures than simply a larger group of similar events? (Is it part of a more inclusive chronological sequence? one more piece of evidence that may point toward a conclusion about history? and so on.)

To what antecedents does the group of events look back? Where can they be found?

What implications, if any, does the group of events have? Does the group point to a need for some sort of action?

II. "Topics" with "Comments" Already Attached

    A. Writing about Propositions (statements set forth to be proved or disproved)

What must be established for the reader before he will believe it?

Into what subpropositions, if any, can it be broken down? (What smaller assertions does it contain?)

What are the meanings of the key words in it?

To what line of reasoning is it apparently a conclusion?

How can we contrast it with other, similar, propositions? (How can we change it, if at all, and still have roughly the same proposition?)

To what class (or classes) of propositions does it belong?

How inclusive (or how limited) is it?

What is at issue, if one tries to prove the proposition?

How can it be illustrated?

How can it be proved (by what kinds of evidence)?

What will or can be said in opposition to it?

Is it true or false? How do we know (direct observation, authority, deduction, statistics, other sources)?

Why might someone disbelieve it?

What does it assume? (What other propositions does it take for granted?)

What does it imply? (What follows from it?) Does it follow from the proposition that action of some sort must be taken?

What does it reveal (signify, if true)?

If it is a prediction, how probable is it? On what observations of past experience is it based?

If it is a call to action, what are the possibilities that action can be taken? (Is what is called for feasible?) What are the probabilities that the action, if taken, will do what it is supposed to do? (Will the action called for work?)

B. Writing about Questions (interrogative sentences)

Does the question refer to past, present, or future time?

What does the question assume (take for granted)?

In what data might answers be sought?

Why does the question arise?

What, fundamentally, is in doubt? How can it be tested? Evaluated?

What propositions might be advanced in answer to it? Is each proposition true? If it is true: What will happen in the future? What follows from it? Which of these predictions are possible? Probable? What action should be taken (avoided) in consequence?

(Most of the other questions listed under "Propositions" also apply.)

One way of introducing students to Larson's questions might be to conduct a discussion with the entire class on the topic "television commercials," using the questions in ID, "Writing about Collections of Items." During the discussion, students will frame propositions ("Most commercials contain misleading slogans") and questions ("How are commercials made?"), which can be probed individually or by breaking the class into groups. One group might use the questions in IIA to develop material on the topic "Most commercials contain misleading slogans." Another group can investigate the process of making commercials by using the questions in IB. Students who want to analyze a specific commercial can begin working with questions in IA. And so on. Of course, not all of the questions need to be used; some questions might be modified; there are no right or wrong answers; some answers will generate additional questions. Since most students are accustomed to answering questions, not asking them or exploring open-ended questions, they probably will feel more comfortable working their way through the heuristic in groups before attempting the procedure on their own.

The last heuristic we will discuss in this chapter is adapted from Richard Young, Alton Becker, and Kenneth Pike's *Rhetoric: Discovery and Change*. What makes this heuristic so useful is that it permits us to examine a subject systematically from several perspectives. Although we customarily consider a subject from only one point of view, tagmemic invention forces us to shift mental gears to see it differently. According to Young, Becker, and Pike, anything—an object, event, concept—can be viewed from three perspectives. We usually regard an oak tree, to use their example, as an isolated, static entity, as a "thing" or particle. But we could also view the oak as a process (wave), as a participant in the natural growth cycle which begins with an acorn and ends when the tree rots or is cut into lumber. Or we may regard the tree as a system (field) of roots, trunk, branches, and leaves. These three perspectives—particle, wave, field—permit us to consider the same subject from three angles: as a static entity, as a dynamic process, and as a system.

Furthermore, in order to "know" this oak tree, we must be able to figure out three aspects of its existence (regardless of which perspective we assume):

1. How is it unique? As an entity, process, or system, how does it differ from everything else? Young, Becker, and Pike label this aspect "contrast."
2. How much can it change and still be itself? How much "variation" is possible in the oak (viewed as entity, process, or system) before it becomes something other than an oak?
3. How does it fit into larger systems of which it is a part? What is its "distribution"? In other words, the oak tree not only *is* a system, but it also belongs to other systems. It is affected by a system of seasonal changes; it participates in the ecosystem of the surrounding countryside; it plays a role in an economic system to which lumber production, tourism, and national parks belong.

The six concepts—particle, wave, field, contrast, variation, and distribution—can be arranged to produce a nine-cell chart, often referred to as a "tagmemic grid" or "matrix" (see *Rhetoric: Discovery and Change*, p. 127).

Although the nine-cell matrix can generate enormous amounts of material about a subject, most students need considerable practice using it before they find it helpful and comfortable. For this reason, you may prefer to introduce students to a simplified version of the matrix, like the one W. Ross Winterowd includes in *Contemporary Rhetoric* (p. 94):

The Los Angeles freeway system, for instance, can be viewed

1. *As an Isolated, Static Entity*

   We ask, What features characterize it? We can draw a map of it; we can measure its total length; we can count the number of overpasses and underpasses. We can describe it in great detail. In fact, such a description could well demand a number of thick volumes. But the point is that we can view anything as an isolated, static entity and begin to find those features that characterize it.

2. *As One Among Many of a Class*

   We ask, How does it differ from others in its class? From this point of view, we would compare the Los Angeles freeway system with others like it. I, for instance, immediately think of the differences between the L.A. freeway system and the turnpikes of the East and Midwest, as well as the German Autobahnen.

3. *As Part of a Larger System*

   We ask, How does it fit into larger systems of which it is a part? The L.A. freeway system would be worthless if it did not integrate with national, state, and county highway systems; therefore, its place in these larger systems is crucial.

4. *As a Process, Rather Than as a Static Entity*

   We ask, How is it changing? In regard to the L.A. freeway system, this question brings up the whole problem of planning for the future, which implies the problem of history, or how the system got to be the way it currently is.

5. *As a System, Rather Than as an Entity*

   We ask, What are the parts, and how do they work together? Now we are focusing on the L.A. freeways as a transportation system, each part of which must integrate and function with the whole.

Eventually, writers must stop generating answers to questions and begin organizing their raw material. They must evaluate what prewriting has yielded, identify hierarchies and classes, assign importance to some ideas and abandon others, and tentatively arrange whatever they want to include in a draft. It's difficult to say when generating material stops and shaping it begins because prewriting, writing, and rewriting don't follow a strict linear sequence. Sometimes prewriting activities generate material that reveals its own implicit organizational plan. Sometimes writers don't discover the best way to organize their material until they've completed two or three drafts. Furthermore, as writers draft and rewrite their work, they often discover "holes" in the discourse. They stop work and return to prewriting, generating additional material to fill the gaps they overlooked earlier.

For most students, the danger is that they begin drafting too soon, before they have sufficiently probed the subject, developing their own point of view and making a commitment to the message. Their papers remain pointless and general because they haven't found enough rich, interesting possibilities to pursue in the raw material.

To correct these problems, we must teach prewriting. We need to give students a repertoire of planning strategies which, used in various combinations, will yield abundant raw material. Of course, to be effective, these planning strategies must be used consistently. Students need specific instruction in how to use a particular prewriting technique and enough practice with it to gain a sense of its potential. We can also structure writing assignments in such a way that students move from brainstorming and freewriting to research and notetaking in response to a heuristic, from role-playing to talking out their ideas to writing them down. Students should view these activities, not as isolated events, but as parts of a process which always looks ahead to drafting and revising. Above all, we can give students time to let a piece of writing grow, time to find a topic but also time to let the topic find them.

7

What do teachers need to know about linguistics?

It is still our custom unhesitatingly and unthinkingly to demand that the clocks of language all be set to Central Standard Time.

MARTIN JOOS

Because we use English every day, we all know quite a bit about how it functions. We've developed an intuitive, largely unconscious ability to create and comprehend statements that conform to the rules of English. That intuitive knowledge—linguists call it *competence*—enables us to understand sentences we've never heard or read before, sentences we may read or hear only once in a lifetime. As writing teachers, however, we have a professional need to know considerably more about language than our experiences as language-users provide. As Charles Hockett points out in *A Course in Modern Linguistics*, "Native control of a language does not in itself imply conscious understanding of how the language works, or ability to teach it—any more than having cancer automatically makeṣ one a specialist in cancer diagnosis and therapy" (p. 2). To *teach* English requires a second kind of knowledge, a "conscious understanding" of linguistic principles.

One purpose for this chapter, then, is to examine the role language plays in the composing process, especially at the writing and rewriting stages. That is when students are principally concerned with manipulating language, putting ideas into words and examining the words to determine if they express ideas effectively. The more we know about how English works, the more linguistic options we can suggest to students struggling to get the words right.

Hockett's analogy suggests another reason why writing teachers need a secure knowledge of linguistic principles. Many people, including English teachers, would characterize student writing as "diseased" prose. Shocked by what they diagnose as a "literacy crisis" in American education, they expect writing teachers to become therapists, remedying students' deficiencies and thereby restoring the English language to its former healthy state. Perhaps the most controversial questions writing teachers confront focus on language: By what standards should we judge student writing? Is it an English teacher's primary responsibility to teach standard English? What right have we to force a particular dialect on speakers of other dialects? If there really is a literacy crisis in this country, what can we do about it? What's the best way to test the language skills of students? We can't answer questions like these responsibly without an understanding of linguistic principles.

A second purpose for this chapter then is to examine some assumptions people make when they discuss language. Many notions about language have no basis in linguistic fact. Instead, they derive their strength from tradition and from the enormous value we attach to our own personal variety of English. Linguists, who analyze languages objectively and systematically, can help us sort through these assumptions, question the methods we use to discuss language with our students, and revise those practices which research has shown to be unproductive. Some of us may not agree with all of their findings, or we may want to adapt their discussions to the particular needs of our students, but we must be familiar with the signficant contributions linguists have made in their study of language.

Linguistics, of course, comprises a large body of organized information about language, not only English but other languages as well.[1] Linguists study how we learn language (language acquisition), what features characterize a language (descriptive or synchronic linguis-

1. A useful bibliographic survey of linguistic theories which bear on the teaching of composition is W. Ross Winterowd's "Linguistics and Composition," *Teaching Composition: Ten Bibliographical Essays* (Fort Worth, Tex.: Texas Christian University Press, 1976), pp. 197–221. Although language acquisition is not discussed in this chapter, teachers, especially at elementary levels, will find useful Roger Brown, *A First Language: The Early Stages* (Cambridge, Mass.: Harvard University Press, 1973) and Courtney B. Cazden, *Child Language and Education* (New York: Holt, Rinehart and Winston, 1972).

tics; phonology, morphology, and syntax), what characteristics languages have in common (comparative linguistics), how languages change (historical or diachronic linguistics), how we attach meaning to sounds (semantics), even how dictionaries are made (lexicography). In this chapter we will limit our discussion of linguistic principles to four topics: the relationship between writing and speech; the nature of language; grammar and usage; and three approaches to grammar. These topics focus on areas of linguistics most beginning writing teachers want to know something about. They also allow us to construct a theoretical framework for Chapters 8–12, which apply linguistic principles to the teaching of writing.

Writing and speech

In Chapter 2, we discussed *code* as one of the elements of Jakobson's diagram. The English graphic system, we noted, comprises 1. alphabet letters and conventions for arranging them into words, sentences, and paragraphs; 2. a system of punctuation marks which separate the structural units of a message; and 3. mechanical customs which determine what the text looks like. The most important thing to remember about codes is that they're arbitrary and conventional. To illustrate this principle, see if you can crack the made-up codes in the following sentences;

1. txetnoc morf sesseug redaer ehT
   spiks tsuj esle ro ,sdrow railimafnu
   .meht
2. The as he reader reads or though sense text the make expects she to.
3. gsv ivzwvi nzpvh fhv lu ivwfmwzmxrvh—ligsltizksrx, hbmgzxgrx, zmw hvnzmgrx—gl ivwfxv fmxvigzmgb zylfg nvmrmt.

Which of the sentences is easiest to read? Why? Although all three sentences use English alphabet letters and punctuation marks, what conventions govern their use? The first sentence arranges English alphabet letters from right to left across the page. The second sentence rearranges whole English words in an unconventional, random order. The third sentence, like many secret codes children devise, assigns new values to English alphabet letters: $z = a$, $y = b$, $x = c$, and so on.

Although some writers—e. e. cummings and George Herbert, for example—deliberately manipulate graphic conventions, we generally agree to use them in certain ways. The shape of the symbols and their order must be observed. The symbols also have linguistic values; that is, they correspond to sounds in spoken English. Writing and speech, however, aren't isomorphic; the graphic symbols and the sounds don't share a strict one-to-one correspondence. For example, the single sound at the beginning and end of *church* (/č/ in the phonemic alphabet linguists use) must be represented by two alphabet letters. Conversely, the alphabet letters *th* represent two different "th" sounds in words like *thigh* (/θaɪ/) and *thy* (/ðaɪ/). Likewise, one symbol *a* represents at least six sounds: *fa*ther, *a*sk, *a*ll, sens*a*-tion, *a*round, m*a*re.

One of the reasons alphabet letters and speech sounds don't "fit" is that writing systems change much more slowly than languages do. When printing presses made books available to an educated middle class, spelling became relatively fixed, even though the language continued to change. We still spell *know* with an initial *k,* a sound speakers of Old English once pronounced. Speakers of Middle English would have pronounced *hope* as a two-syllable word, whereas today we regard the *e* as "silent." And some so-called silent *e*'s were simply added to words by printers who wanted to justify lines of type, to make the margins even.

Although writing and speech share some characteristics, they're different systems. People often confuse the two systems, however. A kind woman once approached me after a talk I'd given and quietly, so as not to embarrass me, encouraged me not to "drop the *g*'s" at the ends of my words. "After all," she whispered, "you're an English teacher." I thanked her, of course, but was reminded that many people assume that words should be pronounced as they're spelled. They rarely are. Even Shakespeare's compositors seem to have had some difficulty determining when the final *g* should be spelled where it was no longer pronounced. They "corrected" the pronunciations of *napkin* and *javelins* by spelling them as *napking* and *javelings*.

Because we all value language as a means of expressing ourselves, we naturally make value judgments about what "sounds good" and "looks right." We all could name the most beautiful and ugliest sounding languages, for example, even justifying our preferences with statements like "Russian sounds harsh; French sounds melodious." Such statements, however, represent opinions, not facts. Many people would say that French and Italian, the languages of love and opera, sound beautiful, whereas German and Russian sound ugly, perhaps because our tastes have been influenced by World War II and Cold War propaganda. Like all matters of taste, our assumptions of what language should and shouldn't be reflect personal and cultural values. Consequently, it's difficult, if not impossible, to discuss English spoken or written systems without bias. It's even more difficult to avoid imposing our values on the students we teach. As teachers our best defense may be acknowledging the problem. Students need to know that all writers make choices based on what they believe constitutes "effective English." They can't make those choices freely if we treat language as absolute, as a system of right and wrong rules. Not only are such notions linguistically inaccurate; they also increase our students' fears of making mistakes, discourage their curiosity about language, and prevent them from appreciating the very power of expression which so attracted us to the study of English in the first place.

The nature of language

Most linguists define *language* as "a learned system of sounds that have an arbitrary value and meet a social need to communicate." For linguists, then, language is sound, not writing. The sounds (phones) may vary from culture to culture, but the organs used to produce them are common to all human beings. Neither climate nor race has a role in speech production. The southern American drawl, for example, isn't the result of hot weather or inherent laziness among southerners; speakers in equally hot or hotter climates in Africa and South America produce speech at relatively fast tempos.

As the definition notes, language is also a social, not a biological, necessity. The organs used to produce speech have as their primary functions breathing, tasting, chewing, and smelling—biological functions which insure human survival. We don't need language to survive. Feral children, raised in the wild without other human beings around them, and mutes, who for some physiological reason aren't able to speak, are evidence that humans can survive without language. However, we need to cooperate with others, establish mutually sustaining relationships, and share our experiences and ideas. Language is an important way of establishing this contact, of realizing a psychological need to live in societies rather than as isolated individuals.

Language also tells us about our societies. Groups of sounds, called *morphs,* have meaning. They denote realities in our culture and reflect or connote the values we place on those realities. Terms for kinship, colors, technological innovations, even the euphemisms we invent to discuss taboo subjects reveal how we perceive the world. Keep in mind, however, that the sounds of English are themselves neutral; /t/ is neither a "good" nor a "bad" sound. When we say *"Spit* is an ugly word," we really mean that the action of spitting in public is socially unacceptable in our culture, not that the sequence of sounds is ugly. The same sequence is found in the word *hospitality,* which has favorable connotations, not because the sounds are "good" but because the reality to which the sounds refer has a positive value in our culture.

That there's nothing intrinsically "good" or "bad" about the sequence of sounds /spɪt/ brings us to another term in our definition of language, *arbitrary.* The sounds of English "have an arbitrary value." Like the symbols in the English graphic system, speech sounds are conventional. We mutually agree to use the system in certain ways. We might just as well call a student a *klib,* and if all of us agreed that *klib* refers to a student, we'd communicate quite well. Similarly, the entire system of English is arbitrary. Its sounds, its vocabulary, its sentence structures have been sanctioned by history, tradition, and the will of the powerful; yet any of these conventions could change if speakers and hearers agreed to adopt the new arrangement.

Languages do change—constantly. People change them by consenting to different styles of expression. Just as hemlines on women's dresses vary from season to season, so too does what is "acceptable" in speech and writing. In the fourteenth century it was appropriate for Chaucer to write four negatives in the lines, "he *nevere* yet *no* vileynye *ne* sayde/In al his lyf unto *no* maner wight" (*Canterbury Tales,* Prologue, lines 70–71), to intensify the negation. Modern readers, however, won't accept this convention in formal writing, even though we certainly can comprehend "double negatives" in spoken English. Despite the opinions of eighteenth-century grammarians, we also know that double negatives don't make a statement positive. No native speaker of English would understand "He ain' no good" to mean "He's good." Formal styles of written English conventionally avoid ending sentences with prepositions, but in informal writing and spoken English, we often place prepositions at the ends of sentences. Winston Churchill maintained it was "a rule up with which I will not put."

Notions about what is grammatical also change. The writers of the King James Bible (1611) didn't subscribe to the later convention of using *who* as a predicate nominative after the verb "to be." For them, "to be," like any other verb, required the objective case: *"Whom* do men say that I the Son of man am?" (Matt. 16:13). Today the use of *'s* to indicate possession seems to be giving way to possessive constructions involving prepositions. We're more likely to say "the top of the house" than "the house's top." In some dialects of English possession is indicated by juxtaposing the noun and its modifier, as in "Mary hat" for "Mary's hat," or "up on the house top" for "up on the top of the house."

As a rule, innovations or changes in language occur slowly. Usually they become acceptable in speech before they're acceptable in writing. Almost always they must be adopted by politically, socially, and culturally influential speakers and writers before they become preferred usages. For us, changes in vocabulary may be the easiest to observe. As events and inventions change our world, we develop new words—*smog, Watergate, television, cloning*—to talk about them. Conversely, some words diminish in importance as we no longer need them. *Forecastle,* for example, still occurs in written form, but people rarely pronounce it in two syllables /fóksəl/ as an old sailor would. Nor would we now understand, as Winfred Lehmann has pointed out, the technical terms once used in astrology. Changes in vocabulary, lexical changes, aren't the only kind speakers of English make. Change has affected and continues to affect every level of the language. For at least 5000 years linguistic developments have altered our system of meaningful speech sounds (phonemes); how we combine them into units of meaning (morphemes); and how we arrange those units into phrases, clauses, and sentences (syntax).[2]

Paradoxically, change is a constant in all languages. Attempts to alter or slow down linguistic change have never been successful. The speakers of a language will express themselves despite the efforts of others to regulate their communication. As the authors of "Students' Right to Their Own Language" have observed, "past change is considered normal, but current change is viewed by some as degradation. From Chaucer to Shakespeare to Faulkner, the language assuredly changed, and yet no one speaks of the primitive language of Chaucer or the impoverished language of Shakespeare" (p. 18). Language change is neither good nor bad; it simply *is.* English speakers will make such innovations as seem necessary to communicating what they want others to understand. As English teachers, we have no hope of halting or reversing innovations in language. But if we understand the role of change in language, we'll be better able to explain these processes to our students. They need to see language, not

2. Especially thorough introductory surveys of these developments are Albert C. Baugh and Thomas Cable, *A History of the English Language,* 3rd ed. (Englewood Cliffs, N.J.: Prentice-Hall, 1978) and Thomas Pyles, *The Origins and Development of the English Language,* 2nd ed. (New York: Harcourt Brace Jovanovich, 1971).

as rules which manipulate writers, but as a resource they can manipulate to express themselves to others.

Grammar and usage

People who don't understand linguistic principles generally confuse the terms *grammar* and *usage*. English teachers, like linguists, must keep them distinct. *Grammar* has several meanings.[3] First, it denotes that intuitive knowledge of language human beings gain by about age five. In this sense, $grammar_1$ means "a capacity for language," a native ability to create and comprehend English utterances. The term also refers to various formal systems ($grammar_2$) scholars developed to explain our capacity for language. Traditional grammar, for example, represents an accumulation of terms, rules, and methods for analyzing what we do when we use language. $Grammar_2$, the field of study, generates theories about $grammar_1$, an unconscious process or behavior.

Usage, on the other hand, refers to linguistic etiquette, to socially sanctioned styles of language appropriate to given situations and audiences.[4] If I address my class with profanity and obscenity, I am demonstrating an insensitivity to usage. My speech would certainly be grammatical, conforming, that is, to ways native speakers of English construct utterances, but profane and obscene language is socially unacceptable in a classroom. Similarly, lacing my responses to questions in a job interview with double negatives wouldn't be consistent with the formality of that situation. Conversely, answering the telephone with "It is I" instead of "It's me," or using the conventions of formal writing in conversations with a close friend would doubtless create the impression that I'm a snob. Usage, then, refers to language in a context, for a particular audience.

Many people link usage to so-called standard English, implying that there's an absolute right and wrong way to use the language. The wrong way denotes nonstandard English; the right way defines the standard. In practice, however, "the wrong way" also defines standard English; that is, people find it much easier to say what standard English is *not* than to describe what it is. By implying that there's only one way to use the language, such definitions are also linguistically inaccurate. Like many styles of dress appropriate to different

3. See W. Nelson Francis, "Revolution in Grammar," *Quarterly Journal of Speech* 40 (October 1954), 299–312.
4. A helpful discussion of usage is in Robert C. Pooley, *The Teaching of English Usage*, 2nd ed. (Urbana, Ill.: NCTE, 1974).

social occasions, English permits several "standards." Edited American English—often called "standard edited English"—comprises many literary dialects. Its conventions tend to be more conservative than those of spoken English, but they define a spectrum of styles useful in writing everything from very formal essays to informal notes. Similarly, standard spoken English consists of many regional, social, and occupational dialects, each of which has several registers or levels of usage. The speech of Presidents Kennedy, Johnson, and Carter, for example, represents several regional varieties of standard spoken English. We may define standard spoken English as that variety of English used by the educated upper middle class, Americans who historically wield the greatest social, political, and economic clout, but we must remember that the definition incorporates many levels of usage which can be employed in very formal to quite informal situations.

Each of us speaks a variety of English, called an idiolect, which differs in details of pronunciation, vocabulary, and syntax from every other idiolect. Like fingerprints, idiolects are unique; no two people share precisely the same idiolect. Many forces shape these individual language patterns: social, cultural, geographical, economic, and educational influences, even our sex and age. Strictly speaking, dialects represent collections of features idiolects have in common, shared similarities in proununciation, vocabulary, and syntax. Dialectologists, linguistic geographers, as well as sociolinguists study dialects and the forces that propagate them.[5]

Dialectal differences are generally determined by the historical character of settlements, geographical features, political or ecclesiastical boundaries, cultural centers, and routes of migration. Other forces promote uniformity among dialects: mass education, urbanization, industrialization, geographic and social mobility. Unlike England or France, where London and Paris are major cultural centers, the United States has no single dominant cultural capital. Consequently, American English comprises several regional dialects. In a project known

5. An excellent introduction to varieties of American English is Raven I. McDavid's "The Dialects of American English," in W. Nelson Francis, *The Structure of American English* (New York: Ronald Press, 1958), pp. 480–543. McDavid's "American English: A Bibliographic Essay," *American Studies International* 17 (Winter 1979), 3–45, discusses numerous resources for investigating the pronunciation, spelling, grammar, usage, names, slang, and regional, social, and literary dialects of American English. I am indebted to Professor McDavid, Professor Emeritus of English at the University of Chicago, and Raymond O'Cain, Columbia, South Carolina, for making available unpublished materials on which I have based my discussion of American dialects and for developing the maps on pp. 110–111 from Linguistic Atlas records.

as the Linguistic Atlas of the United States and Canada (LAUSC), dialectologists have undertaken to survey the English dialects of North America. LAUSC actually represents several autonomous regional surveys which share a common methodology. Using a finely graded phonetic alphabet and elaborate questionnaires, trained investigators have made firsthand observations of local speechways, data which reveal the normal usage on hundreds of points of grammar, vocabulary, and pronunciation among speakers in a network of communities throughout the United States and Canada. The results of this field work appear in several atlases. The *Linguistic Atlas of New England* (1939–43) was the first to be published, followed by the *Linguistic Atlas of the Upper Midwest* (1973–76) and the *Linguistic Atlas of the Middle and South Atlantic States* (1980–   ). The *Linguistic Atlas of the Gulf States* and the *Linguistic Atlas of the North Central States* are now being prepared for publication. Materials for linguistic atlases of Oklahoma, of Missouri, of the Rocky Mountain States, and of the Pacific Coast are in archival form, and Canadian dialectologists have completed extensive field work. These materials together with other published summaries of information from the Atlas records provide an essential foundation for the study of variation in American speech.

The materials also offer practical guidance to writing teachers. Let's examine a simple, fairly uncontroversial usage problem. Suppose you read in a student's paper, "She dove into the pool." Should you mark out *dove* and replace it with *dived?* Which form is more acceptable? You consult several handbooks and dictionaries to discover conflicting information.[6] Some claim that *dove* is "restricted"; its use is limited to particular contexts or is disapproved altogether. Others label *dove* as "colloquial," which, according to many traditional texts, also means "Don't use it." Still other handbooks judge both forms "acceptable." Despite what some handbooks maintain, the Atlas records reveal that both *dived* and *dove* (even /dəv/ and /dɪv/) are legitimate past tense forms of the verb "to dive." Notice their distribution on the maps below.

Dove has a clearly defined regional distribution which extends from the northeast United States westward along migration routes across the Great Lakes to the North Central States and Upper Midwest. Correcting *dove* amounts to insisting on an *ungrammatical* past tense if the student's dialect permits only *dove,* not *dived. Dived* represents

6. Thomas J. Creswell, *Usage in Dictionaries and Dictionaries of Usage* (Publication of the American Dialect Society, Numbers 63–64; University, Ala.: University of Alabama Press, 1975) examines in detail how contemporary American dictionaries, usage guides, and studies of usage differ in their treatment of usage items.

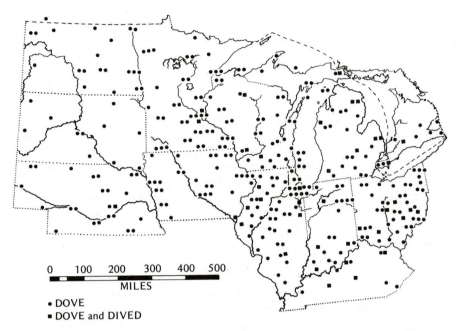

0   100   200   300   400   500
MILES

• DOVE
■ DOVE and DIVED

FIGURE 7.1   Linguistic Atlas Map of Upper Midwest and North Central States

unconventional usage for speakers who grew up in these areas, even though they may no longer live there. On matters of divided or disputed usage, it's best to give student writers options. Send them to *several* dictionaries and usage handbooks. If students can support a usage item with at least one outside reference, permit it. Their investigation, in the meantime, will also have increased their sensitivity to and tolerance for varieties of English.

One of the most difficult issues facing writing teachers is this matter of "linguistic tolerance," which some critics view as the surest course to "corrupting" the English language. Generally, the value judgments we make about another's speech are ethnocentric; that is, they assume the superiority of our own dialect. Few of us, of course, would label our own speech "corrupt" or "unacceptable," but we're all tempted to account for differences in speech—like taste in music, clothes, or food—by questioning the intelligence or heritage of others. The error of their ways is just as obvious as the propriety of ours. It's this tendency we must resist, in ourselves and in our students, for the judgments we make about another person on the basis of language reflect personal values, not linguistic facts. Still, even

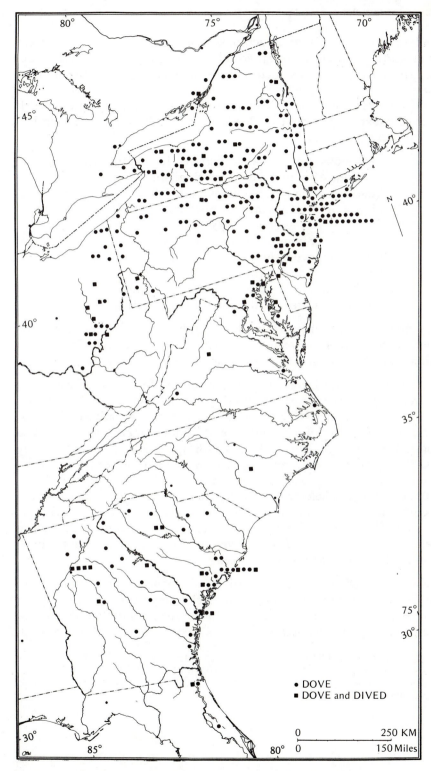

FIGURE 7.2   Linguistic Atlas Map of Middle and South Atlantic States

well-educated people construct elaborate rationalizations to buttress their attitudes about cultural, social, and linguistic differences. Several studies have proven such logic fallacious. Let's examine some of them.

Which of the following statements are true, and which are false? If you consider a statement misleading or believe that "it depends," can you explain why?

1. Textbooks are a reliable resource for determining the conventions of edited American English.
2. Teachers are a reliable resource for determining the acceptability of certain words or phrases, for arbitrating usage.
3. Anybody can learn grammar.
4. Teaching grammar—memorizing parts of speech, diagramming sentences—improves writing ability.
5. Dialects interfere with the ability to read.
6. Dialects interfere with the ability to think.
7. Dialects interfere with the ability to write.

The first six statements are predominantly false either because they confuse the terms *grammar* and *usage* or because they imply that what's true for one language operation is also true for another.

Statement 1: Using Linguistic Atlas findings, Malmstrom[7] compares 57 items of current American usage with the advice of 312 textbooks published between 1940 and 1955. Not only is their advice inconsistent, but their pronouncements about edited American English also contradict what speakers of American English actually do when they use the language. More recently, Creswell has examined the "variations in treatment of usage matters and in judgments about individual locutions in a selected list of recent and contemporary American dictionaries, usage guides, and studies of usage" (*Usage in Dictionaries and Dictionaries of Usage,* p. 7). His study is based on 226 usage items which editors of the *American Heritage Dictionary* (1969) "deemed of questionable acceptability."

Statement 2: Of course, some individual teachers may indeed be reliable usage arbiters. However, Womack[8] demonstrates that English teachers as a group tend to be far more conservative than the rest of the population about *rejecting* usages which current practice and much

7. Jean Malmstrom, "Linguistic Atlas Findings Versus Textbook Pronouncements on Current American Usage," *English Journal* 48 (April 1959), 191–98.
8. Thurston Womack, "Teachers' Attitudes Toward Current Usage," *English Journal* 48 (April 1959), 186–90.

published information support as acceptable. The most conservative judgments about 50 disputed usage items tended to come from high school teachers with B.A. or M.A. degrees who had taught in small towns for more than 10 years; teachers who held a Ph.D. and had been teaching less than 10 years in cities of over 50,000 people were more likely to accept disputed usages. The study also finds that, despite considerable published new information on current American usage, the opinions of English teachers haven't changed dramatically in the light of recent findings.

Statement 3: Meade[9] compares the intelligence quotients of 104 high school seniors to their performance on items from several standarized grammar tests. He concludes that even the brightest students (114–152 I.Q.) have difficulty making a "creditable showing" on the tests; 10 of the 26 students in the "bright" group couldn't complete at least 75% of the test correctly. English teachers who feel confident about "knowing grammar" consequently may assume that their students can also easily master it. Meade's study suggests that perhaps teachers should revise their assumptions and expectations. Most students find learning formal grammar difficult and not very enjoyable. In Donelson's study[10] of effective and ineffective writers in the tenth grade, the students' fondness for grammar instruction was a significant variable. The better writers *least* preferred studying grammar, even though they enjoyed other activities in their English classes. Many experienced teachers won't be startled by these findings. We know our students have trouble learning formal grammar, dislike it, and seem not to retain for very long what they've learned. Nevertheless, we continue to teach it in the belief that "it's good for them," that it improves their writing. But does grammar instruction actually improve writing ability?

Statement 4: Braddock, Lloyd-Jones, and Schoer and many others[11] have repeatedly concluded that formal grammar instruction doesn't improve writing ability, principally because writing involves a great deal more than merely editing a written product. Students learn to

9. Richard A. Meade, "Who Can Learn Grammar?" *English Journal* 50 (February 1961), 87–92.
10. K.L. Donelson, "Variables Distinguishing Between Effective and Ineffective Writers in the Tenth Grade," *Journal of Experimental Education* 35 (Summer 1967), 37–41.
11. Richard Braddock, Richard Lloyd-Jones, and Lowell Schoer, *Research in Written Composition* (Urbana, Ill.: NCTE, 1963). See also the summary of research in Frank O'Hare, *Sentence Combining: Improving Student Writing without Formal Grammar Instruction* (NCTE Research Report No. 15; Urbana, Ill.: NCTE, 1973), pp. 5–18.

write by writing, not by analyzing or diagramming sentences someone else has written, not by memorizing parts of speech which have
been divorced from the context of student prose. Unless grammar
instruction derives from actual discussions of student papers, these
studies conclude, it has no useful connection to the composing process. As Weaver points out, research does not support the notion that
learning grammar is useful in attaining any other goal, except learning grammar:

> As long ago as 1950, the *Encyclopedia of Educational Research* sum-
> marized the available research (pp. 392–96), concluding that the study
> of grammar has a negligible effect in helping people think more clearly,
> and that a knowledge of English grammar does not contribute signif-
> icantly to achievement in foreign language. Furthermore, the results
> from tests in grammar, composition, and literary interpretation led to
> the conclusion that there was little or no relationship between gram-
> mar and composition or between grammar and literary interpretation.
> Further evidence supplementing the early studies indicated that
> training in formal grammar did not transfer to any significant extent
> to writing or to recognizing correct English. In general, the experi-
> mental evidence revealed a discouraging lack of relationship between
> grammatical knowledge and the better utilization of expressional skills.
> Recently grammar has been held to contribute to the better under-
> standing of the sentence. Yet even here, there is discouragingly little
> relationship between sentence sense and grammatical knowledge of
> subjects and predicates. On the whole, the more recent research sup-
> ports the conclusion that the study of grammar in, of, and by itself
> has little positive effect upon anything else. . . . Indeed, even the
> grammatical knowledge itself is not long retained. (*Grammar for
> Teachers*, p. 4)

Statement 5: Gunderson[12] compiles much useful information on theories, research, problems, and practices of teaching reading, and
Baratz and Shuy's collection of articles[13] suggests that the teacher's
attitudes towards dialects, not the dialects themselves, can interfere
with the complex process of learning to read. All of us can understand many varieties of English, even dialects we can't ourselves
speak. It follows then that we don't need to speak Milton's English
to be able to read his work. We read texts to understand their meaning, not to speak them.

12. Doris V. Gunderson, ed., *Language and Reading* (Washington, D.C.: Center for
Applied Linguistics, 1970).
13. Joan C. Baratz and Roger W. Shuy, eds., *Teaching Black Children to Read* (Washington, D.C.: Center for Applied Linguistics, 1969).

Statement 6: Similarly, students who write "he walk" and "Mary hat" aren't deficient thinkers who lack "concepts" of tense or possession. They merely translate those concepts into a written code different from the code we call edited American English. At best "Mary hat" may represent a spelling problem, not a thinking problem which requires endless drilling on the metaphysics of ownership.

The 129-item bibliography appended to "The Students' Right to Their Own Language" cites many useful resources which review the distinctions between speech, writing, thinking, and reading. These authors rightly insist that basing our teaching on value judgments about dialects not only is inconsistent with linguistic fact but also can harm students. It is doubly dangerous, therefore, to assume that particular patterns of speech characterize deficiencies in other, quite different mental processes—thinking, reading, and writing.

Statement 7: Although some students experience difficulty mastering edited American English, a particular written code, they don't have to change their dialect to write effectively. Speaking and writing are different language operations, and if students see a need to write edited American English, they will master it. To cite a previous example, Presidents Kennedy, Johnson, and Carter mastered edited American English, but they did so without changing their speech.

We teach students the conventions of edited American English because many parents, teachers, administrators, and employers believe that it's a code essential to social and professional advancement. But the code, as we know, represents only one element of Jakobson's diagram. To focus our teaching exclusively on code is to ignore other equally important elements of the composing process. Writing that says nothing to no one in particular, regardless of the dialect it's written in, is ineffective.

Approaches to grammar

If teaching grammar per se doesn't improve writing ability, why include in this chapter a section called "Approaches to Grammar"? Because *teachers* do need to know grammar, the theories which explain how English functions systematically. Beginning teachers, especially, should know that the study of grammar can be approached from several perspectives. Each perspective offers ways of helping students expand their powers of expression and increase their linguistic options, especially in editing their work. Furthermore, when teachers understand grammatical theories, they can respond to concerns that parents, administrators, and other teachers express about what should be basic in a writing curriculum. Grammatical knowledge also helps teachers evaluate curricula, instructional materials, and teaching practices.

Many contemporary methods of teaching English originate in past theories about language which ought to be reexamined. The teaching of English as a school subject began in the seventeenth century, when England was filled with foreigners and members of the middle class who wanted to read and write English. Formerly education had belonged to the nobility and the clergy, but in the Renaissance teachers were forced quickly to adapt old methods of teaching Latin and Greek to new students and a new subject, English.

Even though English is structurally quite different from Latin and Greek, nevertheless English instruction was modeled on a classical tradition. As early as 100 B.C., Dionysius Thrax had compiled a grammar of Greek, based on the written, not the spoken, language. He classified Greek into parts of speech. Latin grammar books were based on the Greek classification system. They also included material on metrics and established the practice of imitating literary "models." The tradition of teaching parts of speech, of asking students to memorize verb, noun, and pronoun paradigms, of defining "excellence" with reference to great works of literature, remains virtually unchanged after centuries of employing the classical tradition to teach English.

A second characteristic of English education, making judgments about language, legislating "correctness," stems from classical precepts which were reinforced during the Middle Ages, when the Church fostered education. Christian theology tended to view change negatively, as emblematic of the human condition since the fall from grace in the Garden of Eden. Language was believed to be devolving from Hebrew (erroneously thought to be the oldest language). Language change was seen as further evidence that sin pervaded human existence. To prevent further degeneration, scholars and teachers sought to "fix" language by rigid rules, by establishing classical models and the formal writing of the Church Fathers as standards for correctness. Language study became error-oriented. Students were expected to learn the rules and gain practice in recognizing "deviant" constructions.

The two traditions, a reliance on classical models and an orientation toward correctness, were reemphasized in the eighteenth century, when "scientific rationalism" exerted tremendous influence on the study of language. Scholars of this period sought to make language "logical," reasonable in a scientific, mathematical sense. Wherever possible, they reinforced their explanations of logical rules with examples from classical authors. In an effort to promote and codify the logic of English, eighteenth-century grammarians adopted the following aims: [14]

1. *To devise rules governing "correct" English usage.* Many rules resorted to mathematical principles. For example, writing two negatives in a sentence began to be "incorrect," given the logic of mathematics. Similarly, since the verb *to be* was viewed as a mathematical equals sign, the nominative, not the objective, case became the appropriate form to use after *to be:*

It   is   I (not *me*).

Nominative = Nominative

2. *To refine the language, removing "deviant" constructions and introducing "improvements."* Supposedly inferior words of Anglo-Saxon origin were replaced with Latinate vocabulary. Dr. Samuel Johnson's *Dictionary of the English Language* (1755), the first true English dictionary and a remarkable achievement in its day, often resorts to Latin terms in defining English words. His definition of *network,* for example, reads: "Any thing reticulated or decussated, at equal distances, with interstices between the intersections." Many of the terms we encounter in studying grammar—*antecedent, accusative, intransitive, passive*—originate in this period and reflect a preference for Latin, the "superior" authority as a model.

3. *To fix the English language and prevent further deterioration.* Working from the mistaken notion that Greek and Latin hadn't changed, grammarians wanted to codify the new refinements and rules they had developed for English. In this way, they thought, writers (and speakers) could be guided by the collective wisdom of texts and other reference works. Samuel Johnson's *Dictionary* and the grammar books of Robert Lowth (1762) and Lindley Murray (1795) became important school texts, prototypes of instructional materials used for over 150 years to the present.

Traditional grammar reflects this legacy. It is rules-oriented, Latin-based, prescriptive and proscriptive. It legislates constructions which must be adhered to or avoided. It focuses on the written language. The principal method of teaching traditional grammar is called *parsing,* a rote process which analyzes a given sentence in four steps:

14. For a detailed discussion of these aims, see Baugh and Cable, Chapter 9.

1. By identifying the largest structural components of the sentence (subject and predicate, dependent and independent clauses);
2. By classifying each word as one of eight parts of speech (nouns, pronouns, verbs, adverbs, adjectives, prepositions, conjunctions, interjections);
3. By describing individual words in terms of their inflectional or derivational prefixes or suffixes;
4. By explaining the relationship of each word to other words in the sentence through a "sentence diagram."

Traditional grammarians developed terminology useful to discussing language and codified many conventions governing edited American English. Nevertheless, the traditional approach to grammar has many disadvantages. In the first place, traditional grammarians did not describe what spoken English was but rather legislated what written English ought to be. They failed to respect the role of change in language and refused to recognize that forms appropriate in some kinds of writing might not be appropriate for other audiences.

Second, they based their approach on Latin and Greek, assuming that what was logical for those languages was also logical for English. They failed to recognize English's unique logic and structure. Because English has lost most of its inflectional endings, it differs in many significant ways from its distant Latin and Greek cousins. For example, a paradigm may be useful for teaching the Latin verb *amo* ("I love") in the present tense indicative mood. All the endings are different. In English, however, most verbs show only one inflectional variant in the third person singular; modal verbs show no variants at all.

Latin		English			
am<u>o</u>	am<u>amus</u>	love	love	may	may
am<u>as</u>	am<u>atis</u>	love	love	may	may
am<u>at</u>	am<u>ant</u>	love<u>s</u>	love	may_	may

A paradigm, then, represents a time-consuming, inefficient means of teaching students where English demands final -s on present tense verbs.

Third, traditional grammar's preoccupation with parts of speech leaves little room to study other, equally important, areas of the English language. We've probably memorized the definitions so well that we don't recognize how vague some of them are: "A sentence expresses a *complete thought.*" (What, then, is an "incomplete" thought?) "A verb expresses action or *state of being.*" (How's a tenth grader supposed to understand "being-ness"?) Other definitions are circular: "An adverb modifies a verb, adjective, or *another adverb.*" Still other definitions seem inconsistent; some explain what the part of speech *means,* while others describe what the part of speech *does,* how it functions.

Finally, although traditional grammar claims to study the sentence, the approach focuses on taking language apart, not on putting it together. Students analyze and dissect sentences by diagramming them or labeling each word as a part of speech. Generally, they are someone else's sentences, not the student's. As a result, students may learn terminology and doubtless some principles of editing, but they haven't learned how to *create* discourse, only how to label, diagram, or analyze it. Since the traditional approach doesn't encourage students to apply grammatical principles to the composing process, teachers must. If grammar is taught at all, it should be tied to writing instruction. The student's own prose, not the chapter-by-chapter arrangement of a text, should determine which grammatical principles offer workable solutions to writing problems.

Structural grammar

Although descriptive approaches to the study of language developed more slowly than the traditional prescriptive approach, they have found favor among the majority of modern linguists as well as a good many writing teachers. As long ago as the eighteenth century, Joseph Priestley (*Rudiments of English Grammar,* 1761) and George Campbell (*Philosophy of Rhetoric,* 1776) advanced the theory that contemporary usage, not classical authority, must determine what's appropriate or standard in English. For them, English speakers, not Latin models, were the best authority for describing the grammar of English. When Darwin's studies (1859) asserted that "progress" was beneficial, not harmful, changes in language also began to be viewed more objectively. Scholars began to be more interested in what changes had occurred than in determining whether those changes were right or wrong. In contrast to the prescriptivists, descriptive linguists are primarily interested in examining the language as it is, not advancing notions about what it should be.

In 1933 Leonard Bloomfield, widely regarded as the father of modern linguistics in America, published *Language,* a work which defines the methodology of the descriptive linguist. Working only with data that can be objectively verified, the descriptive linguist must describe, classify, and analyze samples of language before making generalizations about the evidence. Limiting himself only to that which is measurable, Bloomfield relegated the rest of language study, especially thought processes, to other disciplines.

The structural grammarian, one kind of descriptive linguist, sorts language data into three levels: the smallest units of language or individual sounds (phonology), groups of sounds that have meaning (morphology), and the arrangement of morphs which signal complex relationships in phrases, clauses, and sentences (syntax). A major difference between the traditional and structural grammarian can be seen in how they treat parts of speech. Unwilling to classify nouns, for example, on the basis of a word's meaning, structuralists use other evidence. *Gangsters* is a noun, not because it names persons, but because it shows an inflectional plural -*s* and because the derivational suffix -*ster* is a morph reserved exclusively for nouns in English. In addition to form-criteria, position-criteria (syntax) may also determine "nounness." In the sentence, "The gangsters robbed the bank," *gangsters* is a noun because it occupies one of many slots or positions nouns hold in English sentence patterns. Students find these criteria—what a word looks like and where it appears in the sentence—much more reliable and concrete than criteria which resort to a word's meaning.

The structuralists' descriptions of basic English sentence patterns also help students identify the order and arrangement of sentence elements. Without making abstract determinations about a clause's "dependence" or "independence," students can study how words behave in their writing by examining where they appear in sentences. A common technique structuralists advocate for teaching syntax asks students to analyze nonsense sentences like "The trasky gleebers were miffling holps wombly." Deprived of clues to the word's meaning, students must base their understanding of sentence construction on morphological and syntactic evidence.

These and other techniques derived from structural grammar help us teach students about words and sentences more objectively, concretely, and descriptively than the traditional approach permits. We'll examine them in more detail in Chapters 8 and 9. Structural principles also inform Chapter 13, which approaches student papers descriptively, as objective evidence of how the students use language, not as proof that they committed errors.

Generative-transformational grammar

Oddly enough, our ability to decode nonsense sentences points up a shortcoming in the approach and methodology of structural grammar. Dependent on samples of spoken language, the structuralist can't explain how speakers of a language constantly create sentences they've never heard before. Structuralists aren't able to analyze the infinite possibilities of a complex, living language because they limit themselves to investigating only measurable spoken data. They exclude from their studies mental processes, what speakers know, and focus only on performance, the results of speakers' putting what they know to use.

This distinction between *competence* and *performance* is of special interest to generative-transformational grammarians. They attempt to explain how speakers and hearers of English create and understand unique sentences, based on the same code, yet permitting infinite variations. All human beings acquire the ability to use language without formal instruction. We master the code we share with other English speakers long before we know that language has rules, let alone what those rules are. It's this intuitive knowledge that the transformational grammarian seeks to describe.

Noam Chomsky's *Syntactic Structures* sets forth the principles of this recent approach to descriptive linguistics. Chomsky maintains that native speakers know the grammar of their language intuitively. By *grammar* he means not only the rules whereby we combine words into sentences (syntax), but also our knowledge of sounds (phonology) and units of meaning (morphology). A single body of intuitive linguistic knowledge, a grammar, governs all our uses of language, as speakers, hearers, writers, or readers. Whereas the structuralists begin their study with the smallest units of speech, individual sounds, and proceed to analyze ever larger units of language, the transformationalist describes the native speaker's intuitive grammar beginning with the sentence. Defining *sentence* is the heart of transformational grammar. An analogy to mathematics may help to explain the transformationalist's approach.[15]

When we learn mathematics, we don't have to store in our mem-

15. The analogy was suggested by Jeanne Herndon, *A Survey of Modern Grammars* (New York: Holt, Rinehart and Winston, 1970). The second edition (1976) offers an excellent overview of traditional, structural, and transformational approaches to the study of language. For a brief, readable discussion of transformational grammar alone, consult Suzette Haden Elgin, *A Primer of Transformational Grammar: For the Rank Beginner* (Urbana, Ill.: NCTE, 1975).

ories the fact that $126 \times 157 = 19,782$. We simply learn a finite set of multiplication tables and then memorize a few simple rules—how to "carry" numbers, shift columns, add the columns—for reusing the basic tables. Given a finite set of multiplication tables and a finite set of rules for using them, we can perform an infinite number of math problems. Similarly, the transformationalist suggests that we learn, at a very early age, a finite set of phrase-structure rules and a second finite set of transformations which, used over and over or recursively, give us the linguistic capability of generating an infinite number of sentences.

The phrase-structure rules, corresponding to multiplication tables in math, describe the nature and order of the parts in a simple declarative sentence. Written in mathematical notation, the phrase-structure rule $S \rightarrow NP + VP$ reads, "The sentence may be rewritten or defined as 'noun phrase plus verb phrase.'" That is, all declarative sentences *in English* must contain a noun phrase and a verb phrase. A second phrase-structure rule then defines NP:

$$NP \rightarrow \left\{ \begin{array}{c} \text{(Determiner)} + N \\ \text{Pronoun} \end{array} \right\}$$

As the braces indicate, all English noun phrases must contain *either* a pronoun *or* a noun. If a noun is present, a determiner or article *may* also be present. In English, then, we may generate three kinds of noun phrases:

1. N   Dogs
2. Determiner + N   The dogs   barked.
3. Pronoun   They

Notice, too, that the phrase-structure rules prescribe the order of the parts; determiners, if present, always precede the noun. Since the phrase-structure rules are also recursive, a noun phrase, regardless of where it appears in the sentence, will always have the same components.

Long before the sentence is spoken, the speaker selects items from the phrase-structure rules to generate mentally a simple declarative sentence, called a *kernel sentence*. Once the kernel sentence has been generated, a series of operations, called *transformations*, may be applied to the declarative sentence. Transformations are analogous to the multiplication rules for carrying numbers, shifting columns, and adding them up. Each transformation modifies the kernel sentence in a specific way. Some transformations are obligatory; others remain optional; all of them add to, delete from, or reorder the elements of the kernel sentence. The negative transformation, for example, adds *not* to the kernel sentence in a specific place depending on the nature of the verb phrase. Transformations performed on a single kernel sentence are known as *single-base transformations.* Transformations which embed one kernel sentence within a second kernel sentence are called *double-base* (or *multiple-base*) *transformations.* The following sentences, then, are said to be transformationally related to the simple declarative sentence, "Michael painted the picture":

Single-Base Transformations

Michael did not paint the picture. (Negative transformation)

Did Michael paint the picture? (Yes-No question transformation)

The picture was painted by Michael. (Passive transformation)

What was Michael painting? (Wh-question transformation)

Double-Base Transformations (Embedding or sentence combining)

Michael, who painted the picture, won first prize. (Relative clause transformation)

The picture that Michael painted was beautiful. (Relative clause transformation)

Michael's painting the picture took time. (Gerund transformation)

For Michael to paint the picture took time. (Infinitive transformation)

That Michael painted the picture was obvious. (Noun clause transformation)

Michael painted the picture and cleaned the brushes. (Conjunctive transformation)

Michael painted the beautiful picture. (Adjective transformation)

Both generating a kernel sentence and transforming it are mental operations which yield ordered slots for vocabulary items. The sentence to this point is said to have a *deep structure,* as contrasted with a *surface structure,* the appearance it has when it's spoken or written. The sentences "Michael painted the picture" and "The picture was painted by Michael" show a difference in surface structure only; underlying both is the same kernel sentence, the same deep structure, the same meanings, and the same relationships between parts. Their surface structures differ because in the second example the kernel sentence underwent a passive transformation which wasn't applied to the first sentence.

A sentence receives a surface structure when the ordered slots of a transformed kernel sentence are filled with appropriate selections from the English *lexicon,* a kind of internalized, mental dictionary in which we store the countless vocabulary items we learn throughout life. When we learn new words, we remember not only their pronunciations and meanings, but also other information about their use. Generative-transformationalists characterize this information by marking the features of words with a plus or minus. Feature analysis assumes importance in the final stages of creating sentences, when transformed kernel sentences are filled with lexical items sharing compatible features. Although "The building is eating a steak" certainly sounds English and conforms to English sentence structure, it doesn't make sense, except perhaps in the context of a children's story. The "sense" is disturbed because *building* carries the features −animate and −human, whereas the verb *eat* shows +animate and +human features. Substituting a +animate and +human noun for *building* rids the sentence of semantic distortions: "The boy is eating a steak."

Generative-transformationalists focus their attention on the creative aspect of language, on the ability of human beings regularly to produce and understand new utterances, on a language system which holds an infinite number of possible sentences. Furthermore, the approach assumes that native speakers intuitively "know" how English works, that students have a competence for language many teachers have ignored. Sentence-combining represents one way of tapping this intuitive resource. Through sentence-combining, students practice transforming simple declarative sentences and constructing increasingly complex sentences, enlarging their repertoire of syntactic options, improving their ability to "perform" sentences. As Frank O'Hare and John Mellon have demonstrated,[16] sentence-combining

16. John C. Mellon, *Transformational Sentence-Combining: A Method for Enhancing the Development of Syntactic Fluency in English Composition* (NCTE Research Report No. 10; Champaign, Ill.: NCTE, 1967) and Frank O'Hare, *Sentence Combining* (1973) describe the effects of this technique on groups of students participating in research studies. Two texts which give students practice with sentence-combining are Frank O'Hare, *Sentencecraft* (Columbus, Ohio: Ginn and Company, 1974) and Donald Daiker, Andrew Kerek, and Max Morenberg, *The Writer's Options: College Sentence Combining* (New York: Harper and Row, 1979). The best resource for sentence-combining practice, of course, remains the students' own papers.

may increase "syntactic fluency" without formal grammar instruction or elaborate terminology.

If grammatical competence is intuitive, why do students have sentence problems? Fragments, run-on sentences, and confused syntax reflect not deficient competence, but difficulties in performance. They represent problems in "code-switching," transferring spoken English into writing. When students understand that both codes are systematic but that the systems don't always overlap, they can bring to their writing a greater conscious awareness of their linguistic options.

Studying grammar in the context of (not in lieu of) writing practice, then, may foster linguistic flexibility and improve students' abilities to edit their work. Whether it does or not depends on how we approach the study of language in a writing class. Students don't need to "know" grammar in the same way their teachers do. If we teach our students grammar as a subject matter, it remains isolated from and irrelevant to writing. If, on the other hand, we apply what we know about grammar to our teaching, we can help students become more effective writers. When we understand grammatical principles and methods, we can examine intelligently how people use language and then design courses which effectively increase our students' awareness of the choices both the spoken and written language allow.

8

Teaching about words

The Tough Talker . . . is a man dramatized as centrally concerned with himself—his style is *I*-talk. The Sweet Talker goes out of his way to be nice to us—his style is *you*-talk. The Stuffy Talker expresses no concern either for himself or his reader—his style is *it*-talk.

WALKER GIBSON

Writing, the second stage of the composing process, requires considerable concentration. It's an activity writers must do pretty much on their own. The best way to teach it is to give students considerable help with prewriting and then step back while they rough out a draft. Advocates of freewriting recommend just such an approach. The teacher's guidance, they suggest, is most useful later, after students have put some words on paper and are ready to review the material.

Most students, however, don't feel free to let their own linguistic resources take over in drafting. Writing, they believe, is constrained by rules. Paragraphs, sentence structures, punctuation, and spelling must all be perfect the first time around. Attempting to manage everything at once, student writers often disrupt the flow of ideas to attend to individual words. Their past experiences have taught them to equate the first draft with the final product, with a perfect performance worthy of a good grade. From their perspective, writing and rewriting are concurrent activities. Only in two circumstances does rewriting represent a separate process: 1. when the teacher insists that a long assignment, like a term paper, be submitted in two "versions," and 2. when the teacher requires a correction of a paper.

In teaching about words, the subject of this chapter, the first lesson must be that words can be changed. All writers rewrite their work many times before it expresses what they want to say. They play with words, recognizing that nothing about the first draft is carved in stone. They compose many drafts, focusing on different problems they have discovered by listening to the previous draft. "The inspiration for writing," says Donald Murray in "The Feel of Writing—and Teaching Writing," "lies within the work. I do not feel like writing when I come to my desk, but then the language begins to move under my pen. It is alive, and I cannot help but watch it because it is the piece of writing which instructs me. The sound of the writing, its shape, its pace, its direction, its emerging form tells me what its meaning may be" (p. 69).

A second principle students need to learn is that writers view words in the context of other words. In one sense, a word, by itself, has no meaning, not even a "part of speech," until the writer relates it to some other word. Most grammar instruction separates words from their context, treating them as isolated entities, whereas writers must do just the reverse, making meaning by putting words together. It's not the word that creates meaning, but rather the writer's ability to relate words. Students must discover what writers like Murray know: "My writing . . . does not come from unusual words, but the explosion of meaning which comes from the unexpected collision of ordinary words. When I watch my writing I often see a miniature fireworks display, as words and phrases collide, explode, and ignite further explosions on the page" (p. 72).

This chapter, then, treats words in a special way. It will *not* outline a typical grammar unit. As a rule, grammar units divorce words from writing, subordinating the needs of students to lock-step treatment of the subject matter. Different assumptions govern the material presented in this chapter. First, discussions about code should focus primarily on student writing, not solely on a handbook or on the professional models in an essay anthology. Second, the language in student papers should be discussed in ways that encourage rewriting, that identify options which realize particular rhetorical effects. Third, as often as possible, instruction in language should be individualized through conferences or group work. Students who don't need help with subject-verb agreement should be free to work on something else. Finally, this chapter assumes two principles discussed in Chapter 7:

1. That students already know intuitively a great deal about how English works. A good way to begin discussing written English is by tapping the native speaker's knowledge of spoken English.
2. That spoken English, nevertheless, differs in many respects from edited American English. The best way to illustrate such differences is to describe them systematically.

Parts of speech

Traditionally, parts of speech are taught deductively. Students learn terminology, definitions, rules, and paradigms and then are expected to reproduce the constructions in their own writing. However, as most teachers know, students can quote the definition for "verb" much more readily than they can remember to write the final -s when they need to. Perhaps, then, we should be teaching inductively, beginning with the students' considerable intuitive competence.

For example, if students have trouble with verbs, we might begin with spoken nonsense verbs that have no meaning, observing how they behave in different contexts. Without knowing if *glork* represents "an action or state of being," students can generate appropriate forms of the word in sentences like the following:

1. I don't like to _____ when I'm sleepy.
2. She always _____ in the morning.
3. As a matter of fact, she _____ yesterday.
4. Tomorrow she will _____ again.
5. She has _____ every day for the past three years.
6. She is _____ all the time.
7. Her _____ doesn't bother anybody.

Now students can work from "correct" forms they've generated, not "errors"; from strengths, not weaknesses. By discussing these sentences, they may derive the "rules" which describe verb behavior in English. They'll be concentrating primarily on how verbs look in various written contexts and how writers manipulate the form and position of verbs to express different meanings. Most important, they'll discover how much grammar they already know.

Active and passive voice

Although passive voice has legitimate uses, generally we encourage students to write in the active voice because it makes the message more emphatic and less wordy. However, students often have difficulty detecting passive constructions because they have been told to focus on the meaning of the sentence: "Who is doing what to whom?" At best, meaning offers slippery clues. Students seem to feel more secure when the words themselves, their form not their meaning, identify the construction. Students can begin the search for passives by finding forms of the verb "to be." Passive sentences always introduce the verb "to be" plus a past participle (a verb form ending in *-ed, -en;* other forms are also possible: *done, hit, had*)

> Passive: The college *was founded* in 1901.
>
> Passive: The books *were taken.*

As we saw in the previous exercise, the verb "to be" also functions as an auxiliary in active voice constructions, but when this is the case, the *be* verb will always be followed by a present participle ending in *-ing:*

> Active: She *is glorking* all the time.
>
> Active: Carlos *was making* good grades.

Most of the time, students can identify passives simply by scanning their papers for *be* verbs *(is/am/are/was/were/being/been)* and then noticing what the next verb looks like. If the verb behind the *be* verb ends in *-ing,* the sentence is active; if the verb following a form of *be* ends in *-ed, -en,* or something else, the sentence is probably passive.

> Active: Carlos has *been making* good grades.
>
> Passive: The candy had *been hidden* all over the house.

Once students have learned how to find passive constructions, they also need specific instruction in *how* to rewrite them. Other clues about the form and position of words in active and passive sentences can help. I generally begin talking about the two kinds of sentences by writing on the board a passive sentence taken from a student's paper and its active counterpart:

> Active: The teacher *graded* our papers fairly.
>
> Passive: Our papers *were graded* fairly by the teacher.

Discussing paired sentences like these, students can easily identify how they differ and how to restore the passive sentence to the active voice. I lead the discussion toward the following conclusions:

1. The passive sentence reverses the order of two noun phrases.

> Active: *The teacher* graded *our papers* fairly.
>
> Passive: *Our papers* were graded fairly by *the teacher.*

2. Even simple passive sentences are wordy because they introduce a form of the verb "to be" and the preposition *by*.
3. The *by* phrase is optional. Some writers deliberately omit the *by* phrase to avoid giving "actors" responsibility for their actions.

Our papers were graded fairly.

Our taxes were increased.

4. To make passive sentences active, writers must begin the revised sentence with the noun(s) in the *by* phrase, inventing a new subject if the *by* phrase has been omitted. They must also delete the *be* verb and must place the first noun phrase in the passive sentence behind the verb phrase in the active sentence.

Passive: *Our taxes were increased (by X).*

Revision: *The city council increased our taxes.*

Passive: *The books were taken (by X).*

Revision: *Someone took the books.*

Passive: *The candy had been hidden all over the house (by X).*

Revision: *Mother had hidden the candy all over the house.*

Because verb phrases represent complex grammatical constructions, their variety gives writers considerable flexibility in composing. Consequently, students need to know not only *how* to make passive sentences active but also *when* such a revision improves the paper. Encouraging students to become conscious of their options means approaching constructions like these descriptively, discussing first the variety of forms and positions verbs assume in sentence patterns. Then, we can label the constructions, explore their meaning, and judge their effectiveness in specific rhetorical contexts.

Derivational and inflectional affixes

Many teachers use a poem like "Jabberwocky" (or their own nonsense sentences) to review the contextual clues readers and writers use to determine the form and position of words:

'Twas brillig and the slithy toves
Did gyre and gimble in the wabe.

How do we know that *slithy* is an adjective? Although we can't decipher its meaning to determine if it tells "how many" or "what kind," its form and position define its "adjectiveness." Like many adjectives *slithy* ends in -*y*, a form clue. *Slithy* also occupies a slot between *the* and *toves*, which looks like a noun; by position, then, *slithy* also appears to be an adjective. How do we know that *toves* is a noun? Although we don't know if it names persons, places, or things, it ends in -*s*, a form clue. Both nouns and verbs, however, may end in -*s*. Still, by position *toves* also appears to be a noun because it appears after *the* and before "did gyre and gimble," in a nominal position common to many English sentence patterns. The form and position of a word yield useful information about its meaning and function in a sentence. When we confront new vocabulary, form and position clues often enable us to comprehend the author's message without referring to a dictionary. We infer roughly what the word means from where it appears and how it looks.

Much of the evidence about a word's form comes from affixes, units of meaning attached to a base or root. English permits affixes to be added in front of the base (prefixes), behind the base (suffixes), or inside the base (infixes; the past tense affix placed inside "irregular verbs" like *ran*, for example). Affixes are said to be *derivational* or *inflectional* depending on their function. Affixes which change a word's part of speech or its meaning are derivational.[1] The suffix -*fy* is derivational because it creates verbs out of nouns: *beautify, liquify.* The prefix *anti-* is also derivational because it changes a word's meaning: *anti-Semitic, antisocial, antitrust.* On the other hand, inflectional affixes (all of them are suffixes) don't change a word's part of speech or meaning; they adapt words to grammatical functions. *Dog* and *dogs* remain nouns denoting "domesticated mammals of the family *Canis familiaris,*" even though *dogs* shows an inflectional plural suffix. In the following sentence, derivational and inflectional affixes have been marked with *D* or *I:*

> The boys slowly walked backwards, carefully dragging the youngest child's
>   I   D   I   D   D D   I   I   I
> wooden sled.
>   D

Although English once had many inflectional endings, now only eight major suffixes remain:

---

1. For a discussion of derivational affixes, see Norman C. Stageberg, *An Introductory English Grammar,* 3rd ed. (New York: Holt, Rinehart and Winston, 1977), Chapter 8.

1. $-s_1$ noun possessive   boy's
2. $-s_2$ noun plural   dogs, cats, oxen
3. $-s_3$ 3rd person pres. sg.   learns
4. -ing   present participle   They were *writing* letters.
5. $-d_1$ past tense   climbed, walked, rode
6. $-d_2$ past participle   She has *walked* home.
                                         She was *chosen* by him.
7. -er   comparative degree   sweeter, deadlier
8. -est   superlative degree   sweetest, deadliest

Few in number, inflectional endings nevertheless present problems for some students. Our use of final -s seems especially confusing and inconsistent.[2] We add -s to verbs to make them singular, but we add -s to nouns to make them plural. Moreover, we only add -s sometimes. English doesn't permit constructions like "He cans walk" or "Two oxes plowed the field." Too, some dialects differ from edited American English on the matter of final -s. As Mina Shaughnessy demonstrates, writers often see no need for the pluralizing -s in phrases like "these two suggestion" and "four year of college" because plurality is already indicated by quantifiers (*these, two, four*). Some students neither write nor pronounce -s in constructions like "many scientist." Since *many* signals plurality, students may avoid adding -s to *scientist* because it is redundant. Or, they may omit -s because they're spelling the word as they pronounce it, with a simplified final consonant cluster.

Possessive final -s is similarly troublesome. Shaughnessy suggests that some students consider phrases like "42% of this nation youth" analogous to compound nouns like "child welfare," "student activities." Possession by juxtaposition is common in English and may explain why a student writes "Mary hat" for "Mary's hat." Conversely, students who write "it's origins" have applied the rule for possessive -s to a pronoun; if possessive nouns end in 's, they reason, so should possessive pronouns. In English, however, possessive pronouns omit the apostrophe. The students' confusion might be addressed more efficiently if we explained the two ways of making nouns ("the book's cover") and pronouns ("its cover") possessive, instead of drawing distinctions between possessive pronouns ("its") and contractions ("it's").

2. Mina Shaughnessy, *Errors and Expectations* (New York: Oxford University Press, 1977) offers important insights to the logic governing students' writing problems. An extensive discussion of final -s appears in Chapter 4, "Common Errors," pp. 90–159.

As a rule, inflectional endings create problems for students because in some ways the conventions of edited American English *are* redundant and inconsistent. The student's "logic" produces an error because the "logic" of the language requires a different form. To help students become confident about these forms, we must remain sensitive not only to the conventional behavior of English words, but also to the ingeniously unconventional ways in which students sometimes use them.

Resources for language study

Although writing teachers depend on dictionaries, handbooks, and anthologies to teach students about language, we can supplement traditional resources with other materials that stimulate interest in reading and writing. Newspapers, magazines, advertisements, editorials, cartoons, memoranda, reports, and junk mail offer countless possibilities for discussing the purposeful word choices writers make. They illustrate rhetorical strategies and linguistic options which, for students, seem somehow more real than the examples in a textbook.

These materials can be especially useful in discussing dishonest uses of language. Doublespeak, gobbledygook, and jargon depend on passive constructions, piled-up prepositional phrases, abstract nouns, and nominalizations (nouns derived from verbs). The impenetrable pretentious prose many students write—Macrorie calls it "Engfish"[3]—also uses language dishonestly. To write honest prose, students must understand what Engfish looks like and why it's phony. The following memorandum, for example, begs for translation and offers generous material for discussing not only word choices but sentence structure, paragraph construction, and rhetorical principles as well:

MEMORANDUM

```
TO:  Executive Director
FROM:  Regional Planning Director
SUBJECT:  PLAN IMPLEMENTATION, COMPREHENSIVE DEVELOPMENT
          PLAN, policy for
    In the course of evolving a distinctively Regional
program responsive to over-all areawide goals and
objectives for attaining the physical, social, and
economic betterment of the Region, we are undertaking
```

3. See Ken Macrorie, *Telling Writing* (New York: Hayden, 1970), especially Chapter 1. An excellent series of classroom exercises focusing students' attention on irresponsible uses of language is *Teaching about Doublespeak,* edited by Daniel Dieterich (Urbana, Ill.: NCTE, 1976).

```
formulation of initial sets of compatible definitions of
basic concepts in support of an optimal approach to the
participatory processes essential for effectuation of
achievable strategies that may demonstrate at least
minimal promise of generating measurable progress toward
alleviation of selected Regional-scale problems of
priority concern, through implementation of an assertive
action-oriented posture regarding topical issues of
Regional import on the part of the Council, through both
formal and informal mechanisms for eliciting and receiving
citizen-participation impact at critical phases of the
decision-making process, in concert with the advisory to
responsible elected officials of units of local general
government, to the maximum extent feasible at each step in
the comprehensive planning process, and in harmony with
areawide functional planning and programming as well as
established State policies having identifiable application
in prescribing broad guidelines for the compatible
ordering of intraregional development trends, all keyed to
initial revised control projections for the horizon year.
Periodically, revisions are considered in accordance with
HUD guidelines.

cc:  Local Planning Chief
     Planning and Management Assistant
```

When we bring these materials into the English class, we also reinforce our contention that writing matters in the world of work. The state driver's handbook, for example, of special interest to high school students, can be mined for reading and writing assignments as well as discussions of language. Many so-called "survival documents" can be translated into styles appropriate for a variety of audiences: income tax regulations, voter registration forms, owner's manuals for small appliances, insurance policies, credit agreements, applications for college admission or for a particular job. Students are likely to enjoy working with these materials because they symbolize adult responsibilities. They also represent a broad range of styles and language choices.

Suggestions for teaching students about language

Teachers who want to help students enlarge their repertoire of stylistic options and master the conventions of edited American English often encounter apathy or resistance to the subject. For most students, the facts of how people use language have become so confused by rules and exceptions to rules, by shifting definitions, by rote memorization, by routine busywork, that language study is neither interesting nor related to anything worth mastering. "The language manipulates me," they conclude, "I can't possibly control it." They're trapped by rules.

But language is not just a set of rules. It's a tool people use to create meaning, an enormously flexible means of expression. To break out of the language-manipulates-me thinking, students must first understand that language-users, not usage guides and handbooks, determine the conventions of English prose. Then, they can more confidently discuss what language really is, what attitudes people have about it, how writers use it to express ideas purposefully to an audience. Of course, writers observe conventions, but excessive concern about them, especially in the early stages of composing, prevents students from recognizing in their language infinite possibilities for expressing ideas. To foster that recognition, the following suggestions may help.

1. Whenever possible, begin discussions about language by asking students what they already know, or assume to be true, about the material you intend to cover. If you discover that they already understand the material, revise your discussion to help students *apply* the principle to their writing.

2. As your students talk about their writing, listen for evidence of misinformation or confusion about rhetorical and linguistic principles. Explain how the confusion might have arisen. Perhaps a "rule" was only partially learned, or misapplied, or confused with some other principle. Since most misunderstandings contain partial truths, you may want to take the time to review the principle when it comes up, that is, when students are most receptive to discussing it. Listen, too, for examples of linguistic and rhetorical principles in the spoken language students use in the classroom.

3. Whenever possible, base discussions of language on student writing instead of textbook examples. Excellent papers show students that they can use language effectively, that what you're asking them to do doesn't require some peculiar magical power granted only to professionals. Average papers permit the class to praise a student's achievements and also suggest improvements. Avoid discussing weak papers, but remember that weak students occasionally write a solid paragraph or sentence which could be used in class. Some teachers discuss student papers by granting the au-

thor anonymity; others select sample papers from one class to show to another class; still others regularly "publish" papers, names attached, from everyone in the class so that students have several opportunities to gain constructive responses to their work. Of course, these discussions must focus on both the strengths and weaknesses of the piece. With practice, students will become better able to articulate the principles of good writing in their own words, more proficient in analyzing and revising their own work, and more self-reliant critics.

4. Conduct discussions about language with a minimum of technical terms, at least at first. Writing, not learning terminology, should always remain the focus of the course. After students have practiced a particular technique or become reasonably comfortable manipulating the language in certain ways, then terminology can be introduced: "These words we've been using to hook sentences together have a name; we call them 'subordinating and coordinating conjunctions.' "

5. To write well, students need practice using language, creating their own discourse. Avoid asking students to spend a great deal of time analyzing someone else's language. Most worksheets, programmed texts, and exercises don't encourage writing: they teach underlining, circling, and filling in blanks. Workbooks, of course, are easy to grade, but they rarely require students to engage in the composing process. Furthermore, they assume that students must master "pieces" of language in isolation—words, sentences, paragraphs—before negotiating "real" writing. This piecemeal approach, argues David Bartholomae, contradicts the assumption that writing is a process of making decisions and exercising options:

> Before students can be let loose to write, the argument goes, they need a semester to "work on" sentences or paragraphs, as if writing a sentence in a workbook or paragraph in isolation were somehow equivalent to producing those units in the midst of some extended act of writing, or as if the difficulties of writing sentences or paragraphs are concepts rather than intrinsic to the writer and his struggle to juggle the demands of a language, a rhetoric, and a task. ("Teaching Basic Writing: An Alternative to Basic Skills," p. 87)

All of us remember teachers who inadvertently attempted to subvert our love of English. Reviewing our own experiences in English classes can strengthen our teaching. What did we like most and least about studying the English language? Some of us may find that looking up all the words we didn't understand in a reading assignment was dreadfully boring. Others may conclude that reading aloud in front of the class was a humiliating torture. Some of us felt proud to have mastered sentence diagramming; others of us never saw the point of tearing up sentences that way. Perhaps only a few of us enjoyed filling out workbooks or doing homework assignments meant to keep us busy.

To be sure, writing is hard work, but it needn't be synonymous with pain and punishment. Writing, like reading, can have quite unpleasant associations for students, as John Holt points out:

> Mark Twain once said that a cat that sat on a hot stove lid would never sit on one again—but it would never sit on a cold one either. As true of children as of cats. If they, so to speak, sit on a hot book a few times, if books cause them humiliation and pain, they are likely to decide that the safest thing to do is to leave all books alone. ("How Teachers Make Children Hate Reading," p. 191)

The study of English doesn't need to be distasteful for our students if we can prevent them from constantly associating their use of language with mistakes, penalties, and humiliation, real or imagined. Most of us became teachers because we appreciate the enormous expressive power of our language. Inviting students to discover and appreciate their language reflects the essence of our teaching.

9

Teaching about sentences

A sentence should read as if its author, had he held a plow instead of a pen, could have drawn a furrow deep and straight to the end.

HENRY DAVID THOREAU

All of us have a considerable intuitive understanding of sentence structures and their use. We've all been talking in sentences since childhood, rarely stopping to consider whether or not our speech represents a "complete thought," contains a subject and predicate, or manifests "dependent" and "independent" clauses. Our sentences, most of which we've never heard or said before, get the message across. All native speakers *do* know what a sentence is; they can create fairly complex sentences without knowing the names for the constructions they produce.

If that's so, why waste time in a writing class on sentences? It's true that classtime is wasted when students spend too much time analyzing sentences someone else has written instead of generating their own. Classtime is also wasted if it's devoted exclusively to labeling sentence types or various phrases and clauses. Such lessons teach terminology—*what* to call the construction—not writing—*how* to create the constructions. Although human beings have an intuitive competence for creating sentences, obviously many student writers need practice translating competence into fluent performance. The potential may indeed be there, but in fact many writers, even adults, don't write "error-free" sentences.

A major reason why "performing" written sentences is difficult stems from differences between speech and writing. Spoken communication, which may be highly elliptical, generally succeeds without complicated syntax. Gestures, facial expressions, and the habit of taking turns reinforce the message. Although high school and college students are capable of writing complicated sentences, they're unaccustomed to using their entire repertoire of syntactic constructions, especially if they habitually write pretty much as they talk. Second, writing sentences presents considerable risk. Students understand that every word they add to a sentence increases the possibility of misspellings or punctuation mistakes or other errors which jeopardize their grade. Short, simple sentences are safest. Third, some students have trouble with sentences because they can't depend on the eye or ear to help them identify prose rhythms. If they read poorly, have rarely been read to, infrequently converse with adults, or passively watch a great deal of television, they may have a limited repertoire of comfortable sentence options. Television commercials, for example, are usually scripted in sentence fragments, a style which may influence our students' "ear" for sentences to a greater extent than we realize.

For these reasons, students need risk-free opportunities to practice more complex sentences. The study of sentences, however, can't profitably be separated from real writing, from composing longer stretches of discourse. Students must apply what they're learning *about* sentences to composing, must translate knowledge into performance. Instead of analyzing sentences in a textbook, students need to discover what kinds of sentences their own writing contains. Instead of drilling students on various sentence shapes, we need to show them how to create those shapes and how to handle the punctuation problems unfamiliar constructions create. Instead of discussing sentence patterns students already know how to write, we need to individualize instruction so that students are practicing sentence types they may be avoiding for fear of making mistakes in punctuation or subject-verb agreement. The goal of our teaching should be to enlarge the student's repertoire of sentence options and rhetorical choices.

Recently, since the late 1960s, two techniques for teaching sentences in the context of composing have gained increasing popularity: sentence combining and generating cumulative sentences. Both techniques can increase the "syntactic fluency" of students' writing. At the same time, however, writing teachers must guard against the exaggerated claims some proponents of these techniques, especially of sentence combining, have made. Kellogg Hunt, for example, suggests that an entire writing course can be structured around sentence combining: "In every sense, sentence combining can be a comprehensive writing program in and of itself, for at least one semester. It is nonsense, rather than common sense, to suggest that sentence combining can't be the one and only instructional strategy, at least for one term."[1] Nonsense or no, many writing teachers and researchers *do* express misgivings about the efficacy of sentence combining as the sole instructional method in a writing course and have doubts about the syntactic gains which have been attributed to sentence-combining practice. Some of these gains, in fact, may result from instruction in semantics and rhetoric which students receive as they discuss sentence-combining problems. More important, since writing involves much more than simply mastering sentences, no single instructional method, including sentence combining or work with cumulative sentences, will transform poor writers into accomplished writers. Although both techniques can be used to advantage, neither should become the exclusive focus of a writing class.

Sentence combining

Generative-transformational theory suggests that we transform sentences intuitively by adding to, deleting from, or rearranging kernel sentences. Sentence-combining applies this principle to writing instruction.[2] As Charles Cooper explains, sentence-combining problems "confront the student with sentences more complex than ones he would be likely to write at that point in his development; they ask the student to write out fully-formed sentences and they provide

1. Kellogg W. Hunt, "Anybody Can Teach English," in *Sentence Combining and the Teaching of Writing,* ed. Donald A. Daiker, Andrew Kerek, and Max Morenberg (Conway, Ark.: L & S Books, 1979), p. 156. Although I disagree with Hunt, I recommend this collection of essays to teachers who want to know more about sentence combining. I also recommend Stephen P. Witte's review of the book in *College Composition and Communication* 31 (December 1980), 433–37, which discusses some of the reservations writing teachers have about sentence-combining research. For a comprehensive bibliography on the theory and practice of sentence combining, see Max Morenberg and Andrew Kerek, "Bibliography on Sentence Combining: Theory and Practice, 1964–1979," *Rhetoric Society Quarterly* 9 (Spring 1979), 97–111.
2. Frank O'Hare, *Sentence Combining: Improving Student Writing without Formal Grammar Instruction* (NCTE Research Report No. 15: Urbana, Ill.: NCTE, 1973) reviews research on the relationship between grammar study and improvement in writing and describes his own investigation. O'Hare's study demonstrates that written and oral sentence-combining exercises helped seventh graders "write compositions that could be described as syntactically more elaborated or mature" and "better in overall quality" (p. 67).

him the content of the sentences so that his attention can remain focused on the *structural* aspects of the problem."[3] To combine the following sentences, for example, students would insert information from the indented sentence into the first sentence:

> The canary flew out the window.
> > The canary is yellow.
>
> (Student's response: The yellow canary flew out the window.)

Some sentence-combining problems offer clues to suggest which words must be added or deleted:

> SOMETHING made her angry.
> > She read something in the note. (what)
>
> (Student's response: What she read in the note made her angry.)

Multiple embeddings are also possible:

> My friends and I enjoy SOMETHING.
>
> We race our bicycles around the paths in the park. (racing)
> > Our bicycles are lightweight.
> >
> > Our bicycles are ten-speed.
> >
> > The paths are narrow.
> >
> > The paths are winding.
>
> (Student's response: My friends and I enjoy racing our lightweight, ten-speed bicycles around the narrow, winding paths in the park.)

Exercises which contain transformation cues require students to combine the sentences in a specified way. Cued exercises can give students risk-free practice generating syntactic structures they may be avoiding or can't handle confidently. The cues also show students *how* to combine the sentences, providing a working vocabulary of connectives which hold phrases and clauses together. As students work through the exercises, we can introduce terminology and whatever punctuation conventions a particular transformation requires.

Open-ended exercises, which offer no cues, may be more difficult for some students, but they permit more choices and encourage students to consider the rhetorical effect of several possible combinations:

3. Charles Cooper, "An Outline for Writing Sentence-Combining Problems," in *Rhetoric and Composition: A Sourcebook for Teachers*, edited by Richard Graves (Rochelle Park, N.J.: Hayden, 1976), p. 119; reprinted from *English Journal* 62 (January 1973), pp. 96–102, 108. The next three sample problems appear in Cooper, pp. 122, 125, and 127 respectively.

Anteaters are mammals.

Anteaters are common to tropical America and Africa.

Anteaters have long snouts.

Anteaters feed on white ants.

White ants are also called termites.

(Possible student responses, each of which achieves a different rhetorical effect: Anteaters, mammals common to tropical America and Africa, have long snouts and feed on white ants, also called termites. Anteaters are long-snouted mammals, common to tropical America and Africa, which feed on white ants or termites. Mammals common to tropical America and Africa, anteaters feed on white ants or termites with their long snouts.)

(Donald A. Daiker, Andrew Kerek, and Max Morenberg,
The Writer's Options: College Sentence Combining, p. 14)

When students combine sentences in as many ways as they know how, read them aloud, and discuss which versions they like best, they're not only exercising syntactic options but also making rhetorical choices. Like professional writers, the students develop an eye and ear for prose rhythms. "In addition to playing with transformations and making their choices," writes William Strong, "professional writers also seem to spend considerable time hearing the way sentences fit together to make up the 'melody' of their writing. They listen for the dips and swaying curves of some phrases, the hard, rhythmic, regular punch of others. They sensitize themselves to avoid sentences where meaning is almost obscured within the lengthy confines of the sentence itself; they study those sentences where pause, and momentary reflection, have their impact" (*Sentence Combining,* p. xv).

Discussing sentence-combining exercises also helps students become confident about punctuation. My own students shun participial modifiers, appositives, and relative clauses because they aren't sure when to set them off with commas. They avoid introductory adverb clauses for similar reasons. Students who have learned to be careful about commas understandably "write around" the problem. Sentence-combining exercises not only illustrate how punctuation organizes sentence elements for a reader but also how to solve punctuation problems which for years have limited a student's range of syntactic options. Furthermore, the exercises sometimes expose misunderstood punctuation rules discussed in previous English classes. A student of mine, for example, consistently placed commas behind words like *because, since,* and *if* when they began a sentence: "Because, I didn't have a car I shouldn't date Susan." When I asked him why he thought the comma belonged there, he explained, "My English teacher told me to set off *because* words; she called them 'introductory' something-or-other." Doubtless, his teacher encouraged him to set off the entire introductory clause, but the student had heard only part of the message. He solved the problem by practicing a few sentence-combining exercises. My student's problem also illustrates another point: that grammatical labels sometimes create punctuation problems. Sentence combining allows teachers to dispense with terminology altogether or, if they wish, to name constructions *after* students have practiced them.

Other students may need practice "decombining" sentences. Older students sometimes attempt such extraordinarily complicated sentences that the syntax gets twisted. They may be writing to please the teacher whose implicit praise sanctions "long" sentences; nevertheless, they develop a style which obscures ideas in hopelessly convoluted syntax. Here's an example from a college freshman's paper:

> The things that people go to the pharmacist for sometimes are just to get the pharmacist to prescribe them something for their illness, and he can not do any prescribing for anyone for medicine.

Prepositions are part of the problem here, but Kenny loses his reader by piling too much information into one sentence. When he read the sentence out loud, he said it sounded "weird," but he didn't know how to revise it. I asked him to "decombine" the sentence, breaking it into kernel sentences. We came up with the following list:

> ┌─People go to the pharmacist for things.
> │ People go to the pharmacist sometimes.
> │ People just get the pharmacist to do SOMETHING (to)
> and ┌─└─ The pharmacist prescribes them something for their illness.
> ├─He cannot do any SOMETHING. (-ing)
> │ He prescribes for anyone.
> └─He prescribes medicine.

At this point, Kenny could understand why the sentence seems "weird"; it lacks a single focus. Two or three subjects—"people," "pharmacist," and perhaps "things"—vie for attention. Recombining the kernels to emphasize only one subject, "people" or "pharmacist," might yield the following options:

"People" Sentences
1. People sometimes go to the pharmacist, who cannot prescribe medicine for anyone, just to get him to prescribe something for their illness.
2. Sometimes people go to the pharmacist just to get him to prescribe medicine for their illness, something he cannot do.

"Pharmacist" Sentences
1. The pharmacist cannot prescribe medicine for anyone's illness, even though people sometimes ask him to.
2. Although people sometimes ask the pharmacist to prescribe medicine for their illness, he cannot write prescriptions.

The two-step decombining and recombining procedure now gives Kenny several sentences to choose from in revising his original paragraph.

Decombining and recombining sentences can help students untangle, tighten, and rewrite sentences too complex for a reader to follow easily. After a while, students also discover which transformations create convoluted sentences. For Kenny, beginning sentences with noun clauses and piling up infinitives create problems; for other students, passive constructions or beginning sentences with "There are" and "It is" yield tortured syntax. Different kinds of sentence combining exercises not only help students detect these problems but also to find syntactic alternatives for ineffective sentences.

To improve their skill in manipulating sentence structures, students need regular sentence-combining practice over a long period, ideally two or three times a week throughout the entire course of instruction. We could begin the exercises as early as the fourth grade and increase their complexity through college. However, assigning too many problems too frequently bores students, who begin to consider the exercises busywork. Because they emphasize constructing sentences, not longer stretches of discourse, and because the content of the sentences is determined by the exercise, sentence combining should supplement, not replace, student writing.

All the same, sentence combining has several advantages. Used correctly, the technique *does* increase students' syntactic fluency. The exercises can be assigned as homework or completed in a journal. Teachers can design their own exercises or use those available in several published texts. Students can work on them in groups, individually, or as a class. They should never be graded, however, not if they are to give students a risk-free way of experimenting with syntactic structures they have avoided for fear of making low marks. Some teachers post or pass out answers for the problems so that students can check their sentences against the key.

Besides increasing the complexity of student sentences, the exercises have other advantages. We can demonstrate how sentences are constructed without beginning with grammatical terms or singling out errors in a particular student's paper. We can avoid terminology altogether or introduce it after students understand how to perform the transformations. We can describe punctuation, mechanics, and conventions of edited American English in the context of writing, not isolated from it. Because students will combine sentences in various ways, we can also point out rhetorical choices, differences in emphasis which might work more effectively in some larger contexts than in others. Open-ended exercises work especially well in this regard. They help students discover, not the one "right" sentence, but a range of options. Students can also apply the technique to their own drafts, rewriting its sentences to emphasize different ideas, sharpen their focus, coordinate and subordinate material, and achieve sentence variety.

Cumulative sentences

In *Notes Toward a New Rhetoric,* Francis Christensen expresses considerable dissatisfaction with traditional methods of teaching sentences. "We need," he says, "a rhetoric of the sentence that will do more than combine the ideas of primer sentences. We need one that will *generate* ideas" (p. 26). Christensen's generative rhetoric represents an alternative to teaching sentences on the basis of rhetorical classifications (loose, balanced, and periodic sentences) or grammatical categories (simple, compound, complex, and compound-complex sentences). It's a rhetoric which generates ideas, not words. According to Christensen, students don't need to write longer, more complex sentences simply to produce more words; rather, writers can use the sentence-as-form to examine the ideas expressed by the words, sharpen or add to them, and then reproduce the idea more effectively. The "cumulative sentence," the heart of Christensen's generative rhetoric, compels writers to examine their thoughts, the meanings words convey. Consequently, it aids prewriting as well as rewriting.

Generative rhetoric is based on four principles derived from Christensen's study of prose style and the works of contemporary authors. He maintains, first, that "composition is essentially a process of addition"; nouns, verbs, or main clauses serve as a foundation or base to which we add details, qualifications, new meanings. Second, Christensen's "principle of modification" suggests that we can add these new meanings either before or after the noun, verb, or base clause. The "direction of movement" for the sentence changes, depending on where we've added modifiers and new meaning. When modifiers appear before the noun, verb, or base clause (which Christensen calls the "head" of the construction), the sentence "moves" forward. Modifiers placed after the noun, verb, or base clause, move the sentence backward because they require readers to relate the new details, qualifications, and meanings *back* to the head appearing earlier in the sentence. Christensen's third principle states that, depending on the meanings of the words we add, the head becomes either more concrete or less so. The base word or clause together with one or more modifying additions expresses several "levels of generality or abstraction." Finally, Christensen's "principle of texture" describes and evaluates a writer's style. We characterize style as relatively "dense" or "plain" on the basis of the number and variety of additions writers make to nouns, verbs, and base clauses.

Students, of course, don't need to know the four principles in order to create cumulative sentences. When I introduce my class to cumulative sentences, I simply ask the students to add as many words and phrases as they can to the following sentence, written on the blackboard: "The horse galloped." I give them a base clause and deliberately ask them to "load the pattern," a practice which Christensen would condemn but which I intend to use merely as a starting point. After students suggest additions to the sentence for three to five minutes, it might look like the following monstrosity: "Because Farmer Brown didn't notice the swarm of bees in the appletree and hadn't tightened the cinch on the old, brown leather saddle securely, the horse galloped off through the orchard, throwing the startled rider to the ground, terrified by the bees buzzing around his head, until he reached the weathered board fence, where he stopped."

Although the sentence is unwieldy, students seem pleased to discover that they *can* compose complicated sentences like this one. Initially, quantity not quality intrigues them, and that's fine for now; we'll get to quality soon. Generally, students add material at the end of the base clause first. Then, prompted by prewriting questions (Who? What? When? Where? How? Why?), they begin to place modifiers at the beginning or in the middle of the sentence: appositives, participial constructions, relative clauses, adverb and adjective constructions. After they have created the sentence, we can discuss the kinds of grammatical structures and relationships the sentence expresses and punctuation problems we have encountered. Finally, we assess its rhetorical effectiveness, concluding that writing long sentences per se isn't a virtue and that our example needs revising. So, we tighten it, rearranging and deleting elements, reading versions aloud to evaluate the rhythm of our prose, and finally, imagining the larger context of the paragraph in which revised versions of our sentence might appear. Although the sample sentence has enabled us to take up several grammatical, rhetorical, and mechanical concerns, we will explore them in detail for several class meetings.

In one class period, for example, we might examine the kinds of additions which expand the base clause. Discussing sentences in student papers or in a reading assignment can generate the following list of grammatical constructions:

PP - Prepositional phrase

NC - Noun cluster (appositives)

VC - Verb cluster (present and past participles, infinitives)

Abs - Absolute constructions (a participial construction with its own subject)

Adv - Adverb clauses

AC - Adjective clauses

Rel - Relative clauses

Each of these additions adjusts the meaning of the base clause (or other clauses added to the base). "The main or base clause," Christensen explains, "is likely to be stated in general or abstract or plural terms. With the main clause stated, the forward movement of the sentence stops: The writer instead of going on to something new shifts down to a lower level of generality or abstraction or to singular terms, and goes back over the same ground at this lower level" (*Notes Toward a New Rhetoric,* p. 29).

If we indent and number the levels of generality in the sample sentence discussed earlier, it looks like this:

2 Because Farmer Brown didn't notice the swarm of bees

in the appletree and (Adv)

2 (because he) hadn't tightened the cinch on the old, brown leather saddle securely, (Adv)

1 the horse galloped off through the orchard,

2 throwing the startled rider to the ground, (VC)

2 terrified by the bees buzzing around his head, (VC)

2 until he reached the weathered board fence, (Adv)

3 where he stopped. (Rel)

Christensen calls this a three-level sentence. The base clause is always numbered "level 1," regardless of where it appears in the sentence. All of the level-2 additions modify elements in the base clause or level 1. The level-2 adverb clauses, two preceding the base and one following it, modify "galloped off"; the level-2 verb clusters, one a present participial phrase and the other a (misplaced) past participial phrase, modify "horse." The level-3 relative clause refers back to and elaborates "fence" in the previous level-2 adverb clause. Indenting each level helps students see what kinds of additions have been made, where they appear (before, after, or in the middle of the base), whether or not they are grammatically similar or parallel, and how they relate to each other by qualifying or elaborating material elsewhere in the sentence.

Many student sentences remain 1-, or at best, 2-level sentences. Their "texture" is thin or plain. Here's an example of a 1-level sentence, written by a college freshman. She is describing an advertisement.

    1 The background is a dull, white film while

    1 the caption shows black type.

Because the student had practiced expanding sentences with level-2 and -3 modifiers, she knew how and where to improve the sentence with details. Here's her revision:

    2 Cloudy and misty, (AC)

    1 the background looks like a soft, white film,

      2 draped behind bold, black type (VC)

        3 which catches the reader's eye. (Rel)

In building cumulative sentences, however, students aren't merely creating multi-level constructions that string together modifiers one after another. As Christensen warns,

    1 The cumulative sentence in unskillful hands is unsteady,

      2 allowing a writer to ramble on, (VC)

        3 adding modifier after modifier, (VC)

          4 until the reader is almost overwhelmed, (Adv)

            5 because the writer's central idea is lost. (Adv)

Students must control the placement of modifiers, drawing them out of ideas in the base clause. They must see the idea again, sharpen the image, the object, the action. In exploring the implications of what they've said, they will generate or re-invent additional meanings to express. At the level of the sentence, the new meanings can be phrased as cumulative modifiers. As we'll see in Chapters 10 and 11, the generative principles of Christensen's rhetoric can also shape paragraphs and whole papers.

10

Teaching paragraphing

In every structure we may distinguish the *relation* or *relations,* and
the items *related.*

SUZANNE LANGER

Traditional views of the paragraph

Perhaps nowhere else is the tendency to teach writing-as-product
more evident than in the teaching of paragraphs. We may not be able
to remember *how* we learned to group sentences into paragraphs, but
we know by rote *what* paragraphs are: "a distinct unit of thought,"
"a group of logically related sentences," "a set of sentences, all of
which deal with a common topic." Effective paragraphs, we tell our
students, exhibit "unity, coherence, and emphasis," abstract qualities difficult to define in terms of actual words on a page. Traditionally, paragraphs have been taught as "things," as entities. They represent boxes students must wedge ideas into, adjusting their material
until it fills out the specified shape. Paragraphs have also been taught
through models and imitation. Students examine models in their
reading assignments, label them as one of several "methods of paragraph development," and imitate the method in a series of para-
graph-writing exercises.

Let's examine some of the assumptions governing traditional
methods of teaching paragraphs. Although the methods of paragraph
development discussed in modern textbooks vary, the following cat-

149

alogue is a standard list: narration, description, details, definition, comparison or contrast, cause or effect, examples and illustration, enumeration, classification. The list has a long history. Its origins may be found in Aristotle's *Rhetoric*, which catalogues twenty-eight topics of invention. Although many of Aristotle's topics now identify methods of paragraph development, Aristotle wasn't describing structural units in a finished piece of writing or methods of arranging material. He was discussing means of generating subject matter, lines of inquiry which could be used to invent an argument. Over the years, however, terms which had originally defined techniques of invention or prewriting came to describe structures of arrangement. Terms referring to a process eventually became labels for sections in the written product.

By contrast, the terms we use to evaluate paragraphs—*unity, coherence,* and *emphasis*—are relatively recent. They derive from Alexander Bain's *English Composition and Rhetoric* (1866), which stipulates "seven laws" for effective paragraphs:

1. Distribution into Sentences: The consideration of the Unity of the individual Sentence leads up to the structure of the Paragraph, as composed of sentences properly parted off.
2. Explicit Reference: The bearing of each sentence of a Paragraph on the sentences preceding needs to be explicit.
3. Parallel Construction: When several consecutive sentences iterate or illustrate the same idea, they should, as far as possible, be formed alike.
4. Indication of the Theme: The opening sentence, unless obviously preparatory, is expected to indicate the scope of the paragraph.
5. Unity: Unity in a Paragraph implies a sustained purpose, and forbids digressions and irrelevant matter.
6. Consecutive Arrangement: The first thing involved in Consecutive Arrangement is, that related topics should be kept close together: in other words, Proximity has to be governed by Affinity.
7. Marking of Subordination: As in the Sentence, so in the Paragraph, Principal and Subordinate Statements should have their relative importance clearly indicated. (Pp. 92–134)

Bain's principles serve a useful purpose when students want to examine, in literature or in their own writing, the effectiveness of written paragraphs; however, the laws are not so helpful when students want to know how to draft paragraphs from scratch. In the first place, several of Bain's principles of paragraph construction apply equally well to entire essays and books; Bain himself notes that "the internal arrangement of the paragraph comes under laws that are essentially the same as in the sentence, but on a greater scale" (p. 31). Second, the laws describe *what* characterizes an effective paragraph, not *how* a writer achieves the effect. Although keeping related topics close together is, of course, a commendable goal, the principles don't explain *how* that's to be done. Like those in many contemporary texts, Bain's principles describe the qualities paragraphs-as-products should exhibit but offer student writers inadequate help with paragraphing-as-process.

How writers paragraph

One way to balance the view of paragraphs-as-product is to examine our own writing practices. When and why do we indent material? Sometimes, of course, we want to shift to a different idea, or to a different perspective, or to a new subset of material within the larger subject. Paragraphing signals changes to a reader. At other times, we begin new paragraphs to restate a point, to emphasize it, or to provide additional support for an idea. Paragraphing signals similarities in our treatment of the subject, allowing us to accumulate details. Finally, all of us have begun new paragraphs simply because it seems convenient. In reading over a draft, we may notice that a paragraph contains only two or three sentences; so, we decide to combine those sentences with others to create a longer unit. Or, as I've discovered time and again in drafting this book, a paragraph may simply look too long; so, I find a place to break it into two or three smaller chunks. When we shape paragraphs according to how they look on the page— too long, too short, just right—we're basing our decisions first on formal considerations and only secondarily on the logical connections among ideas. We're approaching the material as a reader does, accustomed to seeing a line indented every so often.

Since readers want to comprehend ideas in manageable chunks, writer attempt to oblige them. How we define "manageable chunks," however, depends very much on convention, as Chapter 3 explains. Medieval monks changed the size of the script to mark the first line or so of a new section of manuscript. Nowadays, the kind of writing we're doing often determines how much material constitutes a "manageable chunk." Informal letters, newspaper articles, and advertising copy contain "overdifferentiated" or short paragraphs. "Underdifferentiated" or long paragraphs occur in formal essays, encyclopedia articles, and some legal documents. Paragraph lengths also seem to reflect cultural and historical preferences. Eighteenth- and nineteenth-century prose may impress us as having extremely long paragraphs, perhaps because we're more used to reading the shorter paragraphs of modern newspapers and news magazines.

Examining our own writing habits also forces us to admit that we don't compose paragraphs as textbooks tell us to. Rarely do we consciously construct a topic sentence and then deliberately choose a method of developing it. We may keep a general plan in mind as we write, but actual drafting requires too much concentration to stop every few sentences and ask, "Now, what will my next topic sentence say, and what method of development will I use for this paragraph?" For most writers, the difficult process of generating words shuts out conscious decisions about form. That's why, it seems, we reparagraph at the rewriting stage, when we're relatively less preoccupied with ideas and can attend to paragraphing.

Despite textbook pronouncements, anywhere from 50 percent to 80 percent of the paragraphs written by accomplished professionals do *not* contain a topic sentence.[1] They also don't observe the methods of development listed in most textbooks, as Richard Meade and Geiger Ellis discovered when they examined 300 paragraphs selected at random from *Saturday Review, English Journal,* and letters to the editor of the *Richmond Times-Dispatch.* Meade and Ellis report that "56 percent (168) of the three hundred paragraphs were not developed by any textbook method. The remaining 44 percent followed only two of the textbook methods to any appreciable extent: reasons and examples" ("Paragraph Development in the Modern Age of Rhetoric," p. 222). The study concludes that, despite the variety of methods textbooks mention, "writers generally use paragraphs which reflect development by additional *comment, reasons,* or *examples,* either separately or in combination" (p. 225).

Although we don't yet understand as much as we'd like to about the process of shaping discourse, apparently writers, in drafting the first sentence of a paragraph, commit themselves to a topic and es-

1. William Irmscher, *Teaching Expository Writing* (New York: Holt, Rinehart & Winston, 1979), p. 98, reports that his graduate students found topic sentences in an average of 40% to 50% of the paragraphs they examined, whereas Richard Braddock found them only 13% of the time [see Braddock's "The Frequency and Placement of Topic Sentences in Expository Prose," *Research in the Teaching of English* 8 (1974), 287–302]. As Irmscher points out (p. 98), "Part of the problem is determining exactly what a topic sentence is"; he also notes that "percentages vary greatly among individual writers."

tablish a purpose for subsequent sentences. The first sentence may suggest a range of possibilities for developing an idea, but with each subsequent sentence the writer has less flexibility, fewer options. A writer who becomes committed to a generalization in the first few sentences of a paragraph, for example, still has some choice about supporting it with reasons or examples. Having chosen to present a reason, the writer is almost obligated to cite a second reason or to support the reason with an example. In this way, each decision dictates the range of choices for writing the next sentence.

In writing paragraphs, as in shaping larger units of discourse, we continually discover form. To use Irmscher's simile, "The writer writes more like a sculptor who finds form *while* sculpting [my italics] than like a bricklayer who piles bricks to construct a wall" (*Teaching Expository Writing*, p. 99). We don't begin with the parts, with paragraph-bricks, but with the whole, with ideas to express and a purpose for communicating them. We may set boundaries for the whole, deciding where we want our subject to begin and end, what we want to include and exclude, but in generating language to express the whole we choose to reveal it a certain way. We discover its parts and pieces and their relationships to each other, shaping paragraphs to demonstrate those relationships. We don't begin with forms, pouring content into paragraph molds; rather, we begin with content, and in the act of drafting discover form.

Relating part to whole

If indenting permits writers to relate parts to wholes, what is the nature of those relationships? As many teachers recognize, methods of paragraph development "overlap." Narrative paragraphs often incorporate description; definition paragraphs are frequently supported by examples; comparison paragraphs may resort to point-by-point classifications. Although the so-called "combination of methods" paragraph occurs frequently, textbooks must treat it as an anomaly because there's no room for it in the traditional scheme for classifying paragraph types.

Frank D'Angelo suggests, however, that overlapping categories seem to be the rule rather than the exception. Paragraph types, he maintains, manifest underlying thought processes and consequently are related to the ways we organize perceptions. Although we can assign labels to logical mental operations, what we're doing when we think transcends terminology:

Description, for example, is related to definition. Describing something provides a means of analyzing and identifying it. Defining is a kind of abstract description. Definition, division into parts, and classification share fundamental relationships: to define is to limit or set boundaries to a thing by separating it from other things (division); to define is to put the thing to be defined into a class (classification): to classify is to divide into categories, so classification and division are related categories. Exemplification is related to definition (giving examples is one way of defining), to division in parts (examples are parts of wholes), and to classification (each example is a member of a group or class of persons and things). (*A Conceptual Theory of Rhetoric*, p. 44)

In other words, thinking is *relational*. When we perceive objects and events, we don't merely isolate or identify them; we relate them to other objects and events, to our own past experiences. If thought processes relate perceptions, organizing them into patterns, then it follows that paragraphs will express those relationships. Not only paragraphs, but also sentences and whole discourse.

Although we can't discuss D'Angelo's theory in detail here, some teachers have been applying it to writing classes for many years. When we teach "comparison" by first discussing word comparisons like similes, showing students how to compound sentences, then how to build them into comparison paragraphs, and finally how to expand comparison paragraphs into essays, we implicitly acknowledge that the forms are related. Words, sentences, paragraphs, and essays all express an underlying thought process, in this case, comparison. Teaching paragraphs-as-process implies, then, that we teach students how to discover relationships among ideas, words, and sentences. Instead of focusing instruction on *what* paragraphs are, we need to teach students *how* to discover relationships and express them in units of discourse. To be sure, it's much easier to teach students "about" paragraphs, isolating the shapes and labels, but if we want them to "do" paragraphs, we must teach not paragraphs but paragraph*ing*.[2]

2. This thesis—that paragraphs, sentences, and essays express relationships—governs my selection of methods for teaching paragraphing. As a result, however, other useful techniques have been omitted. Teachers may also want to consult Sheridan Baker, *The Complete Stylist and Handbook*, 2nd edition (New York: Harper and Row, 1980), especially his discussion of "funnel" paragraphs on pp. 50–75; Alton L. Becker, "A Tagmemic Approach to Paragraph Analysis," *College Composition and Communication* 16 (December 1965), 237–42; Willis L. Pitkin, Jr., "Discourse Blocs," *College Composition and Communication* 20 (May 1969), 138–48; Paul C. Rodgers, Jr., "A Discourse-Centered Rhetoric of the Paragraph," *College Composition and Communication* 17 (February 1966), 2–11; *The Sentence and the Paragraph* (Urbana, Ill.: NCTE, 1966).

Generative rhetoric of the paragraph

In teaching students how sentences may be related to each other, we might begin with speech, a more comfortable medium for most students than writing. Patrick Hartwell suggests recording some informal conversations, "then noting the patterns of connection between sentences."[3] As a rule, the patterns of connection will be one of two kinds: coordination or subordination. Coordinate relationships between groups of words (within as well as across sentences) can be expressed by *and, but,* and *or.* As Ross Winterowd demonstrates,[4] each linking word effects a slightly different kind of coordination, but they all grant equal status to the elements being linked. *And* stresses similarities between equal elements; *but* contrasts equal elements; *or* establishes alternatives between equal elements. Subordinate relationships, Winterowd notes, can be expressed by *because* (literally "by cause"), by *so,* and by the colon. *Because* or *for* subordinates causes to effects (or vice versa, effects to causes); *so* subordinates examples or other evidence to a conclusion; the colon signals a list of objects or events which represent particular members of a more general class.

Intuitively, students have been expressing these subordinate and coordinate relationships in speech for most of their lives. Making them conscious of their tacit knowledge can help them control these relationships in sentences, paragraphs, and even larger units of discourse. In speech, coordination and subordination are often implied rather than stated; that is, the linking words may be omitted. For this reason, it's helpful to analyze spoken conversation to give student writers a vocabulary of linking words which expresses the two kinds of relationships. Once they command the basic vocabulary of linking words, certain sentence-combining problems can give students practice creating subordinate and coordinate relationships of

3. Patrick Hartwell, "Teaching Arrangement: A Pedagogy," *College English* 40 (January 1979), 548–54, outlines a sequence of instruction which "begins with the tacit knowledge of organizing speech that we all share and ends with the 'fixed forms' of certain writing situations" (p. 550).
4. W. Ross Winterowd, "The Grammar of Coherence," in *Contemporary Rhetoric: A Conceptual Background with Readings,* edited by W. Ross Winterowd (New York: Harcourt Brace Jovanovich, 1975), pp. 225–33; reprinted from *College English* (May 1970). Winterowd argues that coherence has three levels which are expressed in case relationships, syntax, and transitions or relationships beyond the sentence. Although he originally posited seven transitions, he labels the six relationships I have listed as follows: coordinate (*and*), obversative (*but*), alternative (*or*), causative (*because* or *for*), conclusive (*so*), and inclusive (colon). Since these relationships can be expressed in a variety of ways, not merely with six conjunctions, beginning teachers will find it helpful to read his article in its entirety.

various kinds. For example, we could ask students to relate the following statements using as many of the six words given above as possible:

> He eats spinach. He likes it.
>
> Jane went to a movie. Harry went to a party.
>
> Men can be teachers. Women can be lawyers.

An exercise like this one permits students to discuss differences in meaning expressed by various linking words. It also allows students to suggest additional vocabulary for expressing coordinate and subordinate relationships.

Having examined these relationships in speech and at the level of the sentence, students can begin to discover them at work in longer stretches of discourse. The same relationships operating between the parts and wholes of sentences may structure paragraphs and essays. As we observed in Chapter 9, Christensen's cumulative sentence consists of a base clause to which supporting material has been added (or related). He diagrams subordinate relationships between the base clause and the supporting material by indenting word groups and numbering them consecutively. In the following sentence, for example, each indented word group is more concrete than the one preceding it and, consequently, is subordinate to it:

> 1 He dipped his hands in the bichloride solution and shook them,
> 2 a quick shake, (NC)
> 3 fingers down, (Abs)
> 4 like the fingers of a pianist above the keys. (PP)
>
> (Sinclair Lewis, *Main Street*)

On the other hand, cumulative sentences may coordinate, rather than subordinate, word groups. When they do, we assign word groups the same number and don't indent them. The level-2 word groups in the following sentence exhibit a coordinate relationship with respect to each other (but a subordinate relationship with respect to the base clause):

> 1 He could sail for hours,
> 2 searching the blanched grasses below him with his telescopic eyes, (VC)
> 2 gaining height against the wind, (VC)

    2 descending in mile-long, gently declining swoops when he
      curved and rode back, (VC)
    2 never beating a wing. (VC)

(Walter Van Tilburg Clark, The Ox-Bow Incident)

So too with paragraphs. "The topic sentence of a paragraph," Christensen maintains, "is analogous to the base clause of such a cumulative sentence, and the supporting sentences of a paragraph are analogous to the added levels of the sentence" (*Notes Toward a New Rhetoric,* p. 75). Stated another way, we create a paragraph by beginning with a sentence. If the paragraph is to have coherence, the second sentence must be somehow related to the first. We must decide whether the second sentence is coordinate with or subordinate to the first sentence. In the following paragraph, for example, the second sentence is subordinate to the first; the rest of the sentences repeat "then . . . now" constructions and, consequently, develop the paragraph by coordination:

  1 Nowhere, at no time, have there been five and a half years so alternately wondrous, compelling, swift and cruel.
    2 As the Sixties began, our aspirant astronauts had yet to enter space; now, they practice giant steps to the moon.
    2 Then, jet travel was a conversation piece; now, we change the flight if we've seen the movie.
    2 Then, we were about to be swamped by a recessionary wave; now, riding history's highest flood of prosperity, we are revising our assumptions about the inevitability of ebbs in our economic life.
    2 Then, our Negroes were still marshaling their forces; now, they have marshaled the conscience of mankind.
    2 Then, we were arguing over the fitness of a Roman Catholic to be President; now, we subdue the nightmare of his murder.
    2 Then, a Southerner in the White House seemed politically unthinkable; now, a Southerner [Lyndon Johnson] builds with the most emphatic mandate we have ever bestowed.
    2 Then, John Birch was an unknown soldier, actresses still wore clothes at work, and dancing was something a man and woman did together.

(Leonard Gross, Look, June 24, 1965)

Although each sentence after the first expresses or implies a *but*-relationship ("then" . . . *but* "now"), sentences two through eight repeat characteristics of the sixties, achieving coherence through *and*-relationships. Because sentences two through eight present evidence to support the generalization in sentence one, a colon-relationship holds the entire paragraph together.

On the other hand, the writer may choose to continue subordinating sentences once the "commitment" (or topic) sentence has been written, as in the following example:

1 The process of learning is essential to our lives.

   2 All higher animals seek it deliberately.

      3 They are inquisitive and they experiment.

         4 An experiment is a sort of harmless trial run of some action which we shall have to make in the real world; and this, whether it is made in the laboratory by scientists or by fox-cubs outside their earth den.

           5 The scientist experiments and the cub plays; both are learning to correct their errors of judgment in a setting in which errors are not fatal.

              6 Perhaps this is what gives them both their air of happiness and freedom in these activities.

(J. Bronowski, *The Common Sense of Science*)

Although the halves of sentences three through five express coordinate relationships, each complete sentence in the paragraph is subordinate to the sentence preceding it. Sentences one and two share a *because*-relationship. Sentence three gives particulars of what the general verb *seek* in sentence two implies, a colon-relationship. Sentence four specifically identifies the more general term *experiment* in sentence three and narrows the meaning of *they* in sentence three to include *scientists* and *fox-cubs;* both functions constitute colon-relationships. Sentence five specifies the meaning of *harmless trial run* in sentence four, another kind of colon-relationship. Sentence six represents a conclusion drawn from sentence five, a *so*-relationship. Although all three subordinate relationships—*because, so,* colon—can join parts of sentences, in this paragraph they relate whole sentences to other sentences. The paragraph illustrates that principles used to build sentences also apply to structuring larger units of discourse.

Notice that Bronowski's paragraph develops its commitment sentence by a variety of methods: by constructing an argument of premises and conclusions, by citing examples of what scientists and fox-cubs do to learn, by comparing scientists and cubs, by defining *experiment* as "a sort of harmless trial run," by suggesting a cause-effect relationship between play and learning. Given the traditional labels for methods of paragraph development, we'd have difficulty assigning one label to a paragraph like this one.

A sequence of lessons

Asking students to dissect model paragraphs, however, isn't the same as getting them to create coherent paragraphs. Describing how some-one else subordinates and coordinates sentences doesn't by itself teach students how to do it. Analyzing the created product doesn't help them practice the creative process. For this reason, the chapter con-cludes with a sequence of lessons that teach students how to group progressively larger amounts of material. The sequence moves from creating single sentences through building paragraphs to rewriting them. Although designed for whole-class discussion, the lessons could be modified to help individual students who need practice develop-ing coherent paragraphs. As with any lesson plan, the ten activities outlined below should be adjusted to meet the needs of a particular writing class. Some activities may warrant considerable classtime; others can be handled quickly if students already know how to do them. Whenever possible, focus the discussion on student writing, using professional models only to supplement or reinforce the stu-dents' work.

1. Begin with the sentence. Record informal conversations and discuss the relationships among groups of sentences. Examine sen-tence-combining exercises students have already completed to derive lists of words which express the coordinate and subordinate relation-ships between word groups. Ask students to link pairs of sentences in various ways using a progressively larger vocabulary of linking (or "transition") words:

Coordinate relationships	*Additional linking words*
and-relationship	furthermore, also, too, again, similarly, in addition
but-relationship	yet, however, still, on the other hand, nevertheless
or-relationship	nor
Subordinate relationships	*Additional linking words*
because-relationship	for, as a result, consequently
so-relationship	therefore, thus, for this reason
colon-relationship	first, second, third; who, which, that; for example, to illustrate

2. Delete the linking words from student (or professional) paragraphs and ask students to fill in the blanks with appropriate choices. Discuss alternate wordings the class may have overlooked. The following paragraph reproduces Theron Alexander's words, but similar relationships within and between sentences could be expressed with different words:

> Social change takes many forms in modern society, *and* people are affected by it in several different ways. *For example,* in the past, a man's prestige *as well as* much of his life satisfaction lay in his occupation *and* in his work. *However,* signs indicate that the traditional basis for satisfaction is changing. *Now,* the source often lies outside of "work." The satisfaction formerly obtained in an occupation is being pursued in clubs, sports, and many kinds of projects. This change in attitude toward work stems *not only* from the character of job duties, *but also* from shorter work hours and higher incomes. [Theron Alexander, "The Individual and Social Change," *Intellect* (December 1974)]

3. After students have completed some prewriting on a topic, let them practice writing topic or commitment sentences, which generally exhibit one or more of the following characteristics:

    a. They express an opinion or fact.
       I live in a poor neighborhood.
    b. They express an attitude toward or give an impression of a whole experience.
       Since my automobile accident, I have learned to drive more carefully.
    c. They specify how many parts are contained in the whole.
       My English class has three types of students.
       My brother did not finish school for four reasons.

4. Using one of the students' commitment sentences, guide the whole class in developing it by coordinating and subordinating other sentences to it. Repeat the procedure several times; then let the students try it on their own, first in groups and then individually. For example, the sentence above, "I live in a poor neighborhood," might be developed in two ways:

Coordinate relationships

    1 I live in a poor neighborhood.
      2 Most of the adults are unemployed.
      2 Almost every house needs major repairs and a coat of paint.
      2 Porter Street has never been paved.

Subordinate relationships

1 I live in a poor neighborhood.

  2 Most of the adults are unemployed.

    3 Consequently, the average income per family remains below the poverty level.

    4 Few families can afford to repair their homes.

5. Reproduce only the first and last sentence of a paragraph and ask students to write four or five sentences which would fill in the middle and relate the two sentences you have given them.

6. Rearrange the sentences of a model student paragraph and type the random order of sentences onto a ditto master, numbering the sentences consecutively. Have students put the sentences into any order that makes sense to them, and ask them to explain what relationships among sentences their arrangement expresses. Then show the class the original paragraph and discuss its arrangement.

7. Diagram the coordinate and subordinate relationships in a model paragraph. Christensen's "A Generative Rhetoric of the Paragraph" offers several examples by professional writers, but student paragraphs should also be used. Then ask students to observe the same sentence relationships as they develop several paragraphs on topics they themselves have chosen.

8. Discuss with the class a model paragraph, like the one below, that could be improved with revision. Draw arrows and circles all over it (rewriting is messy work) to determine how the relationships between sentences could be tightened. Where could linking words be added? How could sentence subjects be made more consistent? Can key words be repeated or pronouns be substituted? Does the commitment sentence need changing? Are sentence patterns disrupting the unity of the paragraph?

Original

Many suburban (homeowners) have become slaves to lawns. The (time and money) spent on lawns are ridiculous. (Weekends and evenings) are devoted to mowing, raking, trimming, watering, weeding, and feeding the grass. (Lawns) are cursed and slaved over.

[Notice that each sentence shifts to a new subject. Sentences are all the same type and about the same length.]

Revision

Many suburban (homeowners) have become slaves to their lawns. (They) spend a ridiculous amount of time and money on their yards, devoting weekends and evenings to the care and feeding of the green monsters. Instead of enjoying their leisure time, (these suburbanites) constantly mow, rake, trim, water, weed, and feed their turf. Although most (property own- ers) curse their lawns, (they) slavishly continue to care for the grass.

(Adapted from William E. Mahoney, *Workbook of Current English*, p. 292)

9. Have students examine their previous writings for paragraphs that need rewriting. Guided by questions similar to those in 8 above, let them work in groups or individually to analyze and revise their paragraphs. Ditto several "before" and "after" paragraphs which successfully employ different strategies to discuss with the entire class.

10. After considerable practice creating paragraphs, students (or their teachers) may want to examine and label various paragraph "shapes," reinforcing a skill they have already acquired. Now would be a good time to clarify myths about topic sentences (not all para- graphs have them) and methods of development (the methods usu- ally overlap or occur in various combinations within a single para- graph). Since textbook authors deliberately select model paragraphs to reflect traditional methods of development, students should have opportunities to examine newspapers, popular magazines, advertise- ments, business letters, and other forms of discourse which will en- large their understanding of how sentences legitimately can be grouped.

One traditional approach to paragraphing merits attention as a way of summarizing what students have already learned to do by manip- ulating intersentence relationships. Paragraph shapes—inverted and regular triangles, diamonds, and hourglasses—represent ways of "stacking" sentences which relate to each other. Like Christensen's indented levels of generality, paragraph shapes depict where writers may place the most general statement and how they may arrange, in relation to it, the subordinating material. The inverted triangle, for example, begins with the topic sentence, the level-1 sentence as Christensen would have it, and subordinates subsequent sentences. For ease of comparison, the following paragraph is reproduced both with indented levels of generality and as a geometric shape:[5]

5. The examples illustrating paragraph shapes have been adapted from Glenn R. Wil- liston, *Understanding the Main Idea, Middle Level* (Providence, R.I.: Jamestown Publish- ers, 1976), pp. 14–17, 43.

1 Typhoon Chris hit with full fury today on the central coast of Japan.

  2 High waves carried many homes into the sea.

  2 Heavy rain from the storm flooded the area.

    3 People now fear that the heavy rains may have caused mud slides in the central part of the country.

      4 The number of victims buried under the mud may climb past the 200 mark by Saturday.

*Typhoon Chris hit with full fury today on the central coast
of Japan.* High waves carried many homes into the sea.
Heavy rain from the storm flooded the area. People
now fear that the heavy rains may have caused
mud slides in the central part of the
country. The number of victims
buried under the mud may
climb past the 200
mark by Saturday.

The regular triangle places the topic sentence last and arranges the subordinate sentences so that they lead up to it:

      2 If the wind becomes gusty suddenly after being calm, you may need to start looking for shelter.

      2 If you see clouds becoming darker, you may need shelter right away.

      2 Naturally, you know that thunder and lightning mean a storm is coming.

        3 Keep in mind that bright lightning doesn't mean a storm is coming.

        3 The number of lightning flashes is important, though.

          4 The more lightning flashes, the worse the storm is likely to be.

  1 The signs of a thunderstorm are many, and being able to understand them can be important.

If the wind becomes gusty
suddenly after being calm, you
may need to start looking for shelter.
If you see clouds becoming darker, you may
need shelter right away. Naturally, you know
that thunder and lightning mean a storm is coming.
Keep in mind that bright lightning doesn't mean a storm
is coming. The number of lightning flashes is important, though.
The more lightning flashes, the worse the storm is likely to be. *The signs of
a thunderstorm are many, and being able to understand them can be important.*

In the diamond-shaped paragraph, the topic sentence appears near the middle, the subordinate sentences leading up to and then away from it:

   2 Dark green, leafy vegetables such as kale and spinach are good sources of vitamin C and iron.

   2 Carrots, squash and sweet potatoes are good sources of carotene, which the body changes to vitamin A.

1 All vegetables are good for us because they provide important vitamins and minerals that build cells and keep us healthy.

   2 Vitamin C, for example, builds strong teeth and helps us resist infections.

   2 Vitamin A keeps skin healthy and protects our eyes.

   2 Iron, also an important part of vegetables, builds red blood cells.

Dark green, leafy
vegetables such as kale and
spinach are good sources of vitamin C
and iron. Carrots, squash and sweet potatoes are
good sources of carotene, which the body changes to vitamin A.
*All vegetables are good for us because they provide important vitamins and
minerals that build cells and keep us healthy.* Vitamin C, for example,
builds strong teeth and helps us resist infections. Vitamin A
keeps skin healthy and protects our eyes. Iron,
also an important part of vegetables,
builds red blood cells.

Hourglass or I-shaped paragraphs begin with the topic sentence and end with a restatement of it, sandwiching the supporting material in between:

1 Houdini, the famous magician, began his career with a traveling circus at the age of nine.

   2 His first trick was to pick up needles with his eyelids while he was hanging by his heels, head downward.

      3 He slowly perfected this trick in secret in the family woodshed.

   2 He was world famous for his escapes—from handcuffs, straitjackets, prison cells and sealed chambers.

      3 He even escaped from a grave six feet in the ground.

1 When he died on October 31, 1926, he had been a public performer for forty-three years.

Houdini, the famous magician, began his career with a traveling circus at the age of nine. His first trick was to pick up needles with his eyelids while he was hanging by his heels, head downward. He slowly perfected this trick in secret in the family woodshed. He was world famous for his escapes—from handcuffs, straitjackets, prison cells and sealed chambers. He even escaped from a grave six feet in the ground. *When he died on October 31, 1926, he had been a public performer for forty-three years.*

The value of studying model paragraphs lies not in labeling *what* shape it has. Rather, we can use models to show students *how* writers link sentences one by one, expressing with each new sentence a coordinate or subordinate relationship to those already written. Models also provide a starting point for imitation, for letting students practice different ways of relating sentences in their own writing. Analyzing professional models together with praiseworthy student writing, students discover useful strategies for rewriting paragraphs by tightening or clarifying intersentence relationships. Moreover, if we discuss sentences and paragraphs with a consistent vocabulary, students are less likely to be confused by terminology. Traditional practice establishes one set of terms for sentence types and a different set of labels for methods of paragraph development. Christensen's generative rhetoric and Winterowd's grammar of coherence, on the other hand, allow us to describe relationships within and between sentences with the same set of terms. The same six relationships—three expressing coordination and three expressing subordination—which link word groups within the sentence also link sentences to each other in shaping coherent paragraphs. As we will see in Chapter 11, the same terms also characterize the relationships among paragraphs in whole essays.

11

Shaping discourse

Prose is architecture, not interior decoration.

ERNEST HEMINGWAY

In college as well as in the professional world, writers often observe formal constraints on their work. Business letters, technical reports, and legal documents, for example, require writers to arrange their material in prescribed ways, according to patterns of organization sanctioned by convention and tradition. In these contexts, effective communication depends, in part, on "writing by formula." Writing-by-formula is also necessary in college, where teachers often specify how they want students to arrange book reports, term projects, and footnote or bibliographical citations. Moreover, when writing under pressure, students who command a repertoire of formulas for organizing answers to essay exams save time. Because they have only a few minutes for prewriting during the examination period, they must plan their essays quickly and efficiently. Prescribed patterns of organization, then, serve a useful purpose, especially when time or tradition limits the choices writers have in shaping their work.

This chapter focuses primarily on ways of organizing another kind of writing, writing which allows students more time to discover their purpose and message and which permits several options for organizing the material. This category includes most personal or self-expressive writing and responses to assignments in many composition, creative writing, and journalism classes. It also covers the kind of writing students and professionals do whenever their audience—a teacher, an employer, a committee, a consumer group—considers any one of several organizational patterns acceptable. This kind of writing confronts students with many possibilities for shaping their work. Students need to know what their options are and how to make effective choices.

Discovering form

As with paragraphing, writers discover the shape of the whole discourse as they write. We may begin with a general plan in mind, but we work out the specific relationships between parts and wholes in the writing and rewriting stages. The general plan develops from prewriting decisions. As we probe the subject to discover what we want to say, as we define our purpose and assess the expectations of our audience, we make choices which ultimately are reflected in the organization of the written work. A subject probed thoroughly enough begins to organize itself, begins to suggest possibilities for arranging its presentation. As we draft the piece, executing some of those preliminary decisions, new possibilities emerge, and we may decide to modify or abandon altogether our original plan. Then in reviewing the draft, we may discover holes or overlapping material; sections may need to be condensed, expanded, or rearranged. Most writers complete several drafts before the shape of the discourse suits them.

Since writers discover form at every stage of the composing process, teachers should stress planning strategies but also encourage students to be flexible about them. Inflexible plans which slavishly follow an outline or cram ideas into a prescribed form, for example, can undermine the effectiveness of a student's work. When students adhere too rigidly to their original intention, they seem less likely to make choices which might improve the piece. They also prevent themselves from discovering the material's organic unity and finding new implications in the subject. When we give students plenty of time for prewriting and frequent opportunities to examine where their writing is taking them, they will be more likely to modify or wisely abandon their original plan when necessary, without feeling that they have failed by not sticking to it.

The college freshman who wrote the following essay obviously kept in mind a common organizational pattern: the five-paragraph theme (an introduction, three body paragraphs, and a conclusion). But the paper suffers because her ideas are disconnected and undeveloped.

She's writing off the top of her head, as if "filling up" five "boxes" were more important than discussing how her life differs from her parents':

> The greatest contribution to ones' life are the exposures in which he or she become familiar with. These exposures are what basically effect ones' life and mold the way a person will live their remaining life.
>
> Exposure is the greatest attribute to ones' life. From what I've seen and what my parents saw at my age, what I saw was more. The world is smaller now because of mass transit. You can now fly all over the world in one day. Drive three hundred miles in one day. To be able to go to more places and see more things affects ones' future.
>
> It all amounts to the constant change in life style. Back in my parents' childhood, they could not have dreamed of having their own car. And my grandmother would have killed my mother for smoking a cigarette or drinking a beer.
>
> Of course there is education. Education is a great contribution to how one is going to live their life. Education has become much better then that of my parents.
>
> In conclusion the exposures that one encounters in the early portion of a life time contribute to ones' latter life. The exposures in which I have encountered are greater than my parents, so my life will be better.

Organizing an essay isn't simply a matter, as one student put it, of "telling them what you're going to tell them, telling them, and then telling them what you've told them." "The job of teaching structure," William Irmscher writes, "is not to prescribe it, but to help students realize how they can perceive and create the patterns of their own thoughts" (*Teaching Expository Writing*, p. 105). In other words, students "need to learn more about linking the 'inner parts' than designing the outer shape" (p. 104). In order to link inner parts, writers must do enough prewriting to develop sufficient material to link. Then they must see the connections among ideas, the relationships parts have to the whole. In the final analysis, teaching students to shape discourse is like teaching them to structure sentences and paragraphs. Although the parts and wholes of a complete discourse encompass larger chunks of material than sentences and paragraphs do, the relationships will be the same. The same patterns of coordination and subordination at work in sentences and paragraphs also link the inner parts of an essay to each other and to the "main idea" or thesis.

Re-inventing Comprone's wheel

Joseph Comprone has devised a useful metaphor for demonstrating the interrelatedness of parts in discourse. His wagon wheel (Fig. 11.2) is intended to help students discover the connections between sections of essays assigned as readings in an English class. It provides a visual scheme of the process whereby readers comprehend ideas and experiences. However, if we shift our perspective on the wheel, it also becomes a useful device for helping students plan their own essays. Comprone argues that the wheel or circle represents more accurately the recursive mental processes involved in structuring essays than a linear model can:

> [An essay] serves as the form within which a writer transcribes and follows the growth of an idea, the building of a central idea from a large number of subordinate ideas and from an even larger number of experiences. It is an artificial, linear medium, setting ideas atop of one another like bricks in the wall of a building; yet, as we write and read essays, we must, to understand and use the form efficiently, understand the medium imaginatively as well. The circle metaphor should help your students to see the organic as well as the linear nature of the essay. A straight line development, sentence by sentence, paragraph by paragraph describes the essay as it appears on the lined, typed or printed page, but the circle better illustrates the mental and psychological processes which go on as a writer manipulates and a reader analyzes the essay form. (*Teaching Form and Substance*, p. 11)

Since Comprone uses the wheel principally for analyzing essays, the four-step procedure he outlines can help students evaluate their drafts to determine where inner parts and outer shape need to be realigned in revision. For now, though, let's examine the wheel reinvented as a planning strategy, each of the four steps leading students to discover relationships among the ideas prewriting has generated. Students can build the wheel—that is, shape their essays—by following the steps described below:

1. *Create the hub.* After students have examined prewriting material—brainstormed lists, freewritings, or answers to heuristic questions—ask them to write a sentence which comes closest to incorporating the most material or which expresses the central idea of the essay they propose to write. The hub represents the thesis or commitment sentence, around which everything else revolves.

2. *Design the spokes.* Students should now reexamine their prewritings and the thesis statement for ways of dividing the central idea into related subtopics, which serve as spokes for the wheel. Just as the spokes strengthen and reinforce the wheel, the prewritings contain ideas which can be used to support the thesis. Just as some spokes may be too long or too short to extend from the hub to the rim, so too writers must decide how much of their material to include. They need to ask, "*What* material in my notes seems most important to developing the central idea, and *how* can I present the material?" Answers to the *what* and *how* questions should be written out as brief sentences.

3. *Arrange the spokes around the hub.* Answers to the *what* and *how* questions can be sorted into two categories: spokes that develop content (*what*) and those that reveal a rhetorical strategy (*how*). Content spokes or topic sentences relate the

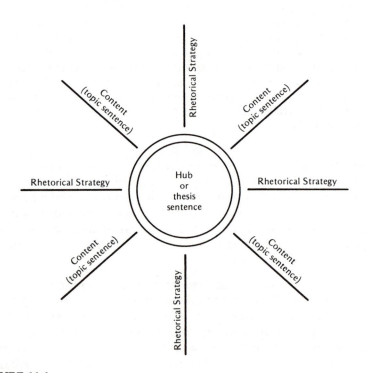

FIGURE 11.1

From Joseph Comprone, *Teaching Form and Substance* (Dubuque, Ia.: Wm. C. Brown, 1976). Reprinted by permission of the publisher.

subtopics to the central idea or thesis. Rhetorical strategy spokes describe how the content can be developed in a paragraph or group of paragraphs. After the spokes have been sorted into these two categories, students can arrange them around the hub, alternating content and strategy sentences. The wheel is now partially completed; it has a hub (thesis), and spokes (topic sentences together with descriptions for developing them).

4. *Build the rim.* Remind students that their essay radiates out from the hub or central idea, along spokes which contain more specific support and explanations, to an even more clearly defined rim of details, statistics, or examples. If the wheel is to roll smoothly, the rim must be connected all the way around and attached firmly to the spokes. In other words, the specific details used to develop each segment of the rim, each section of the essay, must be relevant, arranged in logical order, with adequate transitions between sections. Since each segment of the rim is defined by the content and strategy spokes intersecting it, the writer must fill in the area between the spokes by selecting appropriate details and transitional devices which directly develop each subtopic. Although the prewriting notes may offer specific support for some subtopics, students should expect to do additional prewriting at this stage, generating new details and examples to complete the rim. They might now want to address the following questions: What specific details best develop the subtopics defined by each content spoke? What order and form should the details have to express most effectively the intention represented by each strategy spoke? What transitions can I use to join the segments of the rim and move the reader smoothly through the essay?

The wheel completed (Fig. 11.2), students now have a comprehensive plan for the essay they propose to write. They've created a visual scheme to shape the draft, a blueprint for relating specific details, examples, and transitions (the rim) to subtopics and rhetorical strategies (the spokes) which develop the thesis (the hub).

If Caroline, the student who wrote the essay at the beginning of the chapter, had used this four-step procedure, she could have narrowed the focus of her essay, developed subtopics with a clearer relationship to the central idea, and selected relevant support for each section of the essay. In prewriting her essay, she might have begun

FIGURE 11.2   Comprone's Wheel

From *Teaching Form and Substance* (Dubuque, Ia.: Wm. C. Brown, 1976). Reprinted by permission of the publisher

with several freewritings to help her define "exposures," "lifestyles," or "education." A subject chart with "differences between my life and my parents' lives" in the center would also have generated additional material for the major subdivisions of her topic. As we see, the subject chart drawn from her essay (Fig. 11.3) is skimpy; it contains vague terms and lacks an abundance of details. Caroline simply didn't have enough material to begin drafting her first essay. In rewriting it, she needs to begin at the beginning, probing her subject much more thoroughly using several of the techniques discussed in Chapter 6. Once she has examined her subject through prewriting, she can begin building the wheel, which might look like Figure 11.4 when it is finished.

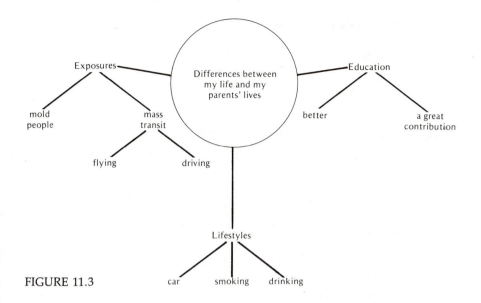

FIGURE 11.3

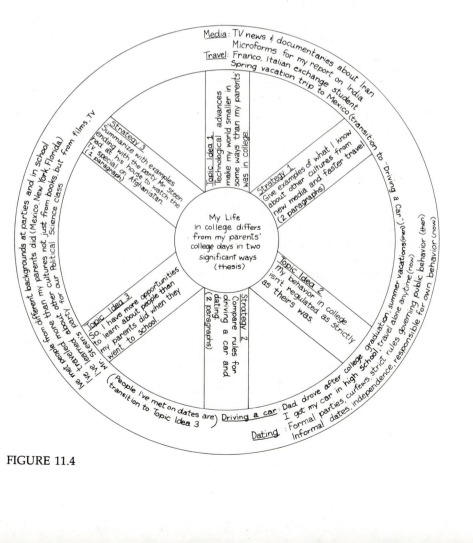

FIGURE 11.4

After Caroline has rewritten her essay, the wheel can suggest additional revisions. By asking questions of the draft, writers can dismantle the wheel, testing its hub, spokes, and rim, strengthening them, rebuilding the essay. Answers to the following questions, adapted from Comprone's *Teaching Form and Substance* (pp. 15, 21), help students detect where the wheel wobbles, where the coherence, emphasis, development, and unity of the essay can be improved:

Coherence: How are the parts of the wheel fitted together (by explicit transitional words, by repetition of key words and phrases)?

Emphasis: How do the main and subordinate ideas relate to each other (by subordination and coordination, by altering syntax and arranging sentences and paragraphs according to some order of importance)?

Development: How are details and specifics used to develop the various parts of the central idea? Does the central idea really become clearer as I read the essay, or have I merely repeated the general idea in slightly different ways, without clarifying it through details, examples, and facts? Does the variety of examples, facts, and specific experiences lead naturally from or work toward the development of a clearly stated thesis?

Unity: Is the central idea suggested in every paragraph and sentence in the essay? When the writer has produced a really complete thesis and a tight, unified essay, the reader can move in many specific directions and still clearly comprehend the presence of the thesis, sometimes by explicit allusion or repetition of it, at other times by more subtle conceptual echoes of it.

Testing the Spokes and Hub: What is the thesis? How is it introduced? How is it developed? Which paragraphs contain general explanations of the thesis? Which paragraphs provide specific support for the thesis? How is the essay concluded so that specifics and generalities are tied together? What logical and emotional appeals does the essay contain? Is the narrating voice believable?

Comprone maintains that many students can't see a significant connection between reading and writing, between skills necessary to analyzing an essay and those necessary to composing it:

> Students are asked to read essays, often with very little attention to the formal qualities of the essays; then they are told simply to take an idea from the essay and write about it. Or, perhaps more frequently, they are told how they might compose an essay of their own, without ever being taught to understand how the essays they have read were themselves composed. (*Teaching Form and Substance*, p. 24)

The wheel encourages students to view reading and writing as inter-dependent processes. As a planning device, the wheel helps writers shape a work by relating its inner parts to a central idea, but it also provides a metaphor for taking apart essays students or professional writers have composed. As a guide to revision or an aid in preparing reading assignments, the four-step procedure examines not only an essay's content but also its rhetorical strategies and formal character-istics.

D'Angelo's paradigms

Another way of looking at form in discourse is to see it as a manifes-tation of thinking. Frank D'Angelo assumes a close connection be-tween invention and arrangement, between thought processes and the organizational patterns or paradigms which express ideas. A par-adigm, as D'Angelo defines it, is "a kind of core structure that bears the main burden of thought."[1] Because the mind composes percep-tions, organizing them into temporal, spatial, and logical patterns, his paradigms reflect those mental processes at work in a piece of writing. The classification paradigm, for example, symbolizes a thought process we use every day. As we perceive the world around us, we constantly create categories, grouping phenomena that share some common characteristic. To express those categories in writing is to reveal how we think: "The same categories that you use to probe a subject you can also use to arrange the details of that subject in an orderly pattern" (p. 70).

D'Angelo divides the paradigms into two groups, "static" and "progressive." The static paradigms arrange topics which can be viewed as entities, fixed *in* time and space; the progressive para-digms order topics, like narration and process, which occur *through* time and space, that is, in several time-states. In their skeletal form, the most commonly used paradigms look like this:

Static Topics

1. Description Paradigm
   Paradigm 1: Vertical Order (bottom to top, top to bottom)
   Paradigm 2: Horizontal Order (left to right, right to left)
   Paradigm 3: Depth Order (inside, outside)
   Paradigm 4: Circular Order (clockwise, counterclockwise)

1. Frank D'Angelo, *Process and Thought in Composition,* 2nd ed. (Cambridge, Mass.: Winthrop, 1980), p. 69. For a fuller explanation of the theory on which D'Angelo's text is based, see his *A Conceptual Theory of Rhetoric* (Cambridge, Mass.: Winthrop, 1975).

2. Definition Paradigm
   Extended Definition A
      1 Introduction (includes logical definition)
      2 Expansion of the genus
      3 Expansion of the differentia
      4 Conclusion (summary or restatement)
   Extended Definition B
      1 Introduction (includes sentence definition)
      2 Supporting details
      3 Supporting details . . .
      4 Conclusion (summary or restatement)

3. Analysis Paradigm
      1 Introduction (states the thesis)
      2 Characteristic 1
      3 Characteristic 2
      4 Characteristics 3, 4, 5, . . .
      5 Conclusion

4. Enumeration Paradigm
      1 Introduction (includes thesis)
      2 First (the first, one)
      3 Second (the next, two)
      4 Third (another, three)
      5 Finally (the final, four)
      6 Conclusion (summary, return to beginning)

5. Classification Paradigm
      1 Introduction (states the thesis)
      2 Type 1
      3 Type 2
      4 Types 3, 4, 5, . . .
      5 Conclusion (summarizes or restates the thesis)

6. Exemplification Paradigm
      1 Introduction (states the thesis)
      2 Example 1
      3 Example 2
      4 Examples 3, 4, 5, . . .
      5 Conclusion (summarizes or restates the thesis)

7. Comparison Paradigms
   Half and Half Pattern
      1 Introduction (includes thesis, sets up comparison)
      2 Subject 1
        a Characteristic 1
        b Characteristic 2 . . .

3 Subject 2
  a Characteristic 1
  b Characteristic 2 . . .
4 Conclusion (summary, return to beginning)
Characteristics Pattern
  1 Introduction (includes thesis, sets up comparison)
  2 Characteristic 1
    a Subject 1
    b Subject 2
  3 Characteristic 2 . . .
    a Subject 1
    b Subject 2
  4 Conclusion (summary, return to beginning)
Point by Point Pattern
  1 Introduction (includes thesis, sets up comparison)
  2 Subject 1 is like (or unlike) Subject 2 in this respect
  3 Subject 1 is like (or unlike) Subject 2 in this respect . . .
  4 Conclusion (summary, return to beginning)

Progressive Topics

1. Narration Paradigm
  1 Introduction (contains time, place, agent, and beginning of action)
  2 Event or Incident 1
  3 Events or Incidents 2, 3, 4, . . .
  4 Conclusion (falling action)

2. Process Paradigm
  1 Introduction (states thesis)
  2 Step or Phase 1
  3 Steps or Phases 2, 3, 4, . . .
  4 Conclusion

3. Cause and Effect Paradigms
  Cause to Effect Pattern A
    1 Introduction (includes thesis)
    2 Cause
    3 Effect
    4 Conclusion (summary or restatement)
  Cause to Effect Pattern B
    1 Introduction (includes thesis)
    2 Cause 1
    3 Causes 2, 3, 4, . . .
    4 Effect
    5 Conclusion (summary or restatement)

Cause to Effect Pattern C
1 Introduction (includes thesis)
2 Cause
3 Effect 1
4 Effects 2, 3, 4, . . .
5 Conclusion (summary or restatement)
Effect to Cause Pattern A
1 Introduction (includes thesis)
2 Effect
3 Cause
4 Conclusion (summary or restatement)
Effect to Cause Pattern B
1 Introduction (includes thesis)
2 Effect 1
3 Effects 2, 3, 4, . . .
4 Cause
5 Conclusion (summary or restatement)
Effect to Cause Pattern C
1 Introduction (includes thesis)
2 Effect
3 Cause 1
4 Causes 2, 3, 4, . . .
5 Conclusion (summary or restatement)

(*Process and Thought in Composition,* 2nd ed., pp. 70–71,
114–15, 124, 167, 179–80, 190, 200, 217)

Like any model, the paradigms are means to an end. Students should view them as options for discovering inherent organizational possibilities in ideas and experiences; "each of these paradigms can be shortened, lengthened, or modified to suit your own purposes," advises D'Angelo (p. 71). Depending on the material, students may need several paragraphs for introductions and conclusions. They may want to subordinate one paradigm to another. For example, each "type" in the classification paradigm could be developed by a series of examples, definitions, comparisons, and so on.

Notice that the paradigms reveal the same coordinate and subordinate relationships paragraphs do. In the classification paradigm, for example, the "types" all share coordinate relationships with each other and are subordinate to the introduction and conclusion. D'Angelo suggests, in "A Generative Rhetoric of the Essay," that an essay can be a kind of extended paragraph, all of its sentences and paragraphs linked to each other by coordination and subordination. These relationships can be seen either in grammatical structures or in meaning. Grammatical coordination occurs when sentences or paragraphs show parallel structures; meaning coordination is reflected by groups of similar examples, reasons, or details. Subordination, on the other hand, either within or between sentences and paragraphs can be detected in several ways:

> Some typical examples of grammatical subordination are the use of a pronoun in one sentence to refer to a noun or pronoun in a previous sentence; the use of transitional markers, such as *thus, therefore,* and *nevertheless,* to tie sentences together; the repetition of a word or a part of a word in a sentence to link it to a similar word in the previous sentence; and the use of a synonym to refer to an equivalent word in a previous sentence. Meaning relationships are much more difficult to determine, but in general, if a sentence gives an example, a fact, a detail, a reason, a qualification, or support of any kind, then consider it to be subordinate to a more general statement that precedes it. (*Process and Thought in Composition,* 2nd ed., p. 81)

Not only does D'Angelo see similarities between the relationships which organize essays and those which hold sentences and paragraphs together, but he also draws connections between invention and arrangement. Because the paradigms reflect thought processes, they also have a heuristic function. The subdivisions of each paradigm can be converted into questions which generate subject matter.[2] By the same token, several prewriting techniques discussed in Chapter 6 imply patterns of arrangement. Larson's problem-solving heuristic, for example, suggests an organizational scheme in eight parts, each discussing one question or step in a process we can use to assess and solve problems. Corbett's heuristic implies a scheme for organizing a discussion of a literary work: analyze the work, interpret the work, evaluate the work. Both Larson and Corbett would argue that these schemes aren't the only ones we can use to discuss problems or works of literature, and they would urge us, furthermore, not to view any organizational model as a rigid formula, incapable of accepting revisions a writer must make because the subject demands them.

Nevertheless, all of these models—Comprone's wheel, D'Angelo's paradigms, and the organizational schemes implicit in heuristics—illustrate that the process of shaping discourse begins with prewriting and continues through rewriting. As means to an end, the models help students plot, at least tentatively, the progress of a draft prior to

2. D'Angelo, *Process and Thought in Composition,* pp. 44–45.

writing it, encouraging them to find patterns in the material prewriting techniques have generated. The wheel and the paradigms also support careful reading, allowing students to abstract ideas in an essay, discover its underlying patterns and the connections between them. Such a skill of course has value outside an English class, but it also serves revision because writers must read their drafts with eyes open to its organizational possibilities. If we encourage students to find form in discourse at each stage of the composing process, they will understand that a paper's organization derives from a range of choices writers control when they perceive relationships to express.

12

Teaching rewriting

How do I know what I think until I see what I say?

E. M. FORSTER

Changing attitudes

For most students, *rewriting* is a dirty word. They see it as a punishment, a penalty for writing poorly in the first place. Many teachers reinforce this notion by insisting that students correct mistakes in papers already graded or complete workbook exercises on writing problems in someone else's prose. Rewriting the *whole* paper, students believe, means they've failed the assignment. For almost all writers, rewriting remains an unpleasant chore, a process which confronts them with countless inadequacies in the draft and convinces them that words manipulate writers, not the other way around. Students rewrite their papers reluctantly for many reasons, as the following comments attest:

1. I wait until the last minute, so there's no time to rewrite.
2. My first draft is the best I can do. I can't improve it.
3. I don't know whether my first draft is any good or not, so how can I improve it?
4. I don't know where to begin, and I wouldn't know when to stop.
5. Well, frankly, I'm lazy.

6. When I tinker with my sentences, they just turn out worse.
7. I don't really care about what I'm writing, so I just want to get it over with.
8. Rewriting is too messy. I like to work with clean looking pages.
9. I'm such a bad writer I hate to read my own writing.
10. Rewriting is my instructor's responsibility.
11. Rewriting is painful. I can't stand the agony.
12. If I can't get it right the first time, I must be stupid.

(Diana Hacker and Betty Renshaw,
A Practical Guide for Writers, p. 20)

Most of these attitudes developed slowly, as students sat year after year in English classes where rewriting *was* a form of punishment, where the teacher's comments on papers rarely praised effective writing or offered practical suggestions for repairing weaknesses, where students never had opportunities to draft several versions of an assignment before it was due. The techniques discussed in this chapter are meant to correct students' perceptions of rewriting-as-punishment, to encourage the view that rewriting remains crucial to the composing process, not an afterthought.

Many good writers spend considerably more time rewriting their work than drafting it. "I can't write five words," Dorothy Parker claims, "but that I change seven." Bernard de Voto insists that "the best reason for putting anything down on paper is that one may then change it." The changes we make in a draft are fairly simple; we add, delete, substitute, or rearrange material. But each adjustment requires judgment, making choices about what to keep and what to discard. We must decide, first of all, whether what we've written suits us, represents what we honestly want to say; then we've got to determine if a reader can make sense of it. From the students' perspective, this process poses several obstacles.

First, if neatness matters, as it has mattered ever since handwriting was graded in elementary school, students will be reluctant to mess up their drafts with changes. Second, if they mistakenly believe that some mysterious genius explodes clearly articulated, perfectly punctuated sentences onto a page, they'll hesitate to admit their "genius" has failed them. Third, if they've had no opportunities to prewrite the paper, to develop an overabundance of material, they'll be reluctant to tamper with the piece for fear of having to endure again the agony of finding something to say and making the words come out right. Finally, students conclude, rewriting doesn't matter much anyway. Their teachers neglect it, rarely demonstrating *how* rewriting works. They only occasionally request "corrections," often schedule assignments so as to preclude time for rewriting, and harp on the disadvantages of scissors and paste.

Nancy Sommers' research demonstrates that many student writers use rewriting strategies different from those experienced writers employ. In "Revision Strategies of Student Writers and Experienced Writers," she notes that students see rewriting primarily as rewording, approaching the process with what she calls a "thesaurus philosophy of writing": "The students consider the thesaurus a harvest of lexical substitutions and believe that most problems in their essays can be solved by rewording" (p. 381). They worry most about eliminating lexical repetition, are predominantly concerned about vocabulary, and delete or substitute words much more frequently than adding or reordering material. Although occasionally they reword the introduction or reorder ideas, they generally limit themselves to matters covered by editing rules. "At best the students see their writing altogether passively through the eyes of former teachers or their surrogates, the textbooks, and are bound to the rules which they have been taught" (p. 383).

Experienced writers, Sommers concludes, approach rewriting differently, much more concerned about finding the shape of their argument and about the reader's expectations. Although they make changes primarily at the level of the sentence (predominantly by addition and deletion), the changes encompass the whole composition and take several cycles to complete, each cycle embracing a different objective:

> The experienced writers see their revision process as a recursive process—a process with significant recurring activities—with different levels of attention and different agenda for each cycle. During the first revision cycle their attention is primarily directed towards narrowing the topic and delimiting their ideas. At this point, they are not as concerned as they are later about vocabulary and style. The experienced writers explained that they get closer to the meaning by not limiting themselves too early to lexical concerns. (p. 386)

Whereas early cycles concentrate on finding form, discovering the message, and clarifying ideas, later cycles focus on stylistic concerns. Yet even though each cycle may have a primary focus, experienced writers subordinate other concerns to it, keeping the whole in mind as they concentrate on its parts.

Sommers' work helps us redefine *rewriting* to include both revising and editing. When we want students to polish a text, to clean up misspellings, to change punctuation, to straighten out grammatical problems, we're asking them to edit, not revise, their work. Editing usually takes place during one of the later cycles Sommers describes. Revising, however, is not, as many textbooks proclaim, the last stage of composing. "Instead of thinking of revision as an activity at the end of the process, what if we thought of revision as a process of making a work congruent with what a writer intends—a process that occurs throughout the writing of a work?"[1] The composing process is *not* a linear sequence of separable stages; prewriting, writing, and rewriting are concurrent activities, repeated over and over again as writers come progressively closer to resolving incongruities between what they intend to say and what the discourse actually says.

Before I drafted the introductory paragraph for this chapter, for example, I compiled a list of notes and decided roughly what I wanted to do: to present the students' perspective on rewriting. Once I've discussed why students hate rewriting, I reasoned, I can then explain what we can do about the problem. When I wrote the paragraph the first time, in pencil on a long, yellow, legal tablet, I got stuck in several places. Instead of erasing my words, as I usually do, I simply crossed through them so that you could see the changes I made while I composed the first draft. Here's the first version of Chapter 12's opening paragraph:

1. Nancy I. Sommers, "The Need for Theory in Composition Research," *College Composition and Communication* 30 (February 1979), 48. Sommers appears to use the term *revising* with the meaning I attach to *rewriting;* both of us agree, however, that *revising* and *rewriting* amount to much more than "editing," "proofreading," or "correcting" a text.

given the paper their best effort), there is no way to improve it by revision. For almost all writers, rewriting is a frustrating chore, ~~When we contemplate an almost alien draft, we~~ ~~a process that required us to admit~~ tempts us to admit th~~It~~ must admit that, some of our ~~words~~ ideas ~~and words~~ refuse to ~~submit to~~ be governed by ~~words~~ ~~didn't intend to say this and left that point undeveloped~~ ~~our control; that we~~ ~~haven't thought things through, that that~~ ~~in some sense we have failed to communicate~~ ~~didn't mean to say this and left that out;~~ that in ~~some~~ many ways the writing has flaws ~~communication is flawed~~ To protect ourselves from viewing our mistakes as a personal failure, we construct defenses which permit ~~prevent~~ us to ignore the draft altogether. Listen to these students as they ~~rationalize~~ their reluctance to rewrite their papers:

Almost a week later, after I'd drafted the entire chapter, I reread it. What especially displeased me about the first paragraph was its lack of focus. Although I had intended to present the students' perspective on rewriting, I shifted the focus several times from "rewriting" to "students" to "teachers" to "all writers/we" back to "students." I wasn't secure about my audience either. Although I wanted to communicate how students feel about rewriting papers, their teachers would be reading the book. Some readers surely would resent phrases like "swear word" and "teachers bent on beating comma faults out of their students' papers." Some would resent my aversion to handbook exercises. At that point in the paragraph where I've marked through "sweated out," I seem to have shifted my language to "talk up" to an audience of colleagues; words like "contemplate," "alien," "be governed by," and "permit" represent, for me, a formal vocabulary, especially in a first draft. The last sentence didn't please me either; I needed a lead into the students' comments, but the alliterating r's seemed too fancy.

Keeping these judgments in mind, I rewrote the paragraph. Again, instead of erasing options I'd discarded, I left them for you to see:

Rewriting
~~Revision~~ has become a dirty word in most English classes. Most students see it as a punishment, a penalty for writing poorly ~~badly~~ in the

first place. ~~Most~~ Many teachers reinforce this notion by asking students to "correct the mistakes" in journals or on separate sheets of paper the teacher will collect ~~and~~ for review. ~~Sometimes teachers assign~~ Some students are sentenced to complete exercises ~~exercises to teach~~ & that & mend their ways of ~~punctuating sentences~~ misusing commas. Others ~~are~~ remain convinced, that, having done the best they could on the paper, there is no way to improve it by revision. It's too much of a chore. Listen to ~~some of the typical~~ their own typically ~~frustrating~~ ~~typical attitudes~~ frustrated, honest ~~views~~ ~~reluctance~~ reasons for not rewriting ~~their~~ papers: ~~collected by Diana Hacker and Betty Renshaw:~~

The second version is considerably shorter than the first, probably because I kept asking myself as I wrote, "What do *students* think about rewriting?" The last sentence gave me fits; for all my tinkering with it, I just couldn't get from my own paragraph to the quoted material. Changing "Most" to "Many" was necessary to avoid antagonizing my audience. Changing "Sometimes teachers" to "Some students" kept the focus of the paragraph on students (a deliberate passive construction helped). I changed "Revision," written too hastily, to "Rewriting" because the entire book organizes itself around words ending in -*writing,* a handy way to remember what the composing process entails.

Eight months later, when I rewrote the entire manuscript, I changed the paragraph again. That third version now appears at the beginning of the chapter. Although the second version had had the focus I wanted and had satisfied me that I wasn't consciously alienating my readers, I wasn't pleased about the sentences. They were all about the same length and type. Comparing the first and second drafts of the paragraph also forced me to reconsider decisions I'd already made about audience: "If I really don't think that 'correction exercises' help students," I thought, "I should say so honestly and explain why. If, throughout the book, I've asserted that teachers *and* students are writers, why not also make the point here?"

As you read this book, several years after I wrote the first draft, you may recognize other changes I could have made just in that one paragraph; doubtless, I will too. Nevertheless, although days and months separate the different versions, a luxury most student writers can't enjoy, the rewriting process was cyclical. I began with a purpose but didn't discover my message until I'd examined the second draft. Sentence problems occupied my attention the second time I reviewed the paragraph, but I also addressed larger concerns, reconsidering my audience and my own attitudes about teaching writing. In rewriting, then, as Sommers' research describes, writers review decisions they've made throughout the composing process. They redefine their purpose and audience, reassess the message, reshape the discourse, and realign their meaning with linguistic forms. For this reason, several strategies, discussed earlier in the context of prewriting and writing, reappear in this chapter.

Beyond redefining for ourselves what rewriting entails, we can also encourage students to see it differently, dispelling some of their negative attitudes toward reviewing their work. We can adjust course schedules so that students have time for prewriting, writing, and rewriting each assignment. At least one-third of our teaching should emphasize how writers rework drafts. We can discuss successive versions of novels, speeches, or other works by professional writers. We can encourage students to examine each other's drafts and together develop strategies for rewriting them. Students especially enjoy reworking their papers aided by word processors and computers, in part because the terminal provides a clean copy of the text as changes are made, in part because these new devices represent sophisticated toys, and perhaps because students have not yet learned to associate machine-edited texts with the teacher's red pen. We can also share our own writing with students, explaining problems we encountered and how we resolved them. This last suggestion is especially crucial for students who believe writing is a magic talent teachers are born with, who need to see what rewriting looks like with all its false starts, messy pages, and momentary indecision. I frequently discuss my own writing projects with students. They've seen the three versions of the opening paragraph for this chapter and reviewed with me the decisions I made each time about purpose, audience, form, sentences, diction, and punctuation. They're amazed to see how messy rewriting can be, but they also understand why the process is cyclical, what strategies it involves, and how to choose among them. As long as I continue to let them see my work, they're also willing to share theirs with other students.

Writing strategies applied to rewriting: finding the subject

Since rewriting occurs throughout the composing process, affecting every level of the composition, several strategies discussed in previous chapters apply to rewriting. The student whose paper appears in Chapter 11 (p. 168), for example, could begin by re-inventing it, redefining her subject, her audience, and her purpose. Although she includes several concrete examples of how her world differs from her parents' and grandparents', she hasn't yet discovered what she wants to say about those differences in travel, education, and "exposure" (perhaps an empty, fancy word intended to impress the teacher-audience). She might brainstorm "travel" and/or "education," construct a subject chart, or apply heuristic questions to a sentence like "The most important influence on my life has been (person or experience)." Freewriting would also make her more comfortable with her subject; the first and last paragraphs are written in "Engfish," the pretentiously formal style some students think their English teachers want to read. Perhaps addressing the paper to a younger brother or sister would also help. The point is that this version of her paper can't be improved significantly by repairing the sentence fragment and correcting "ones'." She needs to find her message and a purpose for expressing it to a reader. This student, like most, needs to spend some time probing the subject again and developing new rhetorical strategies to govern the essay. Then, using a traditional outline, Comprone's wheel, or one of D'Angelo's paradigms, she can redefine the shape she wants to give her essay.

Rewriting: finding the shape of discourse

The following essay, a description of the student's bedroom, could be improved by reviewing its structure:

The Pink Bedroom

This bedroom is unique. The dresser has handmade items that match each other and contain make-up. The bedspread on the canopy bed matches the wallpaper. Under the bed and in the closet are treasured items. The objects on the walls illustrate the accomplishments made during the years at school.

The handmade items on the dresser are pink, and they match the pink and white striped wallpaper on three of the walls. These containers hold make up such as lotion, foundation base, powder, and lipstick. Also, the dresser is composed of a pink jewelry box. On either side of the jewelry box, consists a pink lamp. The dresser is white and has two drawers. This dresser is delicate and stays neat.

The canopy bed is also white. The top of the canopy and the ruffle on the bottom of the bed matches the flower wallpaper that it faces, and the bedspread is white and quilted. On the inside of the top of the canopy is a red rose, that is attractive to look at while in the bed. A few pillows and collected dolls are set on the bed. The mattress is soft, and the bed is high off the ground. This bed is comfortable and makes a nice picture to look at.

In different storage spots, numerous articles are found. Under the bed, boxes of letters and past schoolwork are kept. A scrapbook of different events that have happened is stored. In the closet, an array of clothing hangs and on the shelves collectors' items such as books, stamps, seashells, and coins are placed. A shoerack is also in the closet, so that shoes are neatly arranged. These items are in safe keeping in these different places.

Several plaques are displayed on the walls. Certain frames contain witty sayings, and others show the awards that were received in school. Some of these awards were for photography, biology, and acceptance into the honor society. Also, on the wall is a picture of the Virgin Mary and a crucifix, which shows a dedication to the church. Each of these objects on the wall is special and has a purpose in being there.

Overall, the room is neatly organized and delicate. Pink is the main color theme for the room, and the furniture is white. Several plaques and scrapbooks are selectively displayed in different parts of the room. The room is comfortable to live in, but it also makes an attractive picture for observers.

If we outline only the first three paragraphs, we can see that the student did have a plan for organizing the essay (although it wasn't an effective one). Each sentence in the first paragraph establishes a subtopic developed in subsequent paragraphs:

I. This bedroom is unique.
   A. The dresser has handmade items.
   B. The bedspread matches the wallpaper.
   C. Treasured items are stored under the bed and in the closet.
   D. Plaques hang on the walls.

II. The items on the dresser are pink.
   A. Several containers hold makeup.
   B. There is a jewelry box.
   C. Pink lamps stand on either side of the dresser.
   D. The dresser is white.
   E. The dresser has two drawers.
   F. The dresser is delicate.

III. The canopy bed is white.
   A. The canopy and ruffle match the wall paper.
   B. The bedspread is quilted and white.
   C. A rose inside the top of the canopy is attractive to look at.
   D. Pillows and dolls are set on the bed.
   E. The mattress is soft.
   F. The bed is high off the ground.
   G. The bed is comfortable and nice to look at.

Some weaknesses in the paper may be attributed to the assignment, "Describe a person by describing his or her room." In all probability, the student wasn't much interested in the topic and, consequently, couldn't muster sufficient enthusiasm for a stronger essay. She completes the paper only to please the teacher, a problem we'll discuss in Chapter 13. However, because she organized the paper deliberately, perhaps that's the best place to begin rewriting it. First, the details outlined in paragraph one aren't "unique," nor does she tell us her purpose for including them. The outline shows that she's merely listing "things" without linking them to a description of a person or supporting the "uniqueness" idea. The thesis, "This bedroom is unique," needs revising. So do her rhetorical strategies for the piece. Essentially, those are prewriting concerns, but she can probably best identify the problem by seeing the paper scaled down into an outline.

As she plans the next draft, she could ask herself some of the following questions about the outline: Do I really want to write about my room? If so, why begin with "dresser" and end with "plaques"? Is there a logic to moving around the room this way? What alternate description paradigms could I use? In what ways do the items I'm talking about reveal the kind of person I am? What's the purpose for each paragraph and how does it support the whole? Does each paragraph establish subordinate and coordinate relationships among its sentences? In answering these questions about the outline she should discover a conflict of interest in paragraph two, where II A–C specify items on the dresser while II D–F describe the dresser itself. Or she might see that paragraph three shifts the reader's attention spatially from the canopy to the ruffle to the bedspread back to the canopy to the pillows and dolls on the bedspread to the mattress to the floor. That order of details could be improved. So could sentence structures, but for now, she shouldn't worry about them, not until she's discovered what she wants to say about the bedroom and how to shape her message. She can concentrate on sentence structure, diction, and mechanics later, in subsequent cycles. As papers-in-miniature, outlines and paradigms show students where organizational tensions occur, where sections are skimpy, where details could be deleted or rearranged. One cycle of the rewriting process, then, should focus on improving the shape of the discourse.

Rewriting: finding relationships in paragraphs

Attending to coordinate and subordinate relationships within and between paragraphs can become the goal of yet another rewriting cycle. As students work through the draft a second or third time, they might examine the density and forward movement of paragraphs. By diagramming a paragraph like the one below, the student can see that it contains only two levels of generality, merely lists details, and establishes few subordinate relationships either within sentences or between them:

1 The inside of my jeep is filthy.
   2 The ashtray hasn't been cleaned in weeks.
   2 The floor is covered with corn and dirt from our farm.
   2 The seats are dusty because I haven't driven it in months.
   2 The ceiling has been spotted by beer and soda pop fights.

This student probably did some prewriting, listing *ashtrays, floor, seats, ceiling* under the general heading "My jeep is filthy," but he didn't probe the subject much beyond that. Consequently, the draft only reproduces his prewriting list.

Fortunately, the draft eventually reveals his purpose for discussing the jeep. In the last sentence of his essay, he writes, "Nevertheless, I'll never part with my jeep." In other words, he intended to describe his jeep in such a way that its imperfections "nevertheless" increase its value. Keeping the "nevertheless" intention in mind, he can begin rewriting the paragraph. First, he must invent new material to point up the contrast between "filth that most people object to" and "filth that gives my jeep character." "If most people object to dirty ashtrays," he might ask himself, "why don't I?" After he has explored these contrasts, he must rework the sentences, incorporating more subordination to express the "nevertheless" relationship. The revised version looks like this:

1 Although most people think my jeep is filthy, I can't bring myself to clean it.
   2 The ashtray hasn't been cleaned in weeks.
      3 I won't empty it though because my parents won't let me smoke in the house, and when I'm in my jeep I can do what I want to.
   2 The floor is covered with corn and dirt from our farm.
      3 All the same, I haven't vacuumed it because I'm proud of being a country boy and don't mind carrying my turf around with me.
   2 The seats stay dusty because I've had too much work to do after school lately to take the jeep out of the driveway.
   2 The interior is a mess, the ceiling and upholstery spotted by beer and soda pop fights.
      3 They remind me of all the good times I've had with my friends on weekends.

Although the paragraph could benefit from yet another revision to tighten and polish its sentences, at least now he's identified the relationships which hold the paragraph together. Furthermore, he's added reasons to support the bald statements in the first draft and decreased the distance between himself and his topic, using the description of his filthy jeep to characterize himself. Rewriting has helped him clarify his purpose for the paper.

Some paragraphs require less substantial rewriting. They can be improved by adjusting the topic or commitment sentence; adding, deleting, substituting, or reordering supporting details; improving transitions; or reorganizing sentences to establish chains of equivalent terms which hold the paragraph together. Notice how many "equivalence chains" unify the following paragraph: [2]

As readers, students of English specialize in the interpretation of literary texts. Poems, stories, and plays epitomize the independent nature of written texts: they challenge readers to live the life portrayed in the text, to think its thoughts, to feel its emotions—in short, to become more human by encountering the soul of the writer in and through the work of literature. Anyone who has traveled with Chaucer to Canterbury, or suffered with Shakespeare the plight of Romeo and Juliet, or stopped by those wintry woods with Robert Frost knows how much imagination and insight literature demands of a reader.

Some paragraphs, however, can't be improved by removing irrelevant material, making sentence subjects similar, or establishing equivalence chains. The following paragraph already has consistent sentence subjects:

Draft: The store went out of business. It did not attract enough customers. It had a good location, but its merchandise was overpriced. Its salespeople were not helpful.

(William Mahoney, *Workbook of Current English*, p. 293)

If the writer were to combine these sentences, he'd realize that he doesn't have enough material for a paragraph:

2. The example appears in John Broderick, *The Able Writer* (New York: Harper and Row, 1982). *Equivalence* is a technical term borrowed from structural linguists who study the recurrence of words, parts of words, and phrases in a whole discourse or large sections of it; see Zellig S. Harris, *Discourse Analysis Reprints* (Papers on Formal Linguistics No. 2; The Hague: Mouton, 1963).

Revision: The store went out of business, in spite of its ideal location, because its overpriced merchandise and rude salespeople drove customers away.

Now the "paragraph" has become a tight topic sentence, which could be developed by re-inventing specific examples to support the phrases "overpriced merchandise" and "rude salespeople."

Rewriting: finding sentence problems

Since most writers have enough trouble simply getting their ideas onto the page in an initial draft, they don't worry about constructing polished sentences the first time around. Sentence work can come later, when students are free to concentrate solely on that level of discourse. Now, sentence-combining can help students rid sentences of deadwood and create varied prose rhythms. Moving through a draft, a few sentences at a time, students can embed one sentence into another, review punctuation, condense piled up prepositional phrases into single modifiers, add adverbs and adjectives, substitute action verbs for lifeless *be* and *have,* weed out unnecessary passive constructions, reorder phrases, and undangle participles.

Rewriting sentences will be especially troublesome for students who believe that fancy vocabulary and wordiness define "good writing." Their prose may contain one-third to one-half "lard," a term Richard Lanham uses to characterize stylistic problems which not only lengthen sentences unnecessarily but also obscure meaning. To reduce the lard factor, he recommends that writers diagnose their sentences by the "Paramedic Method":

1. Circle the prepositions.
2. Circle the "is" forms.
3. Ask, "Who is kicking who?"
4. Put this "kicking" action into a simple (not compound) active verb.
5. Start fast—no mindless introductions.
6. Write out the sentence on a blank sheet of paper and look at its shape.
7. Read the sentence aloud with emphasis and feeling.

(*Revising Prose,* p. 21)

Then, guided by their evaluation, students can rewrite sentences like the following:

Original: For the writer, the practice of bad writing is harmful, for it results in an inhibition of his responses to intellectual and imaginative stimuli.
Revision: Bad writing inhibits a writer's mind and imagination. (Lard factor = 66%)

(Revising Prose, p. 29)

Original: I think that all I can usefully say on this point is that in the normal course of their professional activities social anthropologists are usually concerned with the third of these alternatives, while the other two levels are treated as raw data for analysis.
Revision: Social anthropologists usually concentrate on the third alternative, treating the other two as raw data. (Lard factor = 66%)

(Revising Prose, p. 11)

Finally, writers must devote one reading of the draft to proofreading and editing. Students who tend to overlook misspellings may spot them by reading their papers backwards, beginning with the last word. Reading the paper aloud also helps identify stilted phrases or unreasonably convoluted sentences which went undetected in previous rewriting cycles.

Approached as a series of purposeful cycles, rewriting requires several readings of a draft, each with a different emphasis. We read it first to evaluate our rhetorical purpose and the relationships we're establishing among writer, reader, and subject. Then we read to test the overall organization of the discourse, rediscovering its message and strengthening the relationships between inner parts and outer shape. In another reading, we examine paragraph structure; in another, sentence construction and diction. Finally, we clean up the surface features, attending to punctuation, mechanics, and spelling.

Although experienced writers can juggle two or three objectives simultaneously, students may need to move more slowly until they get the hang of it. Some of my students find it helpful to recopy the draft after they've completed two or three rewriting cycles and before they attend to later cycles. Although recopying takes time and unfortunately isolates each level of discourse from the others, these students seem to want a clean text to work from. All the same, I never insist that students recopy their papers, for two reasons. First, although each cycle permits writers to review a particular set of decisions, ultimately those decisions can't be regarded apart from choices which govern the whole piece. As students examine individual paragraphs, for example, they must necessarily examine sentences, consider the overall organization of the piece, and determine if the paragraph realizes prewriting decisions about purpose and audience.

Second, recopying the draft after each cycle is inefficient. It's boring. It not only reduces the amount of time students devote to reviewing their work, but it also lengthens the time between cycles and consequently may prevent students from applying what they've learned in one reading of the paper to subsequent readings. For these reasons, I encourage students to recopy drafts only when it helps to record on a clean page the changes made during one cycle before going on to the next. Several purposeful *readings* of the draft are necessary; endless drafts aren't. With practice, students can complete the cycles of rewriting in the second or third draft.

Writing workshops

We can guide our students' practice with rewriting in several ways. For example, after we've explained how prewriting and writing techniques apply to rewriting, we can ask students to turn in one or two drafts when they submit final copies of their papers. Scratch work and drafts shouldn't be graded, of course, but looking them over helps us determine what rewriting strategies students find useful and which ones they're avoiding either because they haven't thought to use them or don't know how.

We can also turn our classes into writing workshops to let students help each other develop and rewrite papers. Writing workshops have several benefits.[3] They insure that students take time to compose papers in several stages. They encourage students to teach each other by exchanging solutions to writing problems. They provide opportunities to discuss papers with audiences other than the teacher. When students give each other immediate feedback and work out strategies for expressing the message effectively, they gain a broader sense of audience and an understanding that good writing doesn't just conform to teacher-imposed standards. The teacher meanwhile is free to confer individually with students and to offer help when it's requested. For these reasons, many teachers design the entire writing course around the workshop principle.

Writing workshops must be planned carefully. For one thing, students aren't accustomed to working in groups. They're used to lectures and at least initially need specific directions for using their time

3. For a thorough discussion of how writing workshops encourage collaborative learning, see Kenneth A. Bruffee, "The Brooklyn Plan: Attaining Intellectual Growth Through Peer-Group Tutoring," *Liberal Education* 64 (December 1978), 447–68. Donald Murray also advocates the approach throughout his book, *A Writer Teaches Writing* (New York: Houghton Mifflin, 1968), especially in Section Four.

in groups constructively. Second, when students "play teacher," they often adopt the hypercritical, authoritative tone of the comments they've read on their papers. They have to practice making more helpful, positive suggestions. If workshops are to encourage students to help each other, then we must structure groupwork carefully, stating our expectations clearly, at least until the class has learned to work together. Although workshops can be organized several ways, the following suggestions offer a few guidelines for setting them up:

1. Divide the class into groups of no more than three students at first. Let students work with whomever they please so long as they get the work done. Discussing their papers with trusted friends removes the risk of criticism from strangers. Dialogues and trialogues also help students control their comments; they'll be able to learn the language of constructive criticism without embarrassing a student in front of a larger group.

2. Give the groups specific work to do and define it concretely. The first time, for example, students could examine the structure of a single paragraph, rewriting it together, or they might evaluate only the verb choices. Begin with the concrete words on the page and ask them to apply only one or two rewriting techniques. Later on, the groups can focus on whole compositions and more abstract concerns of purpose, audience, and message. Sometimes, it may help to duplicate instructions for workshop activities so that every student has a copy. The following questions, for example, could structure a workshop in which students evaluate entire drafts:

Rewriting Workshop

A. Read only the introductory paragraph.
1. Does the introduction really catch your interest? Why?
2. Can you tell what purpose the writer has for discussing the subject of this paper?
3. What attitude does the writer have toward the reader? The subject?
4. Does the introduction make clear, specifically, how the writer will proceed in the paper?
5. Can you find the thesis statement? Underline what you think it is.

B. Preread the paper; that is, read the introductory paragraph again and the first sentence of each subsequent paragraph. Write a short summary or outline of what you expect to find in the entire paper.

C. Finish reading the entire paper.
1. If the thesis was not clear in the introduction, does it become clear later? If so, where does this happen?
2. Does the body contribute to the main idea? If not, which paragraphs do not seem to belong?
3. Is the order of paragraphs suitable to the writer's overall purpose? What changes should be made?
4. Does the conclusion effectively draw together the various parts of the paper? What changes would you recommend?
5. Should any of the details and examples be relocated or changed? Are they all relevant to the thesis? List necessary changes.
6. Write a short comment indicating your reaction to the paper. What do you think its major weakness is? What is its major strength?[4]

3. Give students a language for discussing their work. In the beginning, they won't know what to ask each other or how to express their impressions of the papers they're examining. So before the workshop gets underway, suggest specific questions writers and readers could ask each other about the paper. You may want to write them on the board so that students can refer to them during group-work. Here are some examples:

Writer: "The main point I wanted to get across in this paragraph was _____."

"What do you still need to know that I haven't told you?"

"I could have handled this part several ways; do you think this way or that way is better?"

Reader: "The best thing about this paragraph is _____."

"What part of the paper gave you the most trouble?"

"You lost me here because _____."

As a rule, workshop talk should begin with the writer's explaining some strategy in the paper; this tactic prevents the reader from beginning with you-should-have-done-thus-and-so comments. Discussions should also begin by noting strengths, using them to improve weak sections of the paper. When writers or readers identify a problem, they should also explain *why* it's a problem and *how* to solve it. Otherwise, the workshop deteriorates into a fault-finding rather than a problem-solving activity.

4. I am indebted to Susan Miller, University of Wisconsin-Milwaukee, for this workshop exercise.

4. Monitor the groups to make sure students use their time productively and phrase comments constructively. Listen carefully to the kind of talk going on, intervening only when a group seems uncertain about what it's supposed to be doing or is obviously wasting time. When students request "teacher's opinion," try to avoid giving it, responding instead with a question that helps them examine the paper more closely or enables them to arbitrate the issue themselves. In this way, you wean them from seeing you as the only authority and encourage them to become independent critics of their own prose. Later in the term, you may decide to observe the groups less frequently, but don't assume that groupwork gives you a "free period." Use the time to confer with each student for two or three minutes or to give special help to students who need it most.

Planned carefully, writing workshops realize the primary objective of a writing course: students and teachers writing and discussing each other's work. Even teachers who prefer more traditional course designs still find groupwork helpful, especially when scheduled a few days before a paper is due. Then students seem most receptive to constructive comments on drafts and most likely to incorporate specific suggestions in rewriting the paper. Students who typically postpone drafting until the night before an assignment deadline may still write their drafts the night before "workshop day," but they'll also have a few more days to rewrite it prior to the deadline. At first, we must direct their work closely, cutting off escape routes and making rewriting more attractive than calling the first draft "finished." In time, however, rewriting becomes less novel, a more natural stage of the composing process, a way of insuring that final drafts represent the students' best work.

Student-generated checklists

Rewriting also calls attention to the criteria for good writing. All teachers (or their surrogates, the textbook) spend some time enumerating the qualities of effective papers. The discussion usually remains pretty one-sided though, the teacher like Moses delivering the ten commandments of acceptable English prose. Instead of legislating these stylistic do's and don't's, we can encourage the class to develop its own guidelines. It takes time, and we'll have to pose questions about areas students have overlooked, but in the long run, a student-generated checklist has several advantages. First, it allows us to change roles. Instead of acting as law-givers and rule-enforcers, we become advisors, helping students attain those standards which the class, not the teacher, has established. Second, the checklist urges students to develop their own definitions of "good writing," based on their experiences solving writing problems. Teacher or textbook criteria often prevent students from developing a practical understanding of writing principles, even though during most of our adult life no teacher will look over our shoulder to tell us what to say and how to say it. A student-generated checklist weans students from the security they seek (and unfortunately, have come to expect) by asking us, "What do you want in this paper?"

The hidden agenda, of course, is that we expect students to develop criteria similar to those we'd use in evaluating their work. And they will. Those standards, after all, are communicated implicitly or explicitly in our teaching and as students discuss their papers with each other. Consequently, the checklist synthesizes class discussion and records generalizations students infer from examining their writing. It needn't be generated all at once but can develop gradually, throughout the course, as class discussion defines additional principles of effective writing to add to the list. Although no two classes will develop identical lists, here's a model to shoot for, one that frames its criteria as questions to guide rewriting:

Subject, Audience, Purpose
1. What's the most important thing I want to say about my subject?
2. Who am I writing this paper for? What would my reader want to know about the subject? What does my reader already know about it?
3. Why do *I* think the subject is worth writing about? Will my reader think the paper was worth reading?
4. What verb explains what I'm trying to do in this paper (*tell* a story, *compare* X and Y, *describe* Z)?
5. Does my first paragraph answer questions 1–4? If not, why not?

Organization
6. How many specific points do I make about my subject? Did I overlap or repeat any points? Did I leave any points out or add some that aren't relevant to the main idea?
7. How many paragraphs did I use to talk about each point?
8. Why did I talk about them in this order? Should the order be changed?
9. How did I get from one point to the next? What signposts did I give the reader?

Paragraphing (Ask these questions of every paragraph)
10. What job is this paragraph supposed to do? How does it relate to the paragraph before and after it?

11. What's the topic idea? Will my reader have trouble finding it?
12. How many sentences did it take to develop the topic idea? Can I substitute better examples, reasons, or details?
13. How well does the paragraph hold together? How many levels of generality does it have? Are the sentences different lengths and types? Do I need transitions? When I read the paragraph out loud, did it flow smoothly?

Sentences (Ask these questions of every sentence)

14. Which sentences in my paper do I like the most? The least?
15. Can my reader "see" what I'm saying? What words could I substitute for *people, things, this/that, aspect,* etc?
16. Is this sentence "fat"? (Apply the "Paramedic Method")
17. Can I combine this sentence with another one?
18. Can I add adjectives and adverbs or find a more lively verb?

Things to Check Last

19. Did I check spelling and punctuation? What kinds of words do I usually misspell? What kinds of punctuation problems did I have in my last paper?
20. How does my paper end? Did I keep the promises I made to my reader at the beginning of the paper?
21. When I read the assignment again, did I miss anything?
22. What do I like best about this paper? What do I need to work on in the next paper?

Students need to view rewriting as more than editing, polishing, or proofreading, as more than correcting flaws in papers we've already graded. Although the draft represents an initial attempt to express a message, most writers don't find its meaning and form until they've reviewed the draft. Students need time to let the composition grow. They need to examine every level of the discourse, review the decisions they made, and incorporate responses from teachers and other students. They may rewrite the piece several times until they're satisfied that it says what they mean. But so must all writers, even talented ones like Hemingway, who revised the last page of *Farewell to Arms* thirty-nine times before it suited him. Hearing that, an interviewer asked him, "Was there some technical problem there? What was it that had you stumped?" "Getting the words right," he replied.[5]

5. Murray, p. 238.

THREE
Teaching as rhetoric

13
Making and evaluating writing assignments

> The writing teacher must not be a judge, but a physician. His job is not to punish, but to heal.
>
> DONALD M. MURRAY

Traditional assignments

When teachers confront a set of student papers, they begin evaluating them by reading the first word of the first paper in the stack. That's not the best place to begin. Because each composition represents a response to a specific "invitation" to write, the problems in many papers may be the fault, not of the writer, but of the assignment. So before we discuss what evaluating student writing entails, let's first examine the context in which it takes place.

How would you react if an administrator on whom your job depends insisted that you respond in writing to the following invitations?

1. "My School"
2. Write a letter to one of your students' parents.
3. Describe the top of your desk.
4. Only ten percent of the students in our department fail their English courses.
5. Assume that you're about to be fired. Defend yourself.

If your job really depended on completing these five assignments, you'd have every right to be angry. You've got very little to go on. You've no idea what criteria will be used to evaluate your responses, and each assignment raises so many questions you'd scarcely know where to begin. What about my school? Am I supposed to describe it, praise it, suggest improvements? What kind of letter am I supposed to write, one of praise or one that discusses a weak student's performance? What, for heaven's sake, has the top of my desk to do with anything? And what's the significance of the information in number 4? Does the administrator think we're not failing enough students or that we should be proud so many complete our courses successfully? And how can I defend myself if I don't know why I'm being fired?

Although each assignment raises enough questions to make responding to it an unsavory experience with writing, the five topics are quite similar to those traditionally given students in writing courses.

Group 1: "My Hometown"
"My First Semester of College"
"My Favorite Sport/Teacher/TV Program"

Group 2: Write a friendly letter.
Write a letter applying for a job.
Write a letter to the editor of the school newspaper.
Write a letter to your school principal/mayor/state representative.

Group 3: Describe your bedroom.
Define *freedom*.
Compare Marlow and Kurtz.

Group 4: Jonathan Swift has an unmistakable style.
"One of the great achievements of *Huckleberry Finn* is the 'vernacular voice' of the narrator."[1]

Group 5: Pretend that you are an animal.
Assume that you've wrecked the family car.
"Write a composition defending multiple-choice tests."[2]

---

1. Listed as a topic in "Suggestions for Papers," *Huckleberry Finn: Texts, Sources, and Criticism,* edited by Kenneth Lynn (New York: Harcourt, Brace and World, 1961), p. 217.
2. Listed as a writing assignment following Banesh Hoffman's "The Tyranny of Multiple-Choice Tests," *Language in Uniform: A Reader on Propaganda,* edited by Nick Aaron Ford (New York: Odyssey Press, 1967), p. 171.

But surely all of these topics can't be faulty. No, they're not. In fact, they all contain at least one feature of carefully designed writing assignments. But each group also omits information which would strengthen a student's written response. To evaluate these assignments, let's return briefly to the communication triangle.

Defining a rhetorical problem

Before writers can respond to a particular task, they must define a rhetorical problem. Defining the problem requires, at the least, assessing the writer's relationship to the subject and the reader.

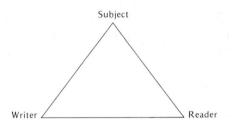

Who am I writing this for and what response am I trying to effect in my reader? Is my audience predisposed toward reading what I have to say on this subject? What do I know about my subject? How do I feel about it? Can I commit myself to addressing it honestly? What angle or point of view can I take in treating the topic? Of course, writers also juggle other constraints: a deadline for the assignment, the demands of a form (letter, essay, report), and an aim (persuasive, referential, self-expressive, literary), and a mode (classification, narration, description, evaluation).

Effective writing assignments encourage students to define progressively more complex rhetorical problems. Since students learn to write by writing, our responsibility is to control and vary the rhetorical demands of writing tasks to give students practice in adjusting relationships among writer, reader, and subject, manipulating more and more complex variables. However, most writing assignments, like those in the five groups, leave too many variables to chance and guesswork. They don't provide enough information to help students define rich rhetorical problems. Instead, they present students with a "paper-writing problem," a meaningless exercise in jumping hurdles for a grade.

The titles in group one, for example, suggest a broad subject but present no additional information. Consequently, students are likely to produce vague, general compositions addressed to the teacher or to no one in particular. Although the topics encourage students to draw on personal experiences, a strength, are they really worth committing oneself to? When, in real life, are writers required to address such topics? What purpose can students find for responding to the assignment?

The assignments in group two are better. They specify an audience and a form of discourse, but neither the subject nor the purpose for writing has been explained. Group three's assignments spell out modes of discourse and a broad subject but fail to address audience, purpose, and form. If students dared question the teacher, they could legitimately ask why it should matter to anyone what their bedrooms look like. The statements in group four represent conclusions about a topic. They're often prefaced by "Comment on the following statement" or followed by "Do you agree or disagree?" The statements usually restrict the subject and express a point of view; they *may* also imply a purpose for the assignment, a mode of development, and the kinds of support students can use. Audience, however, is not specified (or presumed to be the teacher), and the implicit suggestions about aim, mode, and support could be phrased more clearly to give students a complete rhetorical context for planning their response.

The assignments in group five specify a subject—an animal, a car wreck, multiple-choice tests—and suggest a stance to adopt in relation to the subject or a reader. Writing assignments should encourage role-playing because it allows students to imagine rhetorical situations and audiences outside academic contexts. The first assignment, however, suggests a silly role, or at best, one irrelevant to a writing course. Unless it's intended to interest very young writers, the assignment serves no real purpose and doesn't give students practice with the kinds of writing they encounter in school or adult life. The second assignment makes a good beginning but needs development. It doesn't tell students what to do with the situation they imagine themselves to be in. What's the purpose of the assignment? Who's the audience? A parent? A police officer? Someone who can repair the car? What form of discourse does the assignment call for? The third assignment forces students to adopt a stance on multiple-choice testing they may not in fact support, consequently insisting that some students write dishonestly. The assignment could be improved if an audience were specified and if students could choose between attacking or defending the tests.

FIGURE 13.1

Reprinted by permission of the Chicago Tribune—New York News Syndicate, Inc.

All writing assignments must account for more variables than a phrase or even one sentence can identify.[3] If we omit some of the factors which, in real life, help us define rhetorical contexts, we've sentenced students to performing poorly on the assignment. Even if we give students complete freedom in defining some elements of the assignment, in some way we must account for all of the following variables:

1. The students' interest in and understanding of the subject
2. The purpose or aim of the composition
3. The audience (which needn't always be the teacher)
4. A role for the student to take with respect to the subject and audience
5. The form of discourse (which needn't always be an essay)

In addition, the assignment might offer prewriting help by furnishing some data or posing leading questions (too many questions, however, might overwhelm students and provoke incoherent, undeveloped responses). Assignments can also specify how the composition will be evaluated or what particular strategies we expect students to practice this time.

Finally, assignments should be written out so that students can refer to them. Slapping topics on the blackboard or designing them extemporaneously in talking with the class takes less time, of course, but if the assignment is to teach composing, it must be prepared as carefully as each class meeting. In writing it down, we have to decide its function as a teaching tool, assess its relation to other assignments, anticipate problems students might have, and plan other kinds of instruction—class discussions or groupwork—to support the assignment. Although writing assignments vary depending on when in the course they appear and on the abilities of students, the following questions should help you design rich rhetorical problems for students to solve.

A Heuristic for Designing Writing Assignments

1. *What do I want the students to do?* Is it worth doing? Why? What will the assignment tell me about what they've learned? How does it fit my objectives at this point in the course? Does the assignment assess what students can *do* or what they *know?* Am I relating their work to the real world

3. For a discussion of these variables, especially aim and mode, see Eleanor M. Hoffman and John P. Schifsky, "Designing Writing Assignments," *English Journal* 66 (December 1977), 41–45.

(including academic settings) or only to my class or the text? Does the assignment require specialized knowledge? Does it appeal to the interests and experiences of my students?

2. *How do I want them to do the assignment?* Are students working alone or together? In what ways will they practice prewriting, writing, and rewriting? Are writing, reading, speaking, and listening reinforcing each other? Have I given students enough information to make effective choices about the subject, purpose, form, and mode?

3. *For whom are students writing?* Who is the audience? Do students have enough information to assume a role with respect to the audience?

4. *When will students do the assignment?* How does the assignment relate to what comes before and after it in the course? Is the assignment sequenced to give enough time for prewriting, writing, and rewriting? How much time in and outside of class will students need for each stage? To what extent will I guide the students' work? What deadlines do I want to set for collecting the students' papers (or various stages of the project)?

5. *What will I do with the assignment?* How will I evaluate the work? What constitutes a "successful" response to the assignment? Will other students or the writer have a say in evaluating the paper? What problems did I encounter when I wrote my paper on this assignment? How can the assignment be improved?

Students improve their writing skills through practice. Each assignment, then, must incorporate prewriting, writing, and rewriting strategies. By the end of the course, students should have responded to a variety of rhetorical situations in several modes and forms of discourse for diverse purposes and audiences. The writing teacher's primary responsibility, Charles Cooper maintains, is to guide students through the composing process, over and over again.

> To do that the teacher will have to be concerned mainly with the essence of composition, rather than the accidents of transcriptions, to use Janet Emig's terms. Unfortunately, just as we're learning what to do about the essences, some people are using the talk about basic skills to revive misplaced concern with the accidents; but surely the most basic of all the writing skills are matters of persona, audience, and purpose and the word and sentence adjustments the writer makes as he tries to speak with a certain voice to a special audience on a particular topic. ("Responding to Student Writing," p. 2)

The basics and testing

Perhaps no words have generated as much controversy recently among teachers, parents, and the public as "basics," "minimal competence," and "testing." For most people, each word has psychologically comfortable, positive connotations. Who can be opposed to what is basic? Surely none of us supports *in*competence. And how many of us verbally talented English teachers would dispute the numbers which experts attach to tests? As a society we've learned to trust statistics. I.Q. scores reveal how smart we are. SAT and ACT scores determine whether or not we may enter college. "Leading economic indicators" tell us our dollars won't buy what they did ten years ago. Insurance figures predict how we're likely to die. Casualty figures released weekly during the Vietnam war told us we were winning.

With similar illogic, many people believe we can solve educational problems through legislatively mandated competency tests. Test performance presumably will tell us if students learn, teachers teach, and the curriculum is sound. "The effectiveness of minimum competency tests," writes Kenneth Goodman, "depends on the truth of some or all of five propositions:

1. Failure to achieve is due to a lack of school standards.
2. Student failure is largely the result of lack of teacher concern for student success, or teacher mediocrity or both.
3. Solutions for teaching-learning problems are built into current, traditional materials and methods.
4. Test performance is the same as competence; furthermore, existing tests can be used for accurate individual assessment and prediction.
5. If students are required to succeed they will.

None of these propositions, however, is true." ("Minimum Standards: A Moral View," p. 5)

For many educators, going "back to the basics" has become synonymous with going back to the secure good old days, which our selective memories usually depict as having been better than the good old present. In the main, advocates of testing programs are concerned about students, understand the problems teachers face, and want to help solve those problems. Testing students, they believe, will help resolve the literacy crisis.

Many researchers, however, insist that standardized tests aren't valid measures of writing performance. "Although widely used," write Charles Cooper and Lee Odell, "standardized tests measure only editing skills—choosing the best sentence, recognizing correct usage, punctuation, and capitalization" (*Evaluating Writing*, p. viii). Writing teachers, confronted with considerable pressure to submit to accountability-through-testing must educate themselves about the uses and abuses of tests.[4] To support teachers and encourage the responsible use of writing tests, the Conference on College Composition and Communication, a constituent organization of the National Council of Teachers of English, has adopted the following Resolution on Testing and Writing:

RESOLVED: that

1. No student shall be given credit for a writing course, placed in a remedial writing course, exempted from a required writing course, or certified for competency without submitting a piece of written discourse.

2. Responsibility for giving credit, exemption, or accreditation shall rest, not with local administrators or state officials, but with the composition faculty in each institution.

3. Tests of writing shall be selected and administered under the primary control and supervision of representatives of the composition faculty in each institution.

4. Before multiple choice or so-called objective tests are used, the complexities involved in such testing shall be carefully considered. Most important, these tests shall be examined to determine whether they are appropriate to the intended purpose.

5. Before essay tests are used, the complexities of such tests shall be carefully considered. Most importantly, topics shall be designed with great care. Also, readers of the essay tests shall be trained according to principles of statistically reliable holistic and/or analytic reading.

6. The nature and purpose of the test and the various uses of the results shall be clearly explained to all instructors and students prior to the administration of the test.

7. All possible steps shall be taken to educate the universities and colleges, the public and legislatures that, though composition faculties have principal responsibility for helping students develop writing skills, maintenance of these skills is a responsibility shared by the entire faculty, administration, and the public.

4. For a helpful introduction to issues surrounding tests see the report of the NCTE Task Force on Measurement and Evaluation in the Study of English, *Common Sense and Testing in English* (Urbana, Ill.: NCTE, 1975).

8. The officers and Executive Committee of CCCC shall make testing a major concern in the immediate future in order to provide information and assistance to composition instructors affected by a testing situation.

Describing, measuring, judging

The papers in Cooper and Odell's *Evaluating Writing: Describing, Measuring, Judging* provide a comprehensive discussion of techniques for evaluating students' writing performance. Because writing evaluations have many uses, the editors caution, "It is critical for teachers . . . to know *why* they are evaluating before they choose measures and procedures" (p. ix). We may evaluate writing for any one of at least eleven reasons:

Administrative
1. Predicting students' grades in English courses.
2. Placing or tracking students or exempting them from English courses.
3. Assigning public letter or number grades to particular pieces of writing and to students' work in an English course.

Instructional
4. Making an initial diagnosis of students' writing problems.
5. Guiding and focusing feedback to student writers as they progress through an English course.

Evaluation and Research
6. Measuring students' growth as writers over a specific time period.
7. Determining the effectiveness of a writing program or a writing teacher.
8. Measuring group differences in writing performance in comparison-group research.
9. Analyzing the performance of a writer chosen for a case study.
10. Describing the writing performance of individuals or groups in developmental studies, either cross-sectional or longitudinal in design.
11. Scoring writing in order to study possible correlates of writing performance.

(*Evaluating Writing*, p. ix)

This chapter concerns itself principally with the fourth and fifth purposes for evaluating writing. When we diagnose writing problems (item four in the list above), we examine student papers descriptively, not to grade them or to respond with comments students will read, but to determine simply what strengths and weaknesses characterize each paper. "Joan writes simple and compound sentences," we might note, "but she avoids subordination, constructs paragraphs with only two levels of generality, and misspells words with *ance/ence* and *able/ible* suffixes." Such diagnostic evaluations would permit us to design a course of instruction that enhances Joan's development as a writer. For this reason, many teachers treat the first writing assignment in a course diagnostically. It isn't graded; it's mined for information that helps us plan what to teach.

When we respond to student writing (item five in the list above) or encourage students to respond to each other's work, we "guide and focus feedback," helping students understand how a reader perceives the writer's message. Often this is done through written comments. It's a form of teaching; yet, writing comments that enhance learning represents perhaps the most difficult skill an English teacher must master. Traditional methods of hunting errors only identify *what* was wrong with the paper. Comments that teach must do much more. They must also point out what the student did well, why certain problems undermine effective communication, and how to improve the paper. Comments that teach must guide students in developing effective prewriting, writing, and rewriting strategies. Comments are an open-ended form of evaluation; that is, students, guided by responses from the teacher or their classmates, can return to their drafts, rewriting them to adjust the message.

Grading, however, is a closed procedure. Once a paper receives a letter grade, it's been judged, in some way finally classified. Although comments may accompany the grade, most students interpret them not as "feedback" but as a justification of the grade. For them, the paper is "finished," and additional work won't change either the grade or their feelings about succeeding or failing. Grading papers, judging the finished product, represents a necessary form of evaluation of course, but in this chapter we'll discuss ways in which grades need not become the overwhelming concern of writing teachers and their students.[5]

5. Although experienced teachers seem to have internalized the criteria which characterize A, B, C, D, and F papers, beginning teachers may want a more explicit discussion of grades than they will find in this chapter. I recommend the practical advice William F. Irmscher gives in Chapter 13, "Evaluation," in his *Teaching Expository Writing* (New York: Holt, Rinehart and Winston, 1979), pp. 142–78.

Atomistic evaluation

Measures of writing performance can be grouped into two categories: atomistic or holistic measures. Atomistic measures evaluate some part of the composing process, or certain features of the written product, or a skill presumed to correlate with writing ability. A vocabulary test, for example, like the Verbal portion of the SAT assumes that a knowledge of words enhances writing, reading, speaking, and listening. For some students, a relatively high score on the SAT correlates with an ability to write well. At the same time, however, students can score well on vocabulary tests yet produce ineffective compositions (and vice versa, can score poorly on the test and write well) for many reasons, one of them being that composing involves much more than skill with words.

Editing, mechanics, and usage tests are also atomistic measures. They reveal whether or not students recognize conventions of edited discourse, but because composing requires the ability to generate discourse, not merely to analyze it, editing tests can tell us only about some of the skills students use when they write. Similarly, tests of syntactic maturity enable us to evaluate the length and complexity of sentences.[6] If we know what kind of coordination and subordination students achieve in their writing, we can use the information to plan ways of enlarging their repertoire of syntactic options. Although useful, tests of syntactic maturity are atomistic measures because they focus primarily on the student's ability to construct sentences, only one of many skills important to composing.

Atomistic measures aren't inadequate or "bad" tools for evaluating student performance. They measure what they were designed to measure. Because they address part of the composing process or focus on certain features in the product, they isolate problems we can help a student overcome. They're misused when we assume they can tell us everything we need to know about our students' writing ability. Writing evaluations are invalid whenever we measure a student's performance by means of procedures intended to assess only one aspect of it.

Holistic evaluation

Holistic measures assume that all the features of a composition or all the skills which comprise writing ability are related, interdependent.

6. For a description of the procedure developed by Kellogg W. Hunt, see his "A Synopsis of Clause-to-Sentence Length Factors," *English Journal* 54 (April 1965), 300, 305–9, and Kellogg W. Hunt, "Early Blooming and Late Blooming Syntactic Structures," in Cooper and Odell, *Evaluating Writing*, pp. 91–104.

When papers are graded holistically, we assume that their rhetorical effectiveness lies in the combination of features at every level of the discourse, that the whole is greater than the sum of its parts. Charles Cooper describes the procedure this way:

> Holistic evaluation of writing is a guided procedure for sorting or ranking written pieces. The rater takes a piece of writing and either (1) matches it with another piece in a graded series of pieces or (2) scores it for the prominence of certain features important to that kind of writing or (3) assigns it a letter or number grade. The placing, scoring, or grading occurs quickly, impressionistically, after the rater has practiced the procedure with other raters. The rater does not make corrections or revisions in the paper. Holistic evaluation is usually guided by a holistic scoring guide which describes each feature and identifies high, middle, and low quality levels for each feature. (*Evaluating Writing*, p. 3)

Now, as most teachers know, if six of us were to assign individual numbers or letter grades to the same paper, all of us might evaluate it differently. How then, does holistic, "impressionistic" scoring represent an improvement over traditional methods? First of all, holistic scoring is a group activity which requires readers to agree beforehand what criteria determine the ranking of papers. The readers' impressions will be guided by preselected model papers, a scoring guide, or a list of features which define each rank.[7] Second, before readers begin scoring the papers, they practice the procedure, using sample papers written on the same topics by the same kinds of students as those whose work they will score later. The practice session allows raters to "calibrate" themselves to the models, scoring guide, or list of features. When raters consistently agree on what rankings the sample papers should have, the actual scoring can begin. During the scoring session, each student's paper is read at least twice, by two different raters, and assigned a number or letter ranking. When raters disagree on a score, the paper is read by a third reader or given

---

7. For a description of holistic scoring using sample student papers as models see the scale developed by the California Association of Teachers of English, in Sister Judine, ed., *A Guide for Evaluating Student Composition* (Urbana, Ill.: NCTE, 1965), pp. 147–58. Primary Trait Scoring, developed to score the essays for the National Assessment of Educational Progress, uses an elaborate scoring guide, described by Richard Lloyd-Jones, "Primary Trait Scoring," in *Evaluating Writing*, pp. 33–66. The best known "analytic scale" is explained in Paul B. Diederich, *Measuring Growth in English* (Urbana, Ill.: NCTE, 1974). The prominent features of a piece of writing are assigned weighted numerical values, "ideas" and "organization" receiving greater weight than "handwriting" and "spelling." Diederich also constructs an attractive argument for involving the entire English faculty in evaluating writing performance so that bias doesn't unduly affect students' final grades.

to a panel which determines the score. Because raters don't stop to mark the paper, to correct or revise the student's work, they can score a large number of papers in a short time, "spending no more than two minutes on each paper" (*Evaluating Writing*, p. 3). And because they have practiced matching each paper against predetermined criteria, they "can achieve a scoring reliability as high as .90 for individual writers" (*Evaluating Writing*, p. 3).

Holistic evaluation is based on several assumptions many writing teachers find advantageous. First, it assumes that written discourse communicates a complete message to an audience for a particular purpose; consequently, "holistic evaluation by a human respondent gets closer to what is essential in such a communication than frequency counts [of errors or of word or sentence elements] do" (*Evaluating Writing*, p. 3). Rather than single out a few features in the piece, as atomistic measures require, holistic scores reflect all the decisions students made in writing the paper.

Second, holistic measures are flexible. Working together, English teachers can define criteria consistent with a particular course or writing program. Designing and trying out the procedure requires careful work, but once the scale has been developed, large numbers of papers can be read and scored quickly, reliably. Since raters make no comments on the papers, holistic evaluations don't provide feedback for the students; that is, the scores serve an administrative, not an instructional purpose and usually help teachers make decisions about placement or final grades.

Third, holistic evaluation removes much of the subjective static that unavoidably interferes with placement and grading decisions. Although we all try to evaluate our students' work objectively, our judgments are always influenced to some degree by factors that have nothing to do with writing performance. Students who misbehave in class, whose socioeconomic or racial backgrounds differ from ours, whose handwriting is poor, whose past performance has already branded them as D or F students, or whose papers happen to be near the bottom of the stack may receive lower grades than their actual writing ability warrants. However, when papers are coded so that students' names don't appear, when at least two teachers must agree on the score, when all of us in the writing program participate, judgments become considerably more objective and consistent. Furthermore, in developing specific, uniform criteria to guide our scoring, we must discuss, as a faculty, what constitutes "good writing" and how the school's composition program develops the writing abilities of its students. Such questions lie at the center of all writing instruction, and working out the answers together improves both the program and our teaching.

Diagnosing writing problems

The best way to diagnose students' writing problems is to examine carefully samples of their work, ideally two short papers with different discourse aims. Written in class during the first week of the course, the papers can tell us what students have already mastered and what areas we need to emphasize in our teaching. Diagnostic evaluations at midterm help us identify improvements students have made since the course began, new problems which developed in overcoming previous weaknesses, and difficulties which our teaching somehow failed to address and which now need to be approached some other way. At the end of the course, diagnostic evaluations help us determine in what ways students' writing has improved and what elements of the course may need revision.

When we examine a paper diagnostically, we're concerned primarily with describing rather than judging or grading it. Although we inevitably compare it to some mental criteria for effective writing, our primary purpose isn't to determine a letter grade. Rather, we want to know how the students write, what they're having trouble with, and why. To demonstrate the procedure, let's examine David's paper, written in forty-five minutes during the second meeting of a college freshman composition class:

Assignment: Write an essay in which you discuss the way or ways you expect your life to differ from your parents' lives.[8]

As time changes people's views and outlooks on life change with it. My parents grew up with completely diffrent standards in a completely diffrent time. Because of the time I grew up in, and the time I live in, my life differs greatly from the lives of my parents.

Modern society offers more aid to young people—jobs, school, financial—that my parents could never recieve. Because of this aid my life has been more free than theirs ever was. I have more free time on my hands than they ever did. My parents were, and are, always working to keep and get, the things needed for survival in this life.

Also Because of a higher education than the education of my parents I have diffrent outlooks on life. I have a more well-rounded at-

8. The assignment is listed among the "Placement Essay Topics" in Mina F. Shaughnessy, *Errors and Expectations: A Guide for the Teacher of Basic Writing* (New York: Oxford University Press, 1977), p. 295.

titude toward life. I tend to take more things for granted that my parents never would.

We now live in a world of entertainment. My generation has more things in which to occupy their free time that my parents never had.

Because of the time gap seperating my parents an I, I have a diffrent lifestyle than they. Lifestyles change with the change of time, and with that so do people's outlook on life.

First, we need to look at the assignment itself. Since it doesn't specify an audience, we shouldn't be surprised to discover that David addressed the piece to his stereotype of The Teacher or to no one in particular. The assignment specifies or implies the discourse aim ("discuss" should elicit expository or referential discourse), mode ("differ" suggests contrast or classification), and form ("essay"). The topic permits students to draw on personal experience, but it's much too broad. It also doesn't offer any prewriting help and invites a vague, general response (a better topic might be to discuss how students expect this writing course to differ from their senior English course in high school). Given the forty-five-minute time limit, we can also assume that David spent little or no time prewriting and rewriting the paper.

Indeed, David handled the topic fairly generally. Most of the paragraphs contain only one or two levels of generality. Most of the nouns identify abstractions ("views and outlooks," "modern society," "young people," "well-rounded attitude," "world of entertainment," "lifestyle"). However, David does attempt some classification. He subordinates "jobs, school, financial" to "aid" and identifies in the three body paragraphs three ways his life differs from his parents'. More "aid" gives him free time and freedom from worry; more education gives him different outlooks on life; a world of entertainment occupies his free time. At the same time, David maintains considerable distance between himself, his subject, and his audience, a stance characteristic of most "first papers" in a writing course. Although he probably has quite a bit to say about his life, we can understand that he might not choose to discuss it here, certainly not in writing, a more discomfiting medium than speech, and not with a stranger, which is how he must characterize his English teacher at the beginning of the term.

Although David doesn't have sufficient details to develop the paper, it nevertheless has a structure. He's mastered the five-paragraph formula. The first and last paragraphs repeat the idea that "time gaps" separating two generations create different life-styles and outlooks on life. The three body paragraphs attempt to develop separate topics although paragraph three seems to have been prompted by the third sentence of paragraph two. Possibly David discovered that, by the time he began paragraph three, he'd run out of things to say; so, he reread the previous paragraphs and found that he could develop the "free time" idea in paragraph two more fully. Like that of most freshmen, David's writing seems "form-bound"; form precedes content; he thinks first of the five-paragraph mold and then finds enough material to fill it. David probably should be encouraged to identify several ways of organizing the same material, to discover form *in* what he has prewritten rather than impose it *on* the material.

That David stretches himself to find enough to say, a problem prewriting could help him with, is also evident in sentence construction. Students who fear they can't meet a 500-word limit or some self-imposed length requirement often pad their sentences, especially at the end. David does too. The first sentence, for example, might have ended with *change,* but afraid that the paper won't be long enough or that he won't find its message, David adds "with it." Similarly in paragraphs two and three, "in this life" and "toward life" extend sentences that could have closed with *survival* and *attitude* respectively. Although four sentences begin with *because*-clauses (and the first sentence with an *as*-clause), David writes predominantly simple sentences. He probably avoids more complex constructions because they'll create additional comma problems; he plays it safe. Risk-free, ungraded sentence-combining exercises might give him greater confidence in varying sentence structures and punctuating them.

Because David has developed strategies to write his way around comma problems, the paper doesn't offer enough evidence to diagnose the logic governing its mispunctuation. Two introductory *because*-clauses are set off; two aren't. The comma in the last sentence correctly separates two independent clauses joined by *and,* but elsewhere, in the first two paragraphs, *and* may be governing the misuse of commas. To get at the logic behind these errors, we'd need to discuss the paper with David, asking him why he thinks the misused commas belong there, then pointing out where he's used the comma conventionally, using what he's done right to address the mispunctuated sentences.

We'd also have to discuss the logic governing comparisons. David deliberately alternates the conjunction *than* with the relative pronoun *that* to complete comparisons:

That constructions

> Subject + Verb + <u>more</u> aid to young people . . . <u>that</u> my parents could (never)recieve.
>
> Subject + Verb + to take <u>more</u> things for granted <u>that</u> my parents (never) would.
>
> Subject + Verb + <u>more</u> things . . . <u>that</u> my parents (never) had.

Than constructions

> Clause + Subject + Verb + <u>more</u> free <u>than</u> theirs (ever) was.
>
> Subject + Verb + <u>more</u> free time . . . <u>than</u> they (ever) had.
>
> Also Because of a <u>higher</u> education <u>than</u> the education of my parents.
>
> Subject + Verb + a <u>different</u> life style <u>than</u> they.

In English, of course, comparisons are completed by *than* (or *as*), not *that*. The evidence suggests, however, that David completes negative comparisons (signaled by *never*) with *that*; positive comparisons (signaled by *ever* or by affirmative phrases and clauses) with *than*. By discussing with him the chart above, we could help him understand two strategies for rewriting the "that constructions": 1. keep *that* but get rid of *more,* or 2. keep *more* but change *that* to *than*.

The paper contains only a few misspellings. *Diffrent* (four times) and *seperating* (once) are logical transcriptions of how most speakers pronounce these words. *An* (for *and*) may not be a "pronunciation spelling" because David spells *and* correctly elsewhere; he probably just left off the *d* as he hurried to finish the paper. In misspelling *receive* as *recieve,* he logically writes "i before e" but forgets (or never completely learned) "except after c." We might ask him to begin a spelling log, entering these words in one column and their correct spellings in another, so that he can discover which words and sound patterns are likely to give him trouble.[9]

When I analyze a "first paper," I make notes about what I've found on a separate sheet of paper which I keep in each student's folder. Students never see my notes, but I use them throughout the term. They help me decide which writing problems I want each student to work on, and they permit me to record a student's progress in subsequent papers. Having analyzed David's paper, for example, I would jot down on my sheet of notes which writing problems I would want him to work on first. Since he can't work on everything at once without becoming frustrated, I would select only one or two areas to

9. An excellent discussion of types of misspellings and their causes appears in Shaughnessy, Chapter 5.

emphasize as he rewrites this paper or plans the next one. For David (and doubtless other members of the class), practice with prewriting strategies would effect the greatest change in future papers. Writing from an overabundance of material would lengthen paragraphs, help him better support generalizations, and perhaps remove the need to pad sentences. Prewriting might also permit him to find alternative patterns of arrangement in the material, reducing his dependence on the five-paragraph model. In the meantime, he can begin a spelling log and practice ungraded sentence-combining problems which require expanding his inventory of subordinate constructions and which increase his confidence in using commas.

With practice, you can read a paper diagnostically in two or three minutes. At first it helps to describe the features in detail, but after a while, a few brief notes will remind you of problems the student has overcome, new areas to work on, and questions you'll need more evidence to answer. Whether or not you also intend to grade the paper or write comments on it, diagnostic readings reveal not only what the student has done but also how and why, allowing you to hypothesize about the causes of writing problems. Merely to identify a paper's errors and attach a letter grade is to ignore considerable evidence that makes teaching more effective and the student's progress surer.

Responding to student writing

Diagnostic reading is essentially a private response to the paper. We're discussing it with ourselves, explaining its patterns of features and planning a course of instruction for the student. When we respond to the paper by writing comments, we're communicating with a different audience, a student. As with any communication, purpose governs how we express the message and how our audience is likely to respond to it. The only appropriate purpose for comments on student papers is to offer feedback and guide learning. Some comments, however, seem to have been written for other reasons: to damn the paper with faint praise or snide remarks, to prove that the teacher is a superior error-hunter, to condemn or disagree with ideas the paper expresses, to confuse the writer with cryptic correction symbols. Most of us learned how to comment on papers by first surviving and then imitating the responses of teachers to our own work. Few of us, I suspect, looked forward to getting our papers back (except to learn the grade) and could probably sympathize with the following assessment of the experience:

Confused and angry, he stared at the red marks on his paper. He had awked again. And he had fragged. He always awked and fragged. On every theme, a couple of awks and a frag or two. And the inevitable puncs and sp's. The cw's didn't bother him anymore. He knew that the teacher preferred words like courage and contemptible person to guts and fink. The teacher had dismissed guts and fink as slang, telling students never to use slang in their themes. But he liked to write guts and fink; they meant something to him. Besides, they were in the dictionary. So why couldn't he use them when they helped him say what he wanted to say? He rarely got to say what he wanted to say in an English class, and when he did, he always regretted it. But even that didn't bother him much. He really didn't care anymore.

How do you keep from awking, he asked himself. The question amused him for a moment; all questions in English class amused him for a moment. He knew what awk meant; he looked it up once in the handbook in the back of the grammar book as the teacher told him to. But the illustration didn't help him much. He got more awks, and he quit looking in the handbook. He simply decided that he oughtn't awk when he wrote even though he didn't know how to stop awking.

Why not frag now and then, he wondered for almost thirty seconds. Writers fragged. Why couldn't he? Writers could do lots of things. Why couldn't he? But he forgot the question almost as quickly as it entered his mind. No sense worrying about it, he told himself. You'll only live to frag again.

Damn, he whispered. He knew it had to be *damn*. He decided that the teacher didn't have the guts to write damn when she was angry with what he wrote. She just wrote *dm* in the margin. She told the class it meant dangling modifier, but he was sure it meant *damn*.

Choppy! He spat the word out to no one in particular. He always got at least one choppy. "Mature thoughts should be written in long, balanced sentences," the teacher said once. He guessed his thoughts weren't balanced. Choppy again. But he didn't care anymore. He'd just chop his way through English class until he never had to write again.

He stared at the encircled *and* at the beginning of one of his sentences. The circle meant nothing at first. Then he remembered the teacher's saying something about never beginning sentences with a conjunction. He didn't know why she said it; writers did it. But he guessed that since he wasn't a writer he didn't have that privilege.

The rep staggered him. The teacher had drawn a red line from the red rep to the word commitment. He had used it four times. It fit, he thought. You need commitment if you believe in the brotherhood of man, he argued with himself. Why did she write the red rep? He didn't know. But there were so many things he didn't know about writing.

Why do we have to write anyway, he asked himself. He didn't know.

No good reason for it, he thought. Just write all the time to show the teacher that you can't write.

Most of the time he didn't know why he was asked to write on a specific topic, and most of the time he didn't like the topic or he didn't know too much about it. He had written on the brotherhood of man four times during the last four years. He had doubts about man's brotherhood to man. People really got shook about it only during National Brotherhood Week, he had written once in a theme. The rest of the year they didn't much care about their fellow man, only about themselves, he had written. The teacher didn't like what he said. That teacher, a man, wrote in the margin: "How can you believe this? I disagree with you. See me after class." He didn't show up. He didn't want another phony lecture on the brotherhood of man.

That wasn't the only time a teacher disagreed with what he wrote. One even sent him to the principal's office for writing about his most embarrassing moment even though she had assigned the topic. She told the principal he was trying to embarrass her. But all he did was write about his most embarrassing moment, just as she had told him to. And it was a gas.

Another time a teacher told him to write about how a daffodil feels in spring. He just wrote *chilly* on a piece of paper and handed it in. The teacher was furious. But he didn't care. He didn't give a *dm* about daffodils in spring. He didn't care much about what he did last summer either, but the teacher seemed to.

He looked for the comment at the end of the theme. Trite. Nothing else; just trite. He usually got a trite. It would probably mean a D on his report card, but he didn't care. It was hard for him not to be trite when he wrote on the brotherhood of man for the fourth time in four years. He used all the cliches. The teacher wanted them, he thought. So he gave them to her. But he was never sure just what the teacher wanted. Some kids said they had figured out just what the teacher wanted. They said they knew what kinds of words, what kinds of thoughts, and what kinds of sentences she liked. They said they had her "psyched out"; that's why they got A's. But he didn't have her psyched out, and he wasn't going to worry about it anymore.

Every week she told the class to write a theme on some topic, and he knew that she picked out the topics because she liked them. Every week—"Write a theme on such and such." Nothing else—just those instructions. So he gave the topic a few minutes' thought and wrote whatever came to mind. He thought in cliches when he tried to write for her. They were safe, he once thought. But maybe not. Trite again.

He wadded up the brotherhood of man and threw it toward the waste basket. Missed. He always missed—everything.

Drop out, fink, he told himself. Why not? He didn't know what was going on. A dropout. He smiled. Frag, he thought. Can't use dropout all alone. He knew it was a frag. At least he had learned something.

The bell rang. No more awks, no more frags, no more meaningless red marks on papers. No more writing about daffodils and the brotherhood of man—until next week.

(Edward B. Jenkinson and Donald A. Seybold, "Prologue,"
Writing As a Process of Discovery, pp. 3–6)

As this student's plight reveals, comments that simply point out errors or justify a grade tend to ignore the student who reads them. Formative comments, the kind that support learning, however, encourage students to try new strategies, praising what has worked well in the piece and demonstrating how or why something else didn't. In an essay describing several approaches to formative evaluation, Mary Beaven defines six assumptions on which our written responses to student writing should be based:

1. Growth in writing is a highly individualistic process which occurs slowly, sometimes over a much longer period of time than the six-, ten-, or even fifteen-week periods teachers and researchers usually allow.

2. Through their evaluatory comments and symbols teachers help to create an environment for writing. Establishing a climate of trust, in which students feel free to explore topics of interest to them without fear that their thoughts will be attacked, is essential.

3. Risk-taking, trying new behaviors as one writes, and stretching one's use of language and toying with it are important for growth in writing. As writers break out of old, "safe" composing behaviors, they often make *more* mistakes until they become comfortable with new ways of using language. Teachers must encourage and support this kind of risk-taking and mistake-making.

4. Goal setting is also an important process in the development of students. Goals need to be concrete and within reach, and students need to see evidence of their progress. Teachers, then, should urge students to work toward a limited number of goals at a time.

5. Writing improvement does not occur in isolation because writing is related to speaking, listening, reading, and all other avenues of communication, including the experience of living. Prewriting activities, responding to literature, class discussion, revisions, developing a sensitivity to self and

others, experiences both in and out of the English classroom affect growth in writing.

6. Effective formative evaluation depends on our understanding clearly other procedures that encourage growth in writing: diagnosing what students are able to do; arranging for
writing often in many modes; discussing usage, syntactical,
and rhetorical deficiencies by working with the students'
own writing, not by pre-teaching rules; giving feedback and
encouragement; assessing how much growth individuals
have shown, without comparing them to each other and
without expecting "mastery" of some uniform class standard.

(Adapted from *Evaluating Writing*, pp. 136–38)

With these assumptions in mind, let's return to David's paper, not
to read it diagnostically this time, but to respond to it as we would
if we planned to return it to him. The paper has been reproduced
twice so that we can compare the responses of two different teachers.

As time changes people's views and outlooks on

life change with it. My parents grew up with

sp.
Rep.
p
completely diffrent standards in a completely

diffrent time. Because of the time I grew up in

and the time I live in, my life differs greatly

from the lives of my parents.

Modern society offers more aid to young
than
//
people--jobs, school, financial--that my parents
ever
sp.
could never recieve. Because of this aid my life

has been more free than theirs ever was. I have
cliche
more free time on my hands than they ever did. My

p
parents were, and are, always working to keep and

get the things needed for survival in this life.

b   I have more education than my parents do

Also _Because of a higher education than the

education of my parents I have diffrent outlooks on

cliché

life. I have a more well-rounded attitude toward

cliché

life. I tend to take more things for granted that

my parents never would.

not a ¶
awk.

We now live in a world of entertainment. My

?

generation has more things (in) which to occupy their

free time that my parents never had.

Because of the time gap _seperating_ my parents

Sp.
Ref.

an I, I have a _diffrent_ li(fes)tyle than they.

Li(fes)tyles change with the change of time, and with

that so do people's outlook on life.

Avoid clichés and be more specific.
Proofread for spelling and comma problems.

As time changes people's views and outlooks on

Beginning a paper is tough, isn't it? Notice how

life change with it. My parents grew up with

the sentences in this paragraph repeat one basic

✓   completely diffrent standards in a completely

idea three times.

✓   diffrent time. Because of the time I grew up in,

and the time I live in, my life differs greatly

from the lives of my parents.

a good point. Do you have a job? Tell me

Modern society offers more aid to young

about it. Are you on a scholarship?

people—jobs, school, financial—that my parents

Specifically, what did

✓   could never recieve. Because of this aid my life

your parents have to worry about that you don't?

has been more free than theirs ever was. I have

more free time on my hands than they ever did. My

parents were, and are, always working to keep and

You seem to admire them very much; you might

get, the things needed for survival in this life.

want to develop this idea in detail in a future paper.

✓   Also Because of a higher education than the

✓   education of my parents I have diffrent outlooks on

life. I have a more well-rounded attitude toward

Such as?

life. I tend to take more things for granted that

Can you give me an example of how

your attitude toward some issue

my parents never would. *differs from your parents'?*

What does this phrase mean?

We now live in a world of entertainment. My

Which sentence   *Such as?*   *What do you do with*

in paragraph 2

belongs in   generation has more things in which to occupy their

this   *your free time? What did they do?*

paragraph?   free time that my parents never had.

✓   Because of the time gap seperating my parents

✓ ✓   an I, I have a diffrent lifestyle than they.

Lifestyles change with the change of time, and with

that so do people's outlook on life.

You have a strong sense of organization for the whole paper. The

first and last paragraph express the same general idea, and the three body paragraphs break it into "aid," "education," and "entertainment." I would have liked to know more specifically what you like to do with your free time, how your education has changed your attitudes, and what your outlook on life is. Before you start drafting your next paper, spend at least thirty minutes probing each of the sub-topics, jotting down specific examples or incidents to support the general ideas. Then write a rough draft just to get the ideas down. Finally, go back over the draft; ask of each sentence how? why? in what way? such as? to find even more evidence to support each statement. I'd like you to work on ways to let me "see" specifically what you mean by things, attitudes, life-style, outlooks. Please log the spelling problems (each check in the margin represents one misspelling in that line of your paper) in your journal and bring it to your conference next week. If you can't account for all the check marks, I'll be glad to help.

The first set of comments identifies and corrects errors. In addition to placing the symbols and abbreviations in the lefthand margin, the teacher has underlined misspellings, circled punctuation problems, and rewritten some of David's prose. Comments at the end of the paper address in a general way what's wrong with the piece and recommend a few changes (but notice the commanding tone of the imperative verbs). For several reasons, the first set of comments don't teach writing. First, David may not know what the marginal abbreviations refer to; through frustrating trial and error he may have learned that P can mean "passive," "punctuation," "pronoun," "poor phrasing," "point?"—take your pick. *Awk* and its not-so-distant cousin ? communicates only "the teacher didn't like what I said here for some reason"; David is left entirely on his own to figure out *why* the phrasing is awkward and *how* to rewrite it.

Second, the comments don't help David become critical of his own writing. Finding his mistakes underlined again and again, or circled, or corrected, he can easily conclude that he has no responsibility for learning how to find problems he's previously overlooked. The teacher, he believes, will find his mistakes for him. Then, because the teacher *always* discovers a few errors, he's tempted to dismiss the corrections in an effort to protect himself from criticism. Such circular reasoning, which the teacher abets, won't make him an independent editor.

Finally, the comments presuppose that David knew more than in fact he did. They assume that his errors result from careless writing or from failing to apply the rules. Perhaps the teacher believes that David overlooked the mistakes, failed to proofread his paper, or worse, remains defiant toward conventions discussed repeatedly in class. David, however, didn't complete the assignment with the intention of doing poorly; he probably wanted to please his teacher and earn a good grade. Except for mistakes prompted by haste, students write errors because they don't know that they *are* errors.

In *Errors and Expectations,* a book every writing teacher should read cover to cover, Mina Shaughnessy maintains, "The errors students make . . . no matter how peculiar they may sound to a teacher, are the result not of carelessness or irrationality but of *thinking.*" [10] Her study is based on 4000 essays written between 1970 and 1974 by freshmen entering City College in New York, which had just opened its doors to large numbers of remedial students—"Basic Writers," she calls them. She describes and classifies the problems she finds in these papers, devoting chapters to problems of handwriting and punctuation; derailed syntax; common errors of tense, inflection, and agreement; spelling errors; vocabulary problems; and errors beyond the level of the sentence. Her discussion is copiously supported with examples from student papers.

Shaughnessy reads the unique genre called "student writing" in a way that explains how and why errors appear. "Once he grants students the intelligence and will they need to master what is being taught," she argues, "the teacher begins to look at his students' difficulties in a more fruitful way: he begins to search in what students write and say for clues to their reasoning and their purposes, and in what *he* does for gaps and misjudgments" (p. 292). Although errors may appear to us unconventional ways of using language, they are logical; that is, they reflect unique rules and hypotheses students have devised to attempt communication. Errors are also regular; that is, they occur in deliberate, often ingenious patterns.

Instead of isolating mistakes in line after line of a student's work, Shaughnessy encourages us to examine the paper systematically for *patterns* of error, reconstructing the student's unique grammar and formulating hypotheses to explain why or how the patterns devel-

10. Shaughnessy, p. 105. David Bartholomae reviews Shaughnessy's work in *Linguistics, Stylistics, and the Teaching of Composition,* edited by Donald McQuade (Studies in Contemporary Language No. 2; Akron, Ohio: University of Akron, 1979), pp. 209–20.

oped. What the student has done right may also explain the pattern, especially when errors seem to be partially under control or when some textbook pronouncement has been mislearned or misapplied. Whenever our own logic, the logic of the fluent writer, prevents us from discovering the rationale behind a pattern of errors, we must seek an explanation for it by discussing the evidence with the student.

As the second teacher, I responded to David's paper in ways the first teacher didn't. Notice, first of all, that I didn't mark everything. That doesn't mean I overlooked problems. Instead, my comments set one or two reasonable goals. Since David can't work on everything at once, I singled out a significant problem and let the others go for now. Some teachers may feel irresponsible in not marking every mistake, but with practice those pangs of guilt will diminish. Or they can be redirected by helping students log their own errors, signaled by checks in the margin. The purpose of our comments, remember, isn't to compete with other teachers in an error-hunting contest but to guide students' learning. Just as a class meeting organizes discussion around one or two topics, so too limiting the scope of our comments makes learning more efficient.

Second, the comments don't label problems; rather, they emphasize how and why communication fails. The questions create a kind of dialogue between David and me. In answering them, David must reread what he's written, eventually learning to ask similar questions of subsequent drafts. To keep lines of communication open, we ought to balance comments of praise and criticism. We can also encourage students to submit questions or comments together with the paper so that we can know what problems concern them and can offer specific suggestions about matters they want help with.

Responding to papers in ways that enhance learning is as time consuming as locating errors, more so until the procedure becomes comfortable and each student's problems more familiar to us. Although every paper obviously can't be approached in the same way, the following procedure offers some suggestions for planning written comments in much the same way as we prepare classes: 1. assess what the student needs to learn (steps 1–2), 2. plan what to teach and how (steps 3–4), 3. conduct the lesson (steps 4–10), and 4. keep notes to evaluate what's been learned and to plan future lessons (step 11).

Teaching Through Comments on Student Papers

1. Read the paper through without marking on it.
2. Identify one or two problems. In deciding what to teach this time, view the paper descriptively, not to judge it, but

to discover what the text reveals about decisions the writer made. You may want to ask yourself the following questions:

   a. Was the student committed to the assignment?
   b. What did the student intend to do? What was the purpose for writing?
   c. How did the writer define the audience for the piece?
   d. How thoroughly did the student probe the subject?
   e. How are paragraphs arranged?
   f. What are the most frequent types of sentences?
   g. What patterns of errors in spelling, punctuation, grammar, and usage does the paper contain? In what contexts do the errors appear? What makes them similar?

Examining scratch notes and drafts also helps reconstruct how the student created the final draft.

3. Formulate tentative hypotheses to explain the problem you want to focus on. You can assume that there's a logic to what appears on the page, even if it isn't *your* logic. Try to define that logic so that your comments can turn it around or modify it. For example, "I disliked the story because it's ending confused me" assumes (logically but unconventionally) that *'s* marks the possessive pronoun just as it does most nouns. Students who put commas in front of every *and* may be misapplying the rule for punctuating series or conjoining independent clauses; they need to learn that a "series" of two coordinated subjects or verbs doesn't need the comma. Merely labeling the error "misplaced comma," of course, doesn't teach students *why* and *how* your logic and theirs differ.

4. Examine what the student has done well. Can you find evidence elsewhere in the paper that the problem has been handled successfully? How can the student's strengths be used to repair weaknesses?

5. Now you are ready to begin marking the paper. You have examined the evidence, decided what you want to teach, and identified specific examples of the problem (and perhaps its solution) on which to base your lesson.

6. Questions can help call attention to troublespots, but avoid questions which can be answered simply "yes" or "no" and then be dismissed. Preface questions with *why, how,* or *what* so that students must reexamine the paper and become self-critical of their own prose ("How often have

you used this kind of sentence in this paragraph?"). Avoid imperatives ("Proofread more carefully"); they can point out problems, but they don't help students learn *how* to solve them.

7. Avoid labeling problems *unless* you also give students a way of overcoming them. If something is "unclear" or "awkward," let students know the source of your confusion ("Did you mean . . . or . . . ?") or point to other sections of the paper to show *how* the awkwardness could be removed ("You're using abstract words here; why not give me another example as you did in paragraph 2?"). Eschew, when you can, Latinate grammatical terms, abbreviations, and private symbols. They may be clear to you—after all, you've marked hundreds of papers with them—but they might mystify the student.

8. Make praise work toward improvements. Students need to know how a reader responds to their work, but they're rarely fooled by token praise. Avoid "good" or "I like this" unless you add *because*. Remember to commend students for progress they have made since the previous paper.

9. Avoid doing the student's work. Rewriting an occasional sentence can given students a model to imitate, *if* you make it clear what principle the model illustrates. But circled or underlined words (and most marginal symbols) simply locate and label errors; the student probably didn't "see" the problem and needs to practice proofreading and editing. A better strategy might be to place a check in the margin next to the line in which the misspelled word or punctuation problem occurs. Then ask the student to examine the entire line, locate the problem, and determine how to eliminate it. Students who can't find the error on their own should feel free to ask you what the check means. You may want students to log their checks, the error, and a correction for it in their journals so that they develop a sense of what they're overlooking. Logs can be discussed briefly in conference to identify patterns in the errors and work out strategies for anticipating them in future papers.

10. Write a carefully thought-out endnote to summarize your comments on the paper itself and to establish a goal for the next paper. State the goal positively, perhaps mentioning problems in previous papers which now have been solved or pointing to specific strengths in this paper. In-

stead of writing "This paper shows little thought," write "In planning your next paper, spend fifteen minutes freewriting; then fill a page with notes on your subject and decide how to group them under three or four headings." Not, "Your sentences are hopeless"; rather, "You've made considerable progress in organizing the whole essay, but now it's time to work on sentence structures. Draft your next paper to get the ideas down, but study the draft to see where sentences could be combined or made less wordy. Your ideas will come across much more forcefully if you avoid passive voice verbs and sentences which begin with *There are* and *It is*." The goal should be worded to encourage students to experiment and take risks, but don't prescribe additional goals until students have reached those you've already given them.

11. Write yourself a note to chart the student's progress, a reminder you can keep in the student's folder. Describe briefly what areas no longer seem to be problems, what problems your comments on this paper addressed, and what matters need attention later on. If the paper enabled you to teach a principle of paragraphing, remind yourself to evaluate the next paper according to the paragraph-goal you set for the student. But if you also noticed sentence problems, a note can save you time in setting a sentence-goal when you examine a future paper.

Does that sound like an impossible procedure? Perhaps at first reading, but in many ways it saves time. As English teachers, we expect to spend many hours each week commenting on papers.[11] We mark them conscientiously in the belief that students will read what we've written and will profit from our advice. Too often, however, they don't, and consequently, we resent having devoted so much energy to an apparently pointless task. One advantage of the procedure described above is that students *will* read what we've written. They'll expect us to say "bad" things, but they'll discover that we've said "good" things about their work too. They'll read about their weaknesses as they search for comments praising the paper. Second,

---

11. The NCTE Committee on Classroom Practices in Teaching English has compiled a collection of practical essays which suggest ways teachers can evaluate writing constructively even though confronted with unreasonably large classes; see *Classroom Practices in Teaching English 1979–1980: How to Handle the Paper Load* (Urbana, Ill.: NCTE, 1979).

the procedure offers specific help with weaknesses, especially in the goal-setting endnote. When students find out *how* to tackle their writing problems, they'll attempt the techniques we've suggested at least once. If we praise the attempt in marking the next paper, students may try a second time. Third, the procedure saves us time because we're focusing only on one or two problems. With practice, we can develop a mental repertoire of endnotes addressing specific problems. Although the long endnote on page 228 suggests that I spent a great deal of time composing it, I didn't. I want my students to think so, I suppose, but I drew on a stock endnote I've used many times, simply modifying it slightly to fit the particular paper I was marking.

Students must also have a role in evaluating their work. They should respond to their own writing and that of other classmates for several reasons. Because good writers are proficient in addressing varied audiences, students need opportunities not only to write for themselves and others but also to gain responses to their work from audiences other than the teacher. Because the composing process is a highly idiosyncratic affair, students who become conscious of what they're doing by explaining their decisions to other students also learn new strategies for solving writing problems. And because students should become progressively more independent and self-confident as writers, they need to evaluate each other's work and their own frequently, a practice which teaches constructive criticism, close reading, and rewriting.

Writing workshops, of course, enable students to respond to their classmates' writing. Self-evaualuation encourages students to assess their own compositions. As Mary Beaven suggests, "Self-evaluation strengthens students' editing abilities, giving them control over decisions that affect their own writing growth as they learn to trust their own criteria of good writing" (p. 153).

Self-evaluation benefits teachers as well as students. As students become more aware of what they wanted to do and where the writing frustrated their intentions, we can offer help, acting less like a judge and more like an experienced, trusted advisor. We discover how students perceive the composing process, what sorts of risks they're taking as they experiment with new writing techniques, and when to encourage and applaud growth. Self-evaluation realizes an important goal in a writing course: to help students become self-sufficient writers. As Beaven urges, students must have opportunities to decide for themselves "what they are going to learn, how to go about that learning process, and how to evaluate their own progress" (p. 147). Beaven recommends that students evaluate their own papers from the beginning of the course, answering questions we have designed to guide their assessment. At first, we can comment on the quality of their answers, modifying the goals they've set for themselves or suggesting alternative strategies whenever students seem headed in unprofitable directions. Later in the course, as students gain confidence in recognizing the qualities of good writing, we can give them more responsibility for evaluating, even grading, their work. Many teachers, for example, ask students to submit one- or two-paragraph statements which describe the major strengths and weaknesses in their paper. These notes can also explain how students defined their purpose and audience or what organizational and stylistic goals received special attention. Teachers find these statements surprisingly perceptive and extremely useful in composing their own comments. When we urge students to write us notes about drafts or completed papers, we gain a better sense of the problems individual writers confront and encourage an ongoing dialogue about writing through written comments.

Although self-evaluation questions should be changed frequently to reflect the kind of work students are doing, Beaven (p. 143) offers the following questions as a starting point:

1. How much time did you spend on this paper?
2. (After the first evaluation) What did you try to improve, or experiment with, on this paper? How successful were you? If you have questions about what you were trying to do, what are they?
3. What are the strengths of your paper? Place a squiggly line beside those passages you feel are very good.
4. What are the weaknesses, if any, of your paper? Place an X beside passages you would like your teacher to correct or revise. Place an X over any punctuation, spelling, usage, etc., where you need help or clarification.
5. What one thing will you do to improve your next piece of writing? Or what kind of experimentation in writing would you like to try? If you would like some specific information related to what you want to do, write down your questions.
6. (Optional) What grade would you give yourself on this composition? Justify it.

14

Designing writing courses

> For however many models for imitation he may give them from authors they are reading, it will still be found that fuller nourishment is provided by the living voice, as we call it, more especially when it proceeds from the teacher himself, who, if his pupils are rightly instructed, should be the object of their affection and their respect.
>
> MARCUS FABIUS QUINTILIANUS

Teaching as rhetoric

No two writing courses are exactly alike. Even if we begin a new term with the same text and course outline, we'll discover by the second week of class that our original plans must be changed. Just as writers confront unique possibilities in every act of composing, writing teachers discover with each group of students different ways to engage in the process of teaching. The purpose of this chapter is to explore the dimensions of that process and to construct an extended definition of teaching-as-rhetoric.

Teaching, like writing, occurs in a rhetorical context: somebody says something to someone else for a purpose. We can even substitute terms in the communication triangle to diagram these rhetorical elements.

236

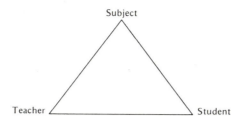

The terms—*teacher, student, subject*—need to be broadly defined though. In a writing class, students often teach each other or themselves, and conversely, the paid professional responsible for the class may learn a great deal about the composing process from students. The subject of a writing course can also vary. In some classrooms, where students and the teacher write, read, and discuss compositions, the subject is the composing process. In other classes, perhaps not properly called writing courses at all, grammar, literature, or a textbook become the subject.

As with writing, teaching brings these elements together in proportions that vary from one teacher and class meeting to the next. Teaching expresses itself in several forms of discourse: lectures, class discussion, conferences, writing workshops, comments on student papers—all of which exhibit special rhetorical strategies. Likewise, pedagogical discourse can have several aims. When we explain a principle of writing, the aim is referential; when we praise student performance, the aim is persuasive; when we share our compositions with the class, the aim is self-expressive (perhaps also referential).

For these reasons, teaching is a complicated rhetorical act, a process of communication. We're constantly realigning our relationship to our students and the subject. As the needs of our students and what we teach change, so does how we teach. We plan, execute, and revise our teaching performance over and over again, eventually developing a style which best expresses our teaching self.

General principles of course design

All writing courses share a common goal: giving students enough guided practice in composing that they become more fluent, effective writers at the end of the course than they were at the beginning. To attain that goal we make pedagogical decisions based on what we know about how students learn to write. Our assumptions about the composing process, in turn, are shaped by theories, research, and classroom practices which experience has validated as "workable." Unfortunately, if we're not thoroughly knowledgeable about theories, research, and practice, the whole pyramid can topple. Throughout our career as teachers, we'll confront questions we can't answer, and if we haven't had time to read and assimilate the theories and research which could reveal the answers, we must look to those who have.

We can find some answers to questions about writing curricula in "Teaching Composition: A Position Statement," developed in 1974 by the NCTE Commission on Composition. Because it provides an important foundation for designing courses, the eighteen-point position paper has been reprinted below in its entirety.

1. *Life in Language.* In many senses, anyone's world is his language. Through language we understand, interpret, enjoy, control, and in part create our worlds. The teacher of English, in awakening students to the possibilities of language, can help students to expand and enlarge their worlds, to live more fully.

2. *Need for Writing.* Writing is an important medium for self-expression, for communication, and for the discovery of meaning—its need increased rather than decreased by the development of new media for mass communication. Practice and study of writing therefore remain significant parts of the school curriculum and central parts of the English course.

3. *Positive Instruction.* Since a major value of writing is self-expression and self-realization, instruction in writing should be positive. Students should be encouraged to use language clearly, vividly, and honestly; they should not be discouraged by negative correction and proscription. They should be freed from fear and restriction so that their sensitivity and their abilities can develop.

4. *Learning by Writing.* Learning to write requires writing; writing practice should be a major emphasis of the course. Workbook exercises, drill on usage, and analysis of existing prose are not adequate substitutes for writing.

5. *Required Writing.* No formula dictates the amount of writing that should be required in a course—a paper a day or a paper a week. Ideally students should be allowed to write when they want to, as much as they want to, and at their own speed. Practically, however, students need class dis-

cipline and class discussion as well as freedom, and they should be frequently encouraged and at times required to write.

6. *Classroom Writing.* Inexperienced writers especially should have an opportunity to compose in school, with help during the actual writing process in clarifying ideas, in choosing phrasing, and sometimes in dealing with mechanical problems. Writing outside the classroom, of course, should be encouraged and sometimes required.

7. *Range of Assignments.* Writing assignments should be individualized, adjusted to the age, interests, and abilities of the student. Particularly in the elementary grades, but also through high school and into college, the teacher should encourage writing from personal experience, sometimes developing classroom experiences to provide material for writing. The expository essay should not be the exclusive form of composition encouraged. Especially for students who have convinced themselves that composition must be boring, a chore to be avoided whenever possible, writing various kinds of narratives, vignettes, dialogues, fables, family folklore, parodies, and the like may create interest.

8. *Alternate Techniques.* Instruction in writing techniques and rhetorical strategies should be part of the writing course, adjusted to the age and need of the students and focused on positive advice, suggestions, information, and encouragement. Instruction can include discussion of various ways in which writing can achieve its ends—in units as brief as a word or two and as long as a book—observations of procedures followed in existing prose, and constructive criticism of student writing.

9. *Composing.* Since there is adequate subject matter for direct study of writing, courses or units of English courses dedicated to composition should not be converted to courses in literature or social problems, with compositions to be written on the side.

10. *Usage.* Usage is an aspect of rhetoric: learning to predict the social effects of different dialects or different linguistic constructions is part of learning how writing can achieve its purposes. Students should be provided with information that will allow them the largest possible body of alternatives from which to choose and will help them to choose

wisely. They should know, for example, that *dragged* and *drug* are both used as past tense forms but that some listeners will react to *drug* by considering it uneducated. Or students should learn that *we was* and *we were* are alternatives but that *we was* is not characteristic of a prestige dialect. Such information should be provided through positive instruction about how dialects develop and why variations occur—not through correction based on notions of right and wrong.

11. *Dialects.* No dialect should be presented as "right" or "pure" or "logical" or better than others. The student should be given an opportunity to learn a standard written English, but the teacher must resist the temptation to allow the cultivation of a standard written English to stifle self-expression or to overshadow emphasis on clear, forceful, interesting writing.

12. *Grammar.* The study of the structure and history of language, including English grammar, is a valuable asset to a liberal education and an important part of an English program. It should, however, be taught for its own sake, not as a substitute for composition and not with the pretense that it is taught only to improve writing.

13. *Support for Composing.* Various kinds of activities related to composition contribute to the student's ability to write— film making, debates, collecting material for notebooks, library investigation, dramatics, field trips, television and film viewing. The attractions of such activities—because of their novelty or because they seem to gain more immediate student interest—should not be allowed to supersede instruction in writing.

14. *Talking and Writing.* Students are influenced by mass media not only as consumers but also as producers. Children, for example, may find it easier to compose orally on tapes, without the labor of handwriting. The teacher can sometimes exploit this interest in oral composition as a step toward writing, but the importance of the written word remains, and practice in oral composition is not sufficient.

15. *Audience.* Although some writing may be intended to be private, writing implies an audience and students should be helped to use a voice appropriate to the interests, maturity, and ability of an audience. Furthermore, since young

writers are especially concerned about response, their writing should be read by classmates as well as the teacher.

16. *Grading.* The mere assignment of grades is rarely an adequate way of encouraging and improving writing; whenever possible grades should be replaced by criticism or detailed evaluation. When grades are required, the teacher should avoid basing them primarily on negative considerations—for example, the number of misspelled words or sentence fragments.

17. *Class size.* Classes in writing should be limited to no more than twenty to facilitate frequent writing, reading of papers, and discussion of written work.

18. *Objectives.* Emphasis on instructional objectives or on accountability should not dictate the content of the course, particularly not to replace writing with attention to measurable skills—mechanics, for example. Teachers should retain responsibility for determining their objectives: demands for accountability should not interfere with independent thought among students.

Some of the statements represent goals we haven't reached yet. For example, most of us teach more than twenty students per class and devote too much attention to essay writing. Though some of the principles sound idealistic, given our students' expectations and the financial constraints on writing programs, nevertheless the goals are worth working toward.

For the most part, the position paper suggests practices we can implement now, without waiting for the system to change. If "writing practice should be a major emphasis of the course," we can reduce substantially the amount of time spent talking about textbooks, assigned readings, and workbook exercises so that students write and discuss their papers. If "writing implies an audience," we can design assignments which give the class practice addressing different audiences, schedule frequent writing workshops, and compose carefully our written responses to student papers. If "various kinds of activities related to composition contribute to the students' ability to write," we can insure that listening, speaking, seeing, reading, and thinking reinforce writing instruction. If "the mere assignment of grades is rarely an adequate way of encouraging and improving writing," we can devise more positive methods of giving students feedback on their work: written comments, conferences, groupwork, self-evaluation. As we plan what we intend to teach and how to go about it, the position statement provides general guidelines for writing curricula and teaching practices.

Course models

Although the position statement implies, generally, that sound writing courses offer students guided practice in composing, it doesn't specify a particular curriculum. There are several ways to structure writing courses, which, like essays, need coherence, a shape that relates parts to the whole in a purposeful arrangement. Models for writing courses can be classified according to which element of the communication triangle receives primary focus.

What-centered courses, perhaps the most common, emphasize the subject matter. To this group belong courses in writing about films or literature or essays. Typically, students see a film or discuss a reading assignment and then write a theme about it. Courses emphasizing linguistic forms are also what-centered; the sequence of instruction begins with words and progresses through sentences to paragraphs to outlines to whole essays (or vice versa, moving from essays "down" to diction). Courses treating rhetorical "modes" (typically, description, narration, exposition, and persuasion) can be what-centered *if* the modes apply to kinds of essays or methods of paragraph development. Occasionally, what-centered courses treat in some systematic progression several forms of discourse: essays, letters, term papers, syllogisms, dialogues, advertisements, poems.

Any course that focuses primarily on Moffett's "it," on forms or models, belongs to the what-centered category. The teacher explains the form, presents several models or examples of it, and gives students opportunities to analyze and imitate the models. The approach assumes that, by imitation, students will internalize the forms and begin to use them on their own. Although a respectable approach, rooted in classical imitation and the *Progymnasmata* of Hermogenes and Aphthonius, it has some disadvantages. Forms practiced by rote or imitation may not become internalized, especially if the teacher explains only *what* the form is but not *how* to reproduce it.

How-centered courses don't emphasize any one element of the communication triangle, but instead focus on the process whereby writers balance all three: the writer's persona, the subject, and the reader. Process-centered courses assume that if students understand the composing process and become conscious of their own writing behaviors, they'll be better able to control those practices. Although the class may spend considerable time discussing student papers and specific prewriting, writing, or rewriting strategies, the course places primary emphasis on students' actually writing. Process-centered courses become writing workshops, students helping each other plan, draft, and rewrite their work. The teacher writes too and shares compositions with the class. The teacher also listens, helping students shape and reshape papers by responding to them in frequent student-teacher conferences. Donald Murray especially advocates the writing workshop as a way of structuring the process-centered course:

> In the usual classroom the teacher speaks and the students listen. In the writing class, the students speak and the teacher listens. The climate of the writing workshop must encourage individual students to bring their own content to the course. During the class the students should not be passive receivers of information. They must be doers, writing and rewriting—discovering what they have to say, discovering what they need to know to say it effectively—until the students complete the act of writing by reaching a reader who understands what they have written. (*A Writer Teaches Writing,* p. 103)

Unless we're careful, process-centered courses can easily assume some other focus, especially if we feel guilty for not being the dominant figure in the classroom. They can become what-centered every time we're tempted to interrupt students engaged in writing with an explanation of some subject matter. For example, if we "explain" prewriting strategies during the first few weeks and then consider the topic closed, we've made prewriting a subject matter, an entity, not an activity, and turned writing into a body of knowledge to be learned rather than a process to be practiced. Sentence-combining also suffers this fate whenever the exercises become the exclusive focus of a writing course. Then, a useful strategy for manipulating sentences becomes an end in itself, not a means of achieving a larger rhetorical purpose.

Process-centered courses also tend to be student- or *who*-centered. But because who-centered courses don't always focus on students, we need to examine what is essentially a third approach to teaching. We've all taken courses in which the significant "who" is the professor. In fact, we deliberately seek out such a mentor as an undergraduate or graduate student because the professor's research, area of specialization, or teaching style appeals to us. As a rule, however, teacher-centered writing courses are ineffective. When lectures or teacher-controlled discussions become the focus of the course, students are shunted to the side. An outside observer, evaluating the visible, outward evidence of the teacher's energetic performance, might conclude that the students in this class are learning to write, that the teacher's salary is well-deserved. But the students probably aren't learning to write, primarily because they're not doing any writing. They're just sitting there.

When students become the significant "who," the observer views quite a different scene.[1] Groups of students discuss papers. Here and there a student works alone on an exercise which addresses some writing problem. One student consults a shelf of handbooks and dictionaries; another talks out the draft of a paper into a tape recorder; another sits beside the teacher's desk having a conference. Although the teacher *appears* to be working with only one student, in fact she's planned, coordinated, and managed activities for every student in her class, lessons which actively involve all the students in writing. In a student-centered course (as in a process-centered course), the class doesn't move through a lock-step curriculum. Instruction is individualized as much as class size permits. Textbooks, if they're used at all, serve as resources or reference works. Teachers are not lecturers but simply more experienced writers acting as models for student apprentices.

Although successful writing courses may focus primarily on a subject matter (*what*), a process (*how*), or students (*who*), most teachers incorporate all three emphases. An excellent illustration of this principle is William Coles' *The Plural "I,"* a dramatic narrative of a freshman composition class at Case Institute of Technology. Each of the book's thirty sections comprises a writing assignment, a classroom dialogue generated by the assignment, and, whenever necessary, Coles' commentary. "Though the real subject of our assignments was going to be language—what it is, how it functions, why it is important—for their nominal subject I decided on the concepts of amateurism and professionalism."[2] Although the course has both a subject matter (language) and a theme (amateurism and professionalism), the assignments also invite the study of traditional rhetorical modes: description, definition, cause-effect, comparison-contrast, narration. Essentially, all of these elements in Coles' course make it *what*-centered. More important, however, is its focus on the process of using language and on students as language-users. Coles views language

1. The student-centered approach is best defined in James Moffett, *Teaching the Universe of Discourse* (Boston: Houghton Mifflin, 1968); see especially Chapter 6, "Learning to Write by Writing," pp. 188–210.

2. William E. Coles, Jr., *The Plural "I": The Teaching of Writing* (New York: Holt, Rinehart and Winston, 1978), p. 6. Teaching and learning is the nominal subject of the thirty assignments in Coles' *Teaching Composing* (Rochelle Park, N.J.: Hayden, 1974).

"as the means by which all of us run orders through chaos thereby giving ourselves the identities we have."[3]; a *professional,* then, is "someone able to use the language of his system to grow as a person" (*The Plural "I,"* p. 213). Coles' students come to learn that language has the power to shape "the plural I," the writer's many selves. As readers of Coles' book, we observe his discussions with students about their papers and come to understand how teaching sounds and feels. We also discover that, in Coles' view, "what we are up to as teachers of writing is to enable students to develop voices or styles of their own, the kind of control of language . . . that will enable them to shape and control, rather than to be shaped and controlled, by their environments."[4]

Course outlines

Having examined a few course models, which we might think of as being analogous to the outer shape of an essay, let's take a look at how to hold the inner parts together, how to discover the relationships between "paragraphs" or units of the course. Most teachers develop course outlines prior to the first day's class meeting. In college courses the outline, usually called a *syllabus,* gives students a one-page list of course "events," a meeting-by-meeting schedule of topics and due dates for papers and reading assignments. In public schools, the terms *curriculum guide* and *lesson plans* denote the written documents which outline the course. The curriculum guide, generally developed by the entire English faculty or mandated by the school's administrators, offers a broad outline of the course (or a series of courses), defining goals and recommending classroom activities, readings, and writing assignments. Daily or weekly lesson plans permit individual teachers to adapt the curriculum guide to the needs of a particular group of students. Whereas lesson plans and curriculum guides provide road maps for the teacher, syllabuses are intended primarily as information for students.

According to Joseph P. Ryan, the syllabus has both an informative and a pedagogical function.[5] It informs students, teachers, and ad-

---

3. William E. Coles, Jr., "The Teaching of Writing as an Invitation to Becoming," paper presented at the Institute on Writing, Iowa City, Iowa, May 1979, p. 1.

4. William E. Coles, Jr., "Teaching the Teaching of Composition: Style for the Sake of Style for the Sake of Style," paper presented at the Institute on Writing, Iowa City, Iowa, May 1979, p. 1.

5. The following paragraph paraphrases "The Function and Format of a Course Syllabus," unpublished faculty development material written by Joseph P. Ryan, University of South Carolina. Ryan also developed the "Checklist for Course Syllabuses" which I have modified to incorporate information unique to writing courses.

ministrators about the course. Administrators view the syllabus as evidence of a teacher's expertise in the field of composition and in teaching. Prospective students can use the information to decide if they're interested in learning what the course teaches; students already enrolled can determine what the course requires and what it offers in return. Other teachers can use the syllabus to acquaint themselves with your interests or to guide their own teaching, especially if they're planning for the first time a course you've taught often. If called on to teach the course in your absence, they can also use the syllabus to plan their presentation. Once the course begins, Ryan maintains, the syllabus serves an important pedagogical function:

> Students in the course use the syllabus to determine what it is they are to learn (course content), in what sense they are to learn it (behavioral objectives), when the material will be taught (schedule), how it will be taught (instructional procedures), when they will be required to demonstrate their learning (exam dates), and exactly how their learning will be assessed (evaluation) and their grade determined. ("The Function and Format of a Course Syllabus," p. 1)

Because the syllabus serves not only as information but also as a teaching tool, it should be designed carefully and revised frequently, each term incorporating improvements based on previous experiences with the course. Although syllabuses generally include information suggested by the following checklist, some points may not be appropriate. Consider the list, not as a series of fixed regulations for composing syllabuses, but as a general set of guidelines. Most of the information can be written out in prose as a "policy statement" for the course; the course schedule (section VII in the checklist), however, may be appended to the policy statement as a one- or two-page list.

Checklist for Course Syllabuses

I. Descriptive Information
- A. Course number
- B. Course title
- C. Catalogue description
- D. Restatement of catalogue description indicating the instructor's emphasis
- E. Credit awarded for the course
- F. Statement of prerequisite (if any)
- G. Specification of intended audience for the course
- H. Instructor's name, office location, office hours, office telephone number

II. Specifications of Course Goals and Content
   A. Course goals—the syllabus should state specifically the purposes of the course and what it teaches students to *do* (e.g., "To help students develop a range of stylistic options for various audiences and rhetorical purposes," etc.)
   B. Course content—the syllabus should list specific terms, principles, and procedures covered throughout the course; if the syllabus lists only general topics or "events," they should be accompanied by a detailed explanation of how the course moves from one topic to the next, of how the parts create a coherent whole.

III. Reading Assignments
   A. A full bibliographical citation for all required texts and supplementary readings (when used)
   B. Specific page references keyed to particular course goals and content
   C. Dates by which time students should have read the assignment

IV. Writing Assignments
   A. The number of writing assignments
   B. A brief description of each assignment
   C. Due dates for assignments
   D. Statement of instructor's policy on revising papers
   E. Statement of instructor's policy on accepting late papers
   F. Description of requirements for special writing activities: journals, term papers, class writing projects
   G. If applicable, a statement of the instructor's preferences about the format of papers (margins, kind of paper to use, and so on)

V. Description of Instructional Procedures—the syllabus should identify approximately how much time will be devoted to lectures, discussion, conferences, in-class writing workshops, student presentations, field trips, guest speakers, and so on.

VI. Course Requirements
   A. Academic requirements—the syllabus should specify all required work (with due dates) and explain how it will be evaluated
   B. Administrative requirements—the syllabus should explain the instructor's policies on class attendance and participation, on granting incompletes, on missing or late assignments

VII. Course Schedule—the syllabus should provide a meeting-by-meeting calendar of events or, at the least, list dates for all assignments

VIII. Evaluation and Grading of Students—the syllabus should specify which assignments will be used to evaluate the student's progress, what criteria will determine if required assignments have been completed satisfactorily, and what formula translates the instructor's assessment of student work into a letter grade.

Lesson plans

Lesson plans, of course, contain much of the same information found on the syllabus. However, their purpose is to guide teachers in managing classtime effectively and efficiently. Most teachers find it helpful to draft weekly lesson plans before the course begins. Then, during the course, they break the week's work into smaller units as they prepare each day's class. Developing the plan in too much detail beforehand locks teacher and students into a course of instruction that may not reflect the needs or interests of the class. "Staying on schedule" assumes greater importance than supporting the diverse rates of development among individual student writers. However, postponing until the first day of class any work on lesson plans leaves teachers without a carefully thought-out blueprint and forces them to design the course hastily, extemporaneously, or not at all. As a result, the course will seem fragmented and incoherent, frustrating for teacher and students alike. Although this section of Chapter 14 offers general advice on developing weekly and daily lesson plans, it is not meant to constrain teachers. With practice, we all develop our own methods for outlining courses as well as shortcuts for reminding ourselves of how we plan to use classtime. Please modify the suggestions given here, depending on how much experience you've had in the classroom and on the kind of writing course you're teaching.

A weekly lesson plan may assume whatever format the teacher finds most useful, but informal outlines are common. The plan should answer the following questions: What do I want to teach this week? How will I teach that? How will I know if students have learned what I wanted to teach? The first question helps me determine goals and objectives for the week's work. The second question lets me develop specific assignments and class activities to help students reach the goals. The third question prompts me to decide how I'll evaluate not only my students' progress but also my own teaching. If I conclude that a particular teaching objective wasn't met, I can adjust next week's lesson plan to re-teach a principle by some other route or review work which gave students more trouble than I'd anticipated. Evaluating the weekly lesson plan may simply mean reviewing mentally on Friday what I did in class and jotting down a few notes to suggest how I might have done it better. I can also ask students from time to time what they enjoyed most about the week's work, when I belabored a point they already felt confident about, and what they want help with next week. When the course has ended, these weekly assessments, viewed cumulatively, suggest revisions I can make to improve the course and my teaching.

A weekly lesson plan, drafted before the course begins, might look like this:

Week 1 (three class meetings)

Topics: Introduction to the course
The writing process
Diagnostic paper

Objectives: To introduce students to the work of the course.
To discuss my writing habits and encourage them to become more aware of what they do as writers.
To discuss what the writing process entails and define terms: communication triangle, persona, prewriting, writing, rewriting, aims and modes of discourse.
To complete an in-class diagnostic paper.
To diagnose each student's strengths and weaknesses (writing profiles are for my own information) and select sample papers to discuss in class next week.

Readings: Chapter One, "Planning the Paper," in the text

Writing Assignments: Diagnostic paper (In class—Day 3)

Class Activities: Discuss policy statement and course schedule (Day 1)
Discuss writing habits (Day 1)
Define rhetorical terms (Day 1)
Groupwork to plan diagnostic paper (Day 2)
In-class freewriting (Day 2)
In-class writing (Diagnostic paper—Day 3)

Evaluation: Review rhetorical terms on Day 2 to be sure definitions were clear.
Observe group work (Day 2) to find out if directions were adequate and if groups need to be changed.
Examine notes and freewritings written on Day 2 (and submitted together with the diagnostic paper) to determine what kind of reassurance and help students need with prewriting strategies.
Ask students what was the most and least troublesome part of the diagnostic assignment (Day 3).

Experienced teachers might manage the entire weeks' classes guided only by the weekly lesson plan outlined above. I can't do it and, like most teachers, find it necessary to "prepare" each class the day before I teach it. Usually I "overprepare," mapping out the day's work in such detail that I can still help students reach their destination via detours. For example, in preparing a daily lesson plan for each of the three class meetings, I would expand the plan outlined above in several ways: by listing questions to guide discussion, by apportioning classtime to make sure everything gets done on schedule, by writing out instructions for groupwork, by devising "stand-by" activities in case we finish the planned work before the class period ends, by writing out the assignment for the diagnostic paper. Then, the lesson plan for Day 2 might look like this:

Day 2 (sixty-minute period)

Objectives: To review rhetorical concepts and terms discussed on Day 1, especially "persona," "audience," "aims and modes of discourse," "prewriting."

To plan the diagnostic paper by giving students experience with groupwork and freewriting.

Reading (10 minutes): Discuss Chapter One, "Planning the Paper."
Why is a plan or blueprint important to a carpenter? To a writer? What strategies does the text suggest for planning a piece of writing? In what ways do those strategies help writers make decisions about persona, audience, aims and modes of discourse? Which strategies have you used before? Do you use planning strategies the text didn't mention?

Groupwork (30 minutes): Have students probe the subject of their diagnostic paper, a past English teacher the student liked or disliked.
1. Ask students to work in pairs with someone they don't know.
2. Explain the procedure (3–4 below), writing these questions on the board to guide the group's talk:
   a. What bothered/pleased you most about the individual's teaching? Why?
   b. In what ways does a particular incident capture the teacher's weaknesses/strengths?
3. As one student in each pair responds to question 2a, the other records words and phrases that capture the impression. Then, students should reverse roles. Both students should respond to question 2a before repeating the talking-notetaking procedure for question 2b. Allow 20 minutes for this step.
4. Have students swap their notes, returning them to the person who originally spoke the words and phrases. Give students 5 minutes to review the notes and add details.

Freewriting (15 minutes): After students review the notes, ask them to complete a ten-minute freewriting. Explain the procedure: "Write whatever comes to your mind. Don't worry about punctuation, spelling, or complete sentences; just keep writing whatever ideas occur to you. If you don't know where to start, begin with _____ was my best/worst English teacher.' If you get stuck, just write the teacher's name as often as you need to until you get another idea." After ten minutes, ask students to stop writing. Give them five minutes to read their freewritings and circle words and phrases that especially appeal to them.

Wrap-up (5 minutes): Did they worry about spelling during the free-writing exercise? Did they get at least one good idea or detail? Then, hand out the diagnostic assignment; explain that the papers will be written in class next time. Assign another ten-minute freewriting as homework. Remind students to bring to the next class both freewritings and the notes from the groupwork; they can use these materials as they write the diagnostic paper. Notes and freewritings will be turned in with the diagnostic paper, but they won't be graded. Encourage students to continue planning the paper by adding to the notes.

Assignment for Diagnostic Paper

You've been thinking and freewriting about a past English teacher you liked or disliked. Now, assume that a younger brother or sister or a close friend wants your advice about whether or not to get into that teacher's class. You can also assume that this student could avoid the class if she or he wanted to. What advice would you give?

Write a letter that *persuades* the student to take or avoid the course. Give at least two reasons to support your position. In developing each reason, select from your notes and freewritings the kinds of details that will best convince your reader to agree with your opinion about the teacher.

The daily plan may seem excessively rigid, almost too detailed. No class is quite so willing to follow a teacher's plan to the minute. Indeed, an experienced teacher might write out only the assignment and a few brief phrases to remind herself of what she plans to do. But the value of a lesson plan lies in its preparation, not its execution. Drafting the plan helps you visualize your teaching performance, to pre-teach the class. If you're confident about what you intend to do, you'll feel secure about deviating from the plan when you sense the need to digress. For example, if students begin discussing the text enthusiastically and profitably, you can let discussion continue for another five or ten minutes, knowing that the class will still have enough time for groupwork and freewriting. Making quick decisions like these during class can enhance rather than subvert learning if you know precisely what your objectives are. Instead of representing attempts to save the period from disaster, on-the-spot adjustments permit students to reach the original goal by a different route.

For this reason, course syllabuses and lesson plans must have flexibility. They define the outer shape of the course and the relationships among its inner parts. Like prewriting, designing syllabuses and lesson plans represents a crucial first step. But at the same time, as in drafting a composition, we may find in the act of teaching new messages or some dimension of our student audience that hadn't occurred to us before. If we're willing to let the course grow, more than likely our experiences with each group of students will reshape the original outline and permit us to discover new meaning in what we teach.

The teaching performance

Effective teachers, like effective public speakers, engage their audiences. We can all remember at least one teacher whose enthusiasm and energy made attending class enjoyable. Although the work was difficult, we didn't mind; we respected, and also liked, the teacher. But we've also endured boring classes conducted by a frozen, unsmiling figure seated behind a desk, eyes glued to yellowed lecture notes. We couldn't concentrate on what was being said; we stared out the window; we saved those homework assignments for last, trying to work up enough enthusiasm to do them at all. Despite what the boring teacher knew, we thought to ourselves, it doesn't come across.

Teachers can usually sense when a class runs amuck, when teaching a particular group of students day after day makes us contemplate some other profession. Our natural response is to assume that the class is especially "slow," or lazy, or a lost cause. Actually it may offer an excellent opportunity to evaluate our own performance.[6] It gives us a valid reason for asking a teacher whose advice we trust to

6. Michael C. Flanigan, "Observing Teaching: Discovering and Developing the Individual's Style," *Journal of the Council of Writing Program Administrators* 3 (Winter 1979), 17–24, describes an excellent teacher observation program which focuses "on teachers' needs, not on evaluating teachers for administrative purposes":

> "First, the observer gathers information about the objectives, concerns, and style of the teacher. Second, the observer describes in detail what went on in the teacher's class. And third, the observer connects what the teacher says she or he wants to achieve with what the observer saw and heard in class" (p. 18).

observe what's going on, to make notes describing how we interact with students, and to discuss with us ways of improving the situation. Or we can arrange to have the class videotaped, to study in private the enormous amounts of information a camera reveals about our teaching.

This last section of Chapter 14 offers some suggestions for evaluating our teaching performance. The word *performance* may suggest cheap theatrical tricks, comedy routines, razzle-dazzle. The focus of this section, however, isn't on performances which substitute entertainment for education; rather, we'll examine how teachers can use effectively verbal and nonverbal codes to reinforce instruction and enhance learning—to get the message across. If we can't all become accomplished actors and actresses in the classroom, we can learn nevertheless a few simple techniques for using the props, blocking the scenes, and commanding the dialogue which dresses our message to advantage and holds the attention of our media-sophisticated students.

Most of us feel a little uncomfortable in the presence of an observer or a videotape camera. Our students' performance as well as our own, we reason, will change, becoming to some extent "artificial." That's true, but our logical excuses also mask a natural reluctance to be evaluated, to be judged and perhaps found inferior. Although the procedure outlined here could be applied to discussions with an outside observer, it's designed for examining the evidence a videotape provides. One advantage of videotaping a class is that no one else needs to see the performance. The technician who operates the equipment probably tapes so many classes that ours becomes indistinguishable from the others. Although we and our students doubtless sense the camera's presence and even play to it for the first few minutes, it doesn't change our actions as drastically as we feel it does. After a few minutes, as we become preoccupied with what we're saying and how our students respond, the camera assumes less prominence.

A second advantage is that videotape provides a more or less permanent record of the teaching performance. We can review it days or weeks later, long after our own recollections of the class have faded. We can play back sections of the tape to study in detail what prompted a lively discussion or an unproductive silence. Because the act of teaching requires enormous concentration, we may not be able to see everything the camera does. We can't teach well, record our own perceptions, and evaluate what's happening all at the same time.

A third advantage is that the tape can be destroyed if we fear that it will be used against us. Videotaping, as described here, has a *di-*

agnostic purpose. As a means of self-evaluation, the tape should never be used without our consent to *judge* teaching effectiveness or to influence salary and promotion decisions. If we wish, of course, we may invite someone else to view the tape with us, but our purpose should be to describe what we see, to identify problems, and to examine alternatives that improve teaching and learning.

Most people's initial response to seeing themselves on videotape is similar to hearing their voice on a tape recorder for the first time. Especially if someone else is present to witness our reaction, we become self-conscious, embarrassed—but fascinated, nevertheless. We never ask, except perhaps jokingly, that the tape be turned off. The response is perfectly natural—give in to it—but, if possible, view the tape alone the first time so that you can concentrate on it without feeling obliged to react to it for the benefit of someone else in the room. Once the newness of what you're seeing wears off, you can stop watching what you look like, entertaining yourself, and begin studying other elements of the total picture more objectively.

What "elements" should you study? What can the tape tell you? You might begin by looking at the eight areas discussed on the following pages, where each set of questions implies solutions to problems that beginning as well as experienced teachers face.[7] You'll probably want to view the tape several times, each time concentrating on a different area. Of course, you could also examine each area without referring to a videotape, by trying to recall from memory what happened during the class. Watch for *patterns* in your behavior or in the students' response. And remember that every teaching performance reveals both strengths and weaknesses. Applaud yourself for the strengths and select only one or two weaknesses to work on between now and the next time you videotape another class.

1. *Pre-viewing:* Before you view the tape, go back over the lesson plan for that day. Recall what you intended to do. All in all, do you think you achieved your purpose? Can you recall particular moments during class when you thought you were teaching well? (Those sections of the tape should get close scrutiny.)

2. *Seating Patterns:* Draft a seating chart. As you view the tape, notice the various roles different students take in conversation. Some will initiate discussion; some will talk only after other students have first taken a turn in the discussion; some may not have said anything. Notice where each kind of student-talker sits. As a rule, stu-

7. I am indebted to Joan Allaire for videotaping my writing class, defining the eight areas, and identifying ways to improve my effectiveness as a teacher.

dents who talk most sit near the middle of the class, where they have direct eye contact with the teacher. Students who feel left out (or wish to exclude themselves) may sit in the back of the class or closest to the extreme left and right sides. Now, notice how you interact with each kind of student-talker. Are you drawing reluctant students into the conversation by moving toward them, by establishing eye contact with them, by calling on them (or on a student who seems to speak for them)? How much of the talk is student-to-teacher conversation? How often do you redirect a student's question to another student for an answer? Which students can you depend on to summarize discussion, make connections, or introduce new lines of thought?

3. *Organization:* Examine the structure of the entire lesson and points of transition between activities. Do students have a clear sense of where you are taking them as you move through the period? Do you begin the class with a specific statement of what will be done that day and how the lesson ties in to the previous class meeting? Writing a *brief* outline of the day's work on the blackboard can help students see connections between activities. Furthermore, an outline tells students how much there is to cover and consequently encourages them to observe the time limits you've set for each activity. Do you announce specific transitions from one section of the lesson to the next and comment on how the activities relate to one another? Do you take a few minutes at the end of class to summarize (or let students summarize) the day's work? Do you introduce briefly what will be covered the next time the class meets? Does the class have an ending, or is it interrupted as students collect their books and scramble for the door? How successfully did you budget your time? If you ran out of time, try to determine where and why you departed from the lesson plan. Was the detour unavoidable? Constructive? Should the lesson plan be revised?

4. *Methods:* In addition to teacher-talk, how often did you use other resources and techniques during the class period?

	Frequently	Occasionally	Not at all
Brief conferences with individual students			
Student-to-teacher discussion			
Student-to-student discussion			
In-class writing			
In-class reading			
Work with the text			
Work with student papers			

	Frequently	Occasionally	Not at all
Student-led presentations			
Handouts			
Blackboard			
Overhead projector			
Tape recorder			
Other resources			

5. *Pacing:* Pacing refers to the "tone" a teacher creates by varying class activities. It's perhaps the most difficult element to control in a teaching performance, but it's also extremely important. Because students bring a variety of interests to class, some are easily motivated; others, easily bored. If the pace is too slow, even interested students become inattentive; it it's too fast, most students will feel lost and frustrated. As you watch the tape, notice the students' body language. Are several of them shifting position impatiently? Have usually attentive students broken eye contact with you to stare somewhere else or to doodle in their notebooks? Are they looking at each other, carrying on silent eye-to-eye conversations? When you detect an unmistakable lack of attention, make a note of what you said at that point in the videotape and where you were standing or sitting with respect to the rest of the class. Then rewind the tape and play it back. You may discover that you didn't vary your talk or your position frequently enough. Since young adults have an attention span of only ten to fifteen minutes, they'll lose interest in what's happening unless *something* changes every ten minutes. Pacing is a matter of controlling those changes, and effective teachers develop a "sense" of when to make a change.

Although a change of pace must occur frequently, it needn't be dramatic. Here are some suggestions:

a. Change your position. Stand up, sit down, walk up a side aisle or into a "hole" in the seating pattern.

b. Change activities. Shift from teacher-talk to work at the blackboard to group work to in-class writing to discussing student papers to work with an overhead projector.

c. Change topics. Move from a discussion of a reading assignment to a discussion of a student paper to planning the next assignment.

d. Change the *kind* of talk you are doing. If you've been asking undirected questions addressed to the entire class, shift to directed questions, calling on specific students by name. If you've been discussing *what* a writer says, talk about *how* or *why* the piece is effective; then move students away from the piece altogether, asking them which strategies might be useful in their own writing. Discussions of abstract principles can yield to concrete applications of those principles and vice versa. Cognitive questions, which elicit facts, can be replaced with affective questions, which elicit feelings.

6. *Questioning Strategies:* What kinds of questions do you ask? How often do you address individual students? The class as a whole? How often do questions begin with *who, what, when, where, why,* and *how?* Are you asking too many questions which require simple "yes" or "no" responses and consequently truncate discussion? Some kinds of questions prevent discussion.[8] The pointless question—"We still have a few minutes, so I might as well ask you what the text says about topic sentences"—is obviously a filler, unimportant to the teacher and consequently also to the students. The loaded question—"Doesn't Frank's opening paragraph develop too much material?"—obviously requires a "yes" answer. End of discussion. Using loaded questions to trap students into giving incorrect answers is pedagogically unsound; students may fall into the trap once, but they may never respond to another question. The intimidating question—"We've discussed this strategy before; does anyone need it explained *again?*"—requires students to admit ignorance.

Notice too if you're giving students enough time to respond. Teachers who feel especially uncomfortable with the silence following a question often answer it themselves or pose another just as a student is leaning forward, beginning to raise a hand, or dropping a jaw to speak. See if you can discover similar body language as you view the tape. In fielding questions, do you rephrase them or ask students to? Helping students articulate precise questions suited to a specific audience reinforces principles they're learning in written communication. Whenever students ask a question, make sure you listen to it. If it's confusing or off the topic, if it contains vague terms, encourage the student to clarify the communication. How do you respond to questions you can't answer? Do you bluff an answer or become excessively apologetic, or do you simply say that you don't know and will find out? When students ask questions you can reasonably expect other students to answer, do you redirect the question? Questions not only help you teach new material but also to reinforce what you've already taught. For example, if Sally had trou-

8. The rest of the paragraph paraphrases "Freshman Rhetoric," University of Illinois, Urbana-Champaign, Illinois.

ble understanding *thesis statement,* a directed question later in the discussion might request her to define the term in her own words, to find the thesis in a student paper, or to summarize the discussion.

7. *Routine Matters:* How do you handle routine procedures like taking attendance, collecting or distributing papers, and making assignments? Are administrative chores consuming too much time? Some teachers ask students to write in their journals for the first ten minutes of class, a procedure which gets the class settled and also allows the teacher time to review the roll. Other teachers take roll immediately after class by recalling which seats were vacant or by looking through assignments collected that day to determine whose papers are missing. Unless student papers will be discussed in class, they're best returned at the end of the hour so that students can discuss with you after class any questions they may have about your comments. Handing out papers at the beginning of class means that some students will pay more attention to your comments or the grade than to the lesson. Assignments should be written out and thoughtfully discussed, with sufficient time for questions; they shouldn't be composed on the spot or thrown at the class as the bell rings.

8. *Personal Qualities:* When you've viewed the videotape to assess each of the preceding areas, examine it again, this time to focus on the impression your voice, appearance, and mannerisms may be giving your students. Without meaning to, beginning teachers sometimes undermine their performance by communicating that they're afraid of their students or lack confidence in their ability to teach them. Indeed, you may feel that way, but your students don't need to know it, and by acting confidently you may begin to convince yourself that you are a competent, capable teacher.

Pay attention to the quality of your voice. Do you speak confidently or in timid, barely audible tones? Most teachers discover that their normal speaking voice is less effective in a classroom than in one-to-one conversation. A teaching voice must vary pitch to a greater extent, must project itself across a greater distance to the back of a classroom, must overemphasize slightly (but not too much) words you want to stress, must avoid annoyingly repetitious fillers ("uh," "ya know," "for sure," "ya see"). A teaching voice should feel as if you're overexaggerating your normal conversational tone a little bit.

Second, notice how you use your eyes. Confident teachers establish eye contact with their students and *rarely* break it, unless they need to glance momentarily at a paper or toward the blackboard. A gaze fixed on notes, the back wall of the room, the floor, or only one or two students makes it appear as if the rest of the class, the audience for your discourse, has been excluded.

Third, observe your stance and patterns of movement. Do you consistently hide behind the security of the desk or podium? Do you stand with your back to the class as you write on the board? (Stand with your right or left side toward the class so that you can maintain eye contact and allow students to see what you're writing.) Do you define your "territory" to extend only to the first row of seats, or do you occasionally move into the first few rows and up side aisles? Remember that staying in one place for longer than ten minutes can slow the pace of the class. Leaning carelessly against a chair, the wall, or a window ledge expresses a nonchalance your students may interpret as an excuse to treat their own work cavalierly. To "see" these problems requires viewing the tape dispassionately, if possible, adopting the students' angle of vision and interpreting nonverbal messages as the class might perceive them.

In *A Writer Teaches Writing*, Donald Murray asserts, "The teacher of writing, first of all, must be a person for whom the student wants to write" (p. 16). To be a person requires both honesty and courage. To be honest with students is to acknowledge that writing courses belong to them, not to us. Their ideas, their voices shape the course and become its content. To be honest with ourselves is to recognize that we too are writers and, like our students, wrestle with the difficult process of creating meaning through language. A writing course then is also our opportunity to write, to share with students our voice and our wars with words.

But viewing writing courses this way also takes courage. Although the academic tradition expects us to profess a subject with authority, our first responsibility is to listen with understanding to our students' voices. Our function, first and foremost, is not to tell them what to say or how to express it but to help them find their own meanings and styles. To listen, then, *is* to profess that student voices matter, matter more, in fact, than our own.

It also takes courage to admit that we cannot be authorities, in the usual sense, transmitting a body of knowledge to students. Although age, experience, and training distance us from younger writers, we need not concern ourselves with bridging the gap, with teaching students what we know. Instead we must use our training and knowledge to help them discover their own world, their own ways of sharing it with others in writing. To be a person is much more difficult than being an authority, or a phony, or a mass of sympathies. Yet if we want our students to write well, we must understand what is truly basic to composing—a person writing to another person.

A selected bibliography

Although the "List of Works Consulted" immediately following cites many helpful books, articles, and videotapes, this list represents a baker's dozen of essential resources for writing teachers. If you have not taught writing before or want to make your teaching more effective, these books offer a useful place to begin.

Cooper, Charles R., and Lee Odell, eds. *Evaluating Writing: Describing, Measuring, Judging.* Urbana, Ill.: NCTE, 1977.

Dixon, Peter. *Rhetoric.* London: Methuen, 1971.

Elbow, Peter. *Writing without Teachers.* New York: Oxford University Press, 1973.

Emig, Janet. *The Composing Processes of Twelfth Graders.* NCTE Research Report No. 13. Urbana, Ill.: NCTE, 1971.

Gebhardt, Richard C., ed. *Composition and Its Teaching.* Findlay, Oh.: Ohio Council of Teachers of English Language Arts, 1979.

Graves, Richard, ed. *Rhetoric and Composition: A Sourcebook for Teachers.* Rochelle Park, N.J.: Hayden, 1976.

Irmscher, William. *Teaching Expository Writing.* New York: Holt, Rinehart, and Winston, 1979.

Murray, Donald. *A Writer Teaches Writing.* Boston: Houghton Mifflin, 1968.

Shaughnessy, Mina. *Errors and Expectations: A Guide for the Teacher of Basic Writing.* New York: Oxford University Press, 1977.

Tate, Gary, ed. *Teaching Composition: Ten Bibliographical Essays.* Fort Worth, Tex.: Texas Christian University Press, 1976.

Tate, Gary, and Edward P.J. Corbett, eds. *The Writing Teacher's Sourcebook.* New York: Oxford University Press, 1981.

Weaver, Constance. *Grammar for Teachers: Perspectives and Definitions.* Urbana, Ill.: NCTE, 1979.

Winterowd, W. Ross, ed. *Contemporary Rhetoric: A Conceptual Background with Readings.* New York: Harcourt Brace Jovanovich, 1975.

List of works consulted

Abbreviations: CCC—*College Composition and Communication*
CE—*College English*
EJ—*English Journal*
NCTE—National Council of Teachers of English
PMLA—Publications of the Modern Language Association of America
RTE—*Research in the Teaching of English*

Adams, James L. *Conceptual Blockbusting: A Pleasurable Guide to Better Problem Solving.* San Francisco: W.H. Freeman, 1974.

Algeo, John. *Problems in the Origins and Development of the English Language.* 2nd ed. New York: Harcourt Brace Jovanovich, 1972.

Arbur, Rosemarie. "The Student-Teacher Conference." CCC 28 (December 1977), 338–42.

Aristotle. *The Rhetoric of Aristotle.* Trans. Lane Cooper. Englewood Cliffs, N.J.: Prentice-Hall, 1932.

Bacon, Francis. *Advancement of Learning.* Great Books of the Western World, Vol. 30. Chicago: Encyclopaedia Britannica, 1952.

Bain, Alexander. *English Composition and Rhetoric.* Enlarged edition. 2 vols. New York: American Book Company, n.d.

Baker, Sheridan. *The Complete Stylist and Handbook.* 2nd ed. New York: Harper and Row, 1980.

Baratz, Joan C., and Roger W. Shuy, eds. *Teaching Black Children to Read.* Washington, D.C.: Center for Applied Linguistics, 1969.

Bartholomae, David. "The Study of Error." CCC 31 (October 1980), 253–69.

—————. "Teaching Basic Writing: An Alternative to Basic Skills." *Journal of Basic Writing* 2 (Spring/Summer 1979), 85–109.

Baugh, Albert C., and Thomas Cable. *A History of the English Language.* 3rd ed. Englewood Cliffs, N.J.: Prentice-Hall, 1978.

Beach, Richard. *Writing about Ourselves and Others.* Urbana, Ill.: NCTE, 1977.

Beard, Ruth M. *An Outline of Piaget's Development Psychology for Students and Teachers.* Students Library of Education. London: Routledge and Kegan Paul, 1969.

Beaven, Mary H. "Individualized Goal Setting, Self-Evaluation, and Peer Evaluation." In *Evaluating Writing: Describing, Measuring, Judging.* Ed. Charles R. Cooper and Lee Odell. Urbana, Ill.: NCTE, 1977. Pp. 135–56.

Becker, Alton L. "A Tagmemic Approach to Paragraph Analysis." *CCC* 16 (December 1965), 237–42.

Berthoff, Ann E. "From Problem-Solving to a Theory of Imagination." *CE* 33 (March 1972), 636–49.

——————. "I. A. Richards and the Philosophy of Rhetoric." *Rhetoric Society Quarterly* 10 (Fall 1980), 195–210.

Bloomfield, Leonard. *Language.* New York: Henry Holt, 1933.

Boley, Tommy J. "A Heuristic for Persuasion." *CCC* 30 (May 1979), 187–91.

Booth, Wayne C. "The Rhetorical Stance." *CCC* 14 (October 1963), 139–45.

Braddock, Richard. "The Frequency and Placement of Topic Sentences in Expository Prose." *RTE* 8 (Winter 1974), 287–304.

Braddock, Richard, Richard Lloyd-Jones, and Lowell Schoer. *Research in Written Composition.* Urbana, Ill.: NCTE, 1963.

Britton, James. *Language and Learning.* Harmondsworth, England: Penguin, 1970.

Britton, James, et al. *The Development of Writing Abilities, 11–18.* Schools Council Research Series. London: Macmillan Education, 1975.

Brock, Dee. *Writing for a Reason* (a thirty-program telecourse of writing instruction). Produced by Instructional Television Center, Dallas, Texas.

Broderick, John. *The Able Writer.* New York: Harper and Row, 1982.

Brown, Roger. *A First Language: The Early Stages.* Cambridge, Mass.: Harvard University Press, 1973.

Bruffee, Kenneth A. "The Brooklyn Plan: Attaining Intellectual Growth through Peer-Group Tutoring." *Liberal Education* 64 (December 1978), 447–69.

Bruner, Jerome. *On Knowing: Essays for the Left Hand.* Cambridge, Mass.: The Belknap Press, 1962.

Burke, Kenneth. *A Grammar of Motives.* Berkeley, Calif.: University of California Press, 1969.

——————. *A Rhetoric of Motives.* Berkeley, Calif.: University of California Press, 1969.

——————. "Rhetoric—Old and New." In *New Rhetorics.* Ed. Martin Steinmann, Jr. New York: Charles Scribner's Sons, 1967. Pp. 60–76. Reprinted from *Journal of General Education* 5 (April 1951), 203–9.

Burt, Forrest, ed. *The Effective Writer: A Freshman English Manual.* Boston: American Press, 1978.

Cazden, Courtney B. *Child Language and Education.* New York: Holt, Rinehart and Winston, 1972.

Chase, Stuart. "How Language Shapes Our Thoughts." In *Speaking of Words.* Ed. James MacKillop and Donna Cross. New York: Holt, Rinehart and Winston, 1978. Pp. 29–33.

Christensen, Francis, and Bonniejean Christensen. *A New Rhetoric.* New York: Harper and Row, 1976.

——————. *Notes Toward a New Rhetoric.* 2nd ed. New York: Harper and Row, 1978.

Cicero. *De oratore.* Trans. E.W. Sutton and H. Rackham. In *Readings in Classical Rhetoric.* Ed. Thomas W. Benson and Michael H. Prosser. Bloomington, Ind.: Indiana University Press, 1972.

Coe, Richard. *Form and Substance: An Advanced Rhetoric.* New York: John Wiley and Sons, 1981.

——————. "Rhetoric 2001." *Freshman English News* 3 (Spring 1974), 1–13.

Coles, William E. *Composing: Writing as a Self-Creating Process.* Rochelle Park, N.J.: Hayden, 1974.

——————. *The Plural I: The Teaching of Writing.* New York: Holt, Rinehart and Winston, 1978.

——————. *Teaching Composing: A Guide to Teaching Writing as a Self-Creating Process.* Rochelle Park, N.J.: Hayden, 1974.

——————. "The Teaching of Writing as an Invitation to Becoming." Paper presented at the Institute on Writing. Iowa City, Iowa. May 1979.

——————. "Teaching the Teaching of Composition: Style for the Sake of Style for the Sake of Style." Paper presented at the Institute on Writing. Iowa City, Iowa. May 1979.

Commission on the Humanities. *The Humanities in American Life.* Berkeley, Calif.: University of California Press, 1980.

Comprone, Joseph. *Teaching Form and Substance: A Left-Handed Guide to Teaching Students to Read and Write.* Dubuque, Ia.: Wm. C. Brown, 1976.

Conference on College Composition and Communication. "Resolution on Testing and Writing." Denver, Colorado. 1 April 1978.

——————. Committe on Teaching and Its Evaluation. "Evaluating Instruction in Composition: Approaches and Instruments." Forthcoming in *CCC* (May 1982).

Cooper, Charles R. "An Outline for Writing Sentence-Combining Problems." In *Rhetoric and Composition: A Sourcebook for Teachers.* Ed. Richard L. Graves. Rochelle Park, N.J.: Hayden, 1976. Pp. 118–28.

——————. "Responding to Student Writing." Paper presented at the Annual Conference on Language Arts, State University of New York at Buffalo, 1975. Reprinted in *The Writing Processes of Students.* Ed. Walter T. Petty and Patrick J. Finn. Buffalo: State University of New York, 1975. Pp. 31–39.

Cooper, Charles R., and Lee Odell, eds. *Evaluating Writing: Describing, Measuring, Judging.* Urbana, Ill.: NCTE, 1977.

——————. *Research on Composing: Points of Departure.* Urbana, Ill.: NCTE, 1978.

Cooper, Charles, and Anthony R. Petrosky. "A Psycholinguistic View of the Fluent Reading Process." *Journal of Reading* 19 (December 1976), 184–207.

Corbett, Edward P.J. *Classical Rhetoric for the Modern Student*. 2nd ed. New York: Oxford University Press, 1971.

—————. *The Little Rhetoric and Handbook*. New York: John Wiley and Sons, 1977.

—————. "The Theory and Practice of Imitation in Classical Rhetoric." *CCC* 22 (October 1971), 243–50.

—————. "The Usefulness of Classical Rhetoric." *CCC* 14 (October 1963), 24–26.

Cowan, Gregory, and Elizabeth Cowan. *Writing*. New York: John Wiley and Sons, 1980.

Cowley, Malcolm, ed. *Writers at Work*. New York: Viking, 1958.

Creswell, Thomas J. *Usage in Dictionaries and Dictionaries of Usage*. Publication of the American Dialect Society, Numbers 63–64. University, Ala.: University of Alabama Press, 1975.

Crews, Frederick. *The Random House Handbook*. 2nd ed. New York: Random House, 1977.

Crowhurst, Marion, and Gene L. Piche. "Audience and Mode of Discourse Effects on Syntactic Complexity in Writing at Two Grade Levels." *RTE* 13 (May 1979), 101–9.

Daiker, Donald, Andrew Kerek, and Max Morenberg, eds. *Sentence Combining and the Teaching of Writing*. Conway, Ark.: L & S Books, 1979.

—————. *The Writer's Options: College Sentence Combining*. New York: Harper and Row, 1979.

D'Angelo, Frank. *A Conceptual Theory of Rhetoric*. Cambridge, Mass.: Winthrop, 1975.

—————. "A Generative Rhetoric of the Essay." *CCC* 25 (December 1974), 388–96.

—————. *Process and Thought in Composition*. 2nd ed. Cambridge, Mass.: Winthrop, 1980.

DeBeaugrande, Robert. "Linguistic Theory and Composition." *CCC* 29 (May 1978), 134–40.

Dewey, John. *Experience and Education*. New York: Macmillan, 1938.

Diederich, Paul B. *Measuring Growth in English*. Urbana, Ill.: NCTE, 1974.

Dieterich, Daniel, ed. *Teaching About Doublespeak*. Urbana, Ill.: NCTE, 1976.

Dixon, Peter. *Rhetoric*. London: Methuen, 1971.

Donelson, K.L. "Variables Distinguishing Between Effective and Ineffective Writers in the Tenth Grade." *Journal of Experimental Education* 35 (Summer 1967), 37–41.

Eble, Kenneth. *The Craft of Teaching* (a videocassette). Produced by the University of Georgia Center for Continuing Education, Athens, Georgia.

Elbow, Peter. *Writing with Power: Techniques for Mastering the Writing Process*. New York: Oxford University Press, 1981.

—————. *Writing without Teachers*. New York: Oxford University Press, 1973.

Elgin, Suzette Haden. *A Primer of Transformational Grammar: For the Rank Beginner*. Urbana, Ill.: NCTE, 1975.

Emig, Janet. *The Composing Processes of Twelfth Graders.* NCTE Research Report No. 13. Urbana, Ill.: NCTE, 1971.

—————. "Writing as a Mode of Learning." *CCC* 28 (May 1977), 122–28.

The English Modules (a series of nine videocassettes emphasizing sentence construction). Produced by the New York Network, Albany, New York.

Faigley, Lester L. "Generative Rhetoric as a Way of Increasing Syntactic Fluency." *CCC* 30 (May 1979), 176–81.

Farrell, Edmund J. "The Beginning Begets: Making Composition Assignments." In *Rhetoric and Composition: A Sourcebook for Teachers.* Ed. Richard L. Graves. Rochelle Park, N.J.: Hayden, 1976. Pp. 220–24.

Flanigan, Michael C. "Observing Teaching: Discovering and Developing the Individual's Style." *Journal of the Council of Writing Program Administrators* 3 (Winter 1979), 17–24.

—————. *A Process-Centered Composition Program* (a series of nine videocassettes designed to help train writing teachers). Produced by Indiana University Television, Bloomington, Indiana, 1976.

—————. *Strategies in College Teaching* (a series of four videocassettes designed to help faculty and graduate students improve their teaching). Produced by Indiana University Television, Bloomington, Indiana, 1976.

Flower, Linda S. "Writer-Based Prose: A Cognitive Basis for Problems in Writing." *CE* 41 (September 1979), 19–37.

Flower, Linda S., and John R. Hayes. "The Cognition of Discovery: Defining a Rhetorical Problem." *CCC* 31 (February 1980), 21–32.

—————. "Problem-Solving Strategies and the Writing Process." *CE* 39 (December 1977), 449–61.

Francis, W. Nelson. "Revolution in Grammar." *Quarterly Journal of Speech* 40 (October 1954), 299–312.

—————. *The Structure of American English.* New York: Ronald Press, 1958.

Freedman, Aviva, and Ian Pringle, eds. *Reinventing the Rhetorical Tradition.* Conway, Ark.: L & S Books, 1980.

Fries, Charles C. *The Structure of English: An Introduction to the Construction of English Sentences.* New York: Harcourt, Brace and World, 1952.

Gebhardt, Richard C., ed. *Composition and Its Teaching.* Findlay, Oh.: Ohio Council of Teachers of English Language Arts, 1979.

Gebhardt, Richard C. "Imagination and Discipline in the Writing Class." *EJ* 66 (December 1977), 26–32.

Gelb, I.J. *A Study of Writing.* Rev. ed. Chicago: University of Chicago Press, 1963.

Gibson, Walker. *Tough, Sweet and Stuffy.* Bloomington, Ind.: Indiana University Press, 1966.

Golden, James L., Goodwin F. Berquist, and William E. Coleman. *The Rhetoric of Western Thought.* 2nd ed. Dubuque, Ia.: Kendall Hunt, 1978.

Golden, James L., and Edward P.J. Corbett. *The Rhetoric of Blair, Campbell, and Whately.* New York: Holt, Rinehart and Winston, 1968.

Goodman, Kenneth. "Minimum Competencies: A Moral View." In *Minimum*

Competency Standards: Three Points of View. N.P.: International Reading Association, 1978. Pp. 3–5.

Gorrell, Robert M., ed. *Rhetoric: Theories for Application.* Champaign, Ill.: NCTE, 1967.

Graves, Richard, ed. *Rhetoric and Composition: A Sourcebook for Teachers.* Rochelle Park, N.J.: Hayden, 1976.

Gregory, R.L. *The Intelligent Eye.* New York: McGraw-Hill, 1970.

Gunderson, Doris V., ed. *Language and Reading.* Washington, D.C.: Center for Applied Linguistics, 1970.

Hacker, Diana, and Betty Renshaw. *A Practical Guide for Writers.* Cambridge, Mass.: Winthrop, 1979.

Halliday, M.A.K., and Ruqaiya Hasan. *Cohesion in English.* English Language Series No. 9. London: Longman, 1976.

Harris, Zellig S. *Discourse Analysis Reprints.* Papers on Formal Linguistics No. 2. The Hague: Mouton, 1963.

——————. *Structural Linguistics.* Chicago: University of Chicago Press, 1951.

Harris, Stephen L., and Stephen P. Witte. "Sentence Combining in a Rhetorical Framework: Directions for Further Research." In *Reinventing the Rhetorical Tradition.* Ed. Aviva Freedman and Ian Pringle. Conway, Ark.: L & S Books, 1980. Pp. 89–98.

Hartwell, Patrick. "Teaching Arrangement: A Pedagogy." *CE* 40 (January 1979), 548–54.

Herndon, Jeanne. *A Survey of Modern Grammars.* New York: Holt, Rinehart and Winston, 1970.

Hiatt, Mary P. "Students at Bay: The Myth of the Student Conference." *CCC* 26 (February 1975), 38–41.

Hirsch, E.D., Jr. *The Philosophy of Composition.* Chicago: University of Chicago Press, 1977.

Hochmuth, Marie. "Kenneth Burke and the 'New Rhetoric.' " *Quarterly Journal of Speech* 38 (April 1952), 133–44.

Hockett, Charles F. *A Course in Modern Linguistics.* New York: Macmillan, 1958.

Hodges, John C., and Mary E. Whitten. *Harbrace College Handbook.* 8th ed. New York: Harcourt Brace Jovanovich, 1977.

Hoffman, Eleanor M., and John P. Schifsky. "Designing Writing Assignments." *EJ* 66 (December 1977), 41–45.

Holt, John. "How Teachers Make Childen Hate Reading." In *The Norton Reader.* 4th ed. Ed. Arthur M. Eastman. New York: W.W. Norton, 1977. Pp. 189–97. Reprinted from *Redbook* (November 1967).

Howell, Wilbur S. *Eighteenth-Century British Logic and Rhetoric.* Princeton: Princeton University Press, 1971.

——————. *Logic and Rhetoric in England, 1500–1700.* New York: Russell & Russell, 1961.

Hunt, Kellogg W. *Grammatical Structures Written at Three Grade Levels.* NCTE Research Report No. 3. Urbana, Ill.: NCTE, 1965.

──────. "A Synopsis of Clause-to-Sentence Length Factors." *EJ* 54 (April 1965), 300, 305–9.

Irmscher, William. *Teaching Expository Writing.* New York: Holt, Rinehart and Winston, 1979.

Jakobson, Roman. "Linguistics and Poetics." In *Style in Language.* Ed. Thomas Sebeok. Cambridge, Mass.: The MIT Press, 1960. Pp. 350–77.

Jenkinson, Edward B., and Donald A. Seybold. *Writing as a Process of Discovery: Some Structured Theme Assignments for Grades Five through Twelve.* Bloomington, Ind.: Indiana University Press, 1970.

Johannesen, Richard, Rennard Strickland, and Ralph Eubanks, eds. *Language Is Sermonic: Richard M. Weaver on the Nature of Rhetoric.* Baton Rouge, La.: Louisiana State University Press, 1970.

Joos, Martin. *The Five Clocks.* New York: Harcourt, Brace and World, 1961.

Joseph, Sister Miriam. *Rhetoric in Shakespeare's Time.* New York: Harcourt, Brace and World, 1962.

Judine, Sister M., ed. *A Guide for Evaluating Student Composition.* Urbana, Ill.: NCTE, 1965.

Judy, Stephen, ed. *Lecture Alternatives in Teaching English.* Urbana, Ill.: NCTE, 1971.

──────. *Teaching English: Reflections on the State of the Art.* Rochelle Park, N.J.: Hayden, 1979.

Judy, Stephen N., and Susan J. Judy. *An Introduction to the Teaching of Writing.* New York: John Wiley & Sons, 1981.

Karrfalt, David H. "The Generation of Paragraphs and Larger Units." *CCC* 19 (October 1968), 211–17.

Kennedy, George. *The Art of Persuasion in Greece.* Princeton, N.J.: Princeton University Press, 1963.

──────. *The Art of Rhetoric in the Roman World.* Princeton, N.J.: Princeton University Press, 1972.

──────. *Classical Rhetoric and Its Christian and Secular Tradition from Ancient to Modern Times.* Chapel Hill, N.C.: University of North Carolina Press, 1980.

Kinneavy, James L. "A Pluralistic Synthesis of Four Contemporary Models for Teaching Composition." In *Reinventing the Rhetorical Tradition.* Ed. Aviva Freedman and Ian Pringle. Conway, Ark.: L & S Books, 1980. Pp. 37–52.

──────. *A Theory of Discourse.* Englewood Cliffs, N.J.: Prentice-Hall, 1971.

Kitzhaber, Albert R. *Themes, Theories, and Therapy: The Teaching of Writing in College.* New York: McGraw-Hill, 1963.

Kline, Charles R., Jr., and W. Dean Memering. "Formal Fragments: The English Minor Sentence." *RTE* 11 (Fall 1977), 97–110.

Kolers, Paul A. "Experiments in Reading." *Scientific American* 227 (July 1972), 196–203.

Kroll, Barry M., and John C. Shafer. "Error-Analysis and the Teaching of Composition." *CCC* 29 (October 1978), 242–48.

Lanham, Richard. *Revising Prose.* New York: Charles Scribner's Sons, 1979.

————. *Style: An Anti-Textbook.* New Haven, Conn.: Yale University Press, 1974.

Larson, Richard L., ed. *Children and Writing in the Elementary School.* New York: Oxford University Press, 1975.

————. "Discovery Through Questioning: A Plan for Teaching Rhetorical Invention." *CE* 30 (November 1968), 126–34.

————. *Evaluation of Teaching College English.* Urbana, Ill.: NCTE, 1970.

————. "Problem-Solving, Composing, and Liberal Education." *CE* 33 (March 1972), 628–35.

Lauer, Sister Janice M. "Invention in Contemporary Rhetoric: Heuristic Procedures." Diss. University of Michigan, 1967.

Lefrancois, Guy R. *Of Children: An Introduction to Child Development.* 3rd ed. Belmont, Calif.: Wadsworth, 1980.

Lehmann, Winfred. *Historical Linguistics: An Introduction.* New York: Holt, Rinehart and Winston, 1962.

Lunsford, Andrea. "Aristotelian Rhetoric: Let's Get Back to the Classics." *Journal of Basic Writing* 2 (Fall/Winter 1978), 2–12.

————. "An Historical, Descriptive, and Evaluative Study of Remedial English in American Colleges and Universities." Diss. Ohio State University, 1977.

————. "What We Know—and Don't Know—About Remedial Writing." *CCC* 29 (February 1978), 47–52.

McCrimmon, James M. *Writing with a Purpose.* Short edition based on the 7th ed. Boston: Houghton Mifflin, 1980.

McDavid, Raven I. "American English: A Bibliographic Essay." *American Studies International* 17 (Winter 1979), 3–45.

MacKillop, James, and Donna Cross, eds. *Speaking of Words: A Language Reader.* New York: Holt, Rinehart and Winston, 1978.

Macrorie, Ken. *Searching Writing.* Rochelle Park, N.J.: Hayden, 1980.

————. *Telling Writing.* 3rd ed. Rochelle Park, N.J.: Hayden, 1980.

————. *A Vulnerable Teacher.* Rochelle Park, N.J.: Hayden, 1974.

————. *Writing to Be Read.* 2nd ed. Rochelle Park, N.J.: Hayden, 1976.

Mahoney, William E. *Workbook of Current English.* Glenview, Ill.: Scott, Foresman, 1978.

Malstrom, Jean. "Linguistic Atlas Findings Versus Textbook Pronouncements on Current American Usage." *EJ* 48 (April 1959), 191–98.

Meade, Richard A. "Who Can Learn Grammar?" *EJ* 50 (February 1961), 87–92.

Meade, Richard A., and W. Geiger Ellis. "Paragraph Development in the Modern Age of Rhetoric." *EJ* 59 (February 1970), 219–26.

Mellon, John C. *Transformational Sentence-Combining: A Method for Enhancing the Development of Syntactic Fluency in English Composition.* NCTE Research Report No. 10. Champaign, Ill.: NCTE, 1967.

Memering, Willard Dean. "Recent Theories and Practices in the Teaching of Composition." Diss. Florida State University, 1971.

Menendez, Diane S. *Critical Moments in College Teaching* (a series of four videocassettes discussing problems that college teachers face in and outside the classroom). Produced by the National Center for the Development of Training Materials in Teacher Education, 1976. Distributed by the Indiana University Audio-Visual Center, Bloomington, Indiana.

Miller, Susan. *Writing: Process and Product.* Cambridge, Mass.: Winthrop, 1976.

Moffett, James. "I, You, and It." *CCC* 16 (December 1965), 243–56.

——————. *Teaching the Universe of Discourse.* Boston: Houghton Mifflin, 1968.

Moffett, James, and Betty Jane Wagner. *Student-Centered Language Arts and Reading: A Handbook for Teachers.* 2nd ed. Boston: Houghton Mifflin, 1976.

Morenberg, Max, and Andrew Kerek. "Bibliography on Sentence Combining: Theory and Practice, 1964–1979." *Rhetoric Society Quarterly* 9 (Spring 1979), 97–111.

Murphy, James F. *Rhetoric in the Middle Ages.* Berkeley, Calif.: University of California Press, 1974.

Murray, Donald M. "The Feel of Writing—and Teaching Writing." In *Reinventing the Rhetorical Tradition.* Ed. Aviva Freedman and Ian Pringle. Conway, Ark.: L & S Books, 1980. Pp. 67–73.

——————. "The Listening Eye: Reflections on the Writing Conference." *CE* 41 (September 1979), 13–18.

——————. *A Writer Teaches Writing.* Boston: Houghton Mifflin, 1968.

NCTE Commission on Composition. "Teaching Composition: A Position Statement." *CE* 36 (October 1974), 219–20.

NCTE Committee on Classroom Practices in Teaching English. *Classroom Practices in Teaching English 1979–1980: How to Handle the Paper Load.* Urbana, Ill.: NCTE, 1979.

NCTE Task Force on Measurement and Evaluation in the Study of English. *Common Sense and Testing in English.* Urbana, Ill.: NCTE, 1975.

Neel, Jasper P. *Options for the Teaching of English: Freshman Composition.* New York: Modern Language Association, 1978.

Odell, Lee, and Joanne Cohick. "You Mean, Write It Over in Ink?" *EJ* 64 (December 1975), 48–53.

O'Hare, Frank. *Sentence Combining: Improving Student Writing without Formal Grammar Instruction.* NCTE Research Report No. 15. Urbana, Ill.: NCTE, 1973.

——————. *Sentencecraft.* Columbus, Ohio: Ginn and Company, 1974.

Ohmann, Richard M. *English in America: A Radical View of the Profession.* New York: Oxford University Press, 1976.

Ohmann, Richard M., and W.E. Coley, eds. *Ideas for English 101: Teaching Writing in College.* Urbana, Ill.: NCTE, 1975.

Ong, Walter J., S.J. "Hostility, Literacy, and Webster III." In *Aspects of American English.* 2nd ed. Ed. Elizabeth M. Kerr and Ralph M. Aderman. New York: Harcourt Brace Jovanovich, 1971. Pp. 109–15.

—————. "Literacy and Orality in Our Times." *ADE Bulletin* 58 (September 1978), 1–7.

—————. "The Writer's Audience Is Always a Fiction." *PMLA* 90 (January 1975), 9–21.

Parker, William Riley. "Where Do English Departments Come From?" *College English* 28 (February 1967), 339–51.

Perl, Sondra. "The Composing Processes of Unskilled College Writers." *RTE* 13 (December 1979), 317–36.

Pianko, Sharon. "A Description of the Composing Processes of College Freshman Writers." *RTE* 13 (February 1979), 5–22.

Pitkin, Willis L. "Discourse Blocs." *CCC* 20 (May 1969), 138–48.

Plato. *The Dialogues of Plato.* Trans. Benjamin Jowett. Great Books of the Western World, Vol. 7. Chicago: Encyclopaedia Britannica, 1952.

Pooley, Robert C. *The Teaching of English Usage.* 2nd ed. Urbana, Ill.: NCTE, 1974.

Pyles, Thomas. *The Origins and Development of the English Language.* 2nd ed. New York: Harcourt Brace Jovanovich, 1971.

Robins, Adrienne. *The Writer's Practical Rhetoric.* New York: John Wiley and Sons, 1980.

Rodgers, Paul C. "A Discourse-Centered Rhetoric of the Paragraph." *CCC* 17 (February 1966), 2–11.

Rohman, D. Gordon. "Pre-Writing: The Stage of Discovery in the Writing Process." *CCC* 16 (May 1965), 106–12.

Rohman, D. Gordon, and Albert O. Wlecke. *Pre-Writing: The Construction and Application of Models for Concept Formation in Writing.* USOE Cooperative Research Project No. 2174. East Lansing, Mich.: Michigan State University, 1964.

Rose, Mike. "Rigid Rules, Inflexible Plans, and the Stifling of Language: A Cognitivist Analysis of Writer's Block." *CCC* 31 (December 1980), 389–401.

Ryan, Joseph P. "The Function and Format of a Course Syllabus." Unpublished faculty development material. University of South Carolina. Columbia, S.C., Fall 1978.

Ryle, Gilbert. *The Concept of Mind.* New York: Barnes & Noble, 1949.

Scaglione, Aldo. *The Classical Theory of Composition from Its Origins to the Present: A Historical Survey.* Chapel Hill, N.C.: University of North Carolina Press, 1972.

The Sentence and the Paragraph. Urbana, Ill.: NCTE, 1963, 1965, and 1966.

Shaughnessy, Mina. "Diving In: An Introduction to Basic Writing." *CCC* 27 (October 1976), 234–39.

—————. *Errors and Expectations: A Guide for the Teacher of Basic Writing.* New York: Oxford University Press, 1977.

Sommers, Nancy I. "The Need for Theory in Composition Research." *CCC* 30 (February 1979), 46–49.

—————. "Revision in the Composing Process: A Case Study of College

Freshmen and Experienced Adult Writers." Diss. Boston University, 1978.

——————. "Revision Strategies of Student Writers and Experienced Writers." *CCC* 31 (December 1980), 378–88.

Stageberg, Norman C. *An Introductory English Grammar.* 3rd ed. New York: Holt, Rinehart and Winston, 1977.

Steinmann, Martin M., ed. *New Rhetorics.* New York: Charles Scribner's Sons, 1967.

Stern, Arthur A. "When Is a Paragraph?" *CCC* 27 (October 1976), 253–57.

Stewart, Donald C. "Composition Textbooks and the Assault on the Tradition." *CCC* 29 (May 1978), 171–76.

[Stone, George Winchester]. "The Beginning, Development, and Impact of the MLA as a Learned Society: 1883–1958." *PMLA* 73 (December 1958), 23–44.

Strong, William. *Sentence Combining.* New York: Random House, 1973.

——————. *Sentence Combining and Paragraph Building.* New York: Random House, 1981.

"Students' Right to Their Own Language." *CCC* 25 (Special Fall Issue 1974).

Tate, Gary, ed. *Teaching Composition: Ten Bibliographical Essays.* Fort Worth, Tex.: Texas Christian University Press, 1976.

Tate, Gary, and Edward P.J. Corbett, eds. *Teaching High School Composition.* New York: Oxford University Press, 1970.

——————. *The Writing Teacher's Sourcebook.* New York: Oxford University Press, 1981.

Ulanov, Barry. "The Relevance of Rhetoric." *EJ* 55 (April 1966), 403–8.

Vygotsky, Lev. *Thought and Language.* Cambridge, Mass.: MIT Press, 1962.

Wallace, Karl R. "*Topoi* and the Problem of Invention." *The Quarterly Journal of Speech* 58 (December 1972), 387–95.

Weaver, Constance. *Grammar for Teachers: Perspectives and Definitions.* Urbana, Ill.: NCTE, 1979.

Whorf, Benjamin Lee. *Language, Thought and Reality.* Ed. John B. Carroll. Cambridge, Mass.: The MIT Press, 1967.

Wiener, Harvey S. "Selecting the Freshman English Textbook." *CE* 37 (September 1975), 28–34.

——————. *The Writing Room: A Resource Book for Teachers of English.* New York: Oxford University Press, 1981.

Williston, Glenn R. *Understanding the Main Idea, Middle Level.* Providence, R.I.: Jamestown Publishers, 1976.

Winterowd, W. Ross, ed. *Contemporary Rhetoric: A Conceptual Background with Readings.* New York: Harcourt Brace Jovanovich, 1975.

——————. *Rhetoric: A Synthesis.* New York: Holt, Rinehart and Winston, 1968.

Witte, Stephen P. Rev. of *Sentence Combining and the Teaching of Writing,* ed. Donald Daiker, Andrew Kerek, and Max Morenberg (Conway, Ark.: L & S Books, 1979). *CCC* 31 (December 1980), 433–37.

Womack, Thurston. "Teachers' Attitudes Toward Current Usage." *EJ* 48 (April 1959), 186–90.

Woodson, Linda. *A Handbook of Modern Rhetorical Terms.* Urbana, Ill.: NCTE, 1979.

Young, Richard E., Alton L. Becker, and Kenneth L. Pike. *Rhetoric: Discovery and Change.* New York: Harcourt, Brace and World, 1970.

Zoellner, Robert. "A Behavioral Approach to Writing." *CE* 30 (January 1969), 267–320.

Index